Managerial Skills

Managerial Skills

Explorations in Practical Knowledge

edited by
John D. Bigelow

SAGE PUBLICATIONS
The International Professional Publishers
Newbury Park   London   New Delhi

For information address:

SAGE Publications, Inc.
2455 Teller Road
Newbury Park, California 91320

SAGE Publications Ltd.
6 Bonhill Street
London EC2A 4PU
United Kingdom

SAGE Publications India Pvt. Ltd.
M-32 Market
Greater Kailash I
New Delhi 110 048 India

Printed in the United States of America

Library of Congress Cataloging-in-Publication Data

Managerial skills : explorations in practical knowledge / edited by John
    D. Bigelow.
        p. cm.
    Includes bibliographical references and index.
    ISBN 0-8039-4095-5. — ISBN 0-8039-4096-3 (pbk.)
    1. Management. 2. Executive ability. I. Bigelow, John D.
HD31.M293943   1991
658.4—dc20   90-28271
                                                                   CIP

FIRST PRINTING, 1991

Sage Production Editor: Judith L. Hunter

Contents

Acknowledgments

I would like to first acknowledge the role of the Organizational Behavior Teaching Society (OBTS) in the inception of this book. A number of individuals contributed to its creation, whom I would like to acknowledge. Larry Michaelsen provided much assistance in the earlier stages of pulling the book together. In addition he was the entrepreneur who connected with Sage. Ann West of Sage provided much initial guidance and help in organizing the book. Later, Harry Briggs, Donna Feeney, and Judy Hunter of Sage provided patient editorial help and encouragement during later stages. Craig Lundberg has provided inestimable help in formulating the Introduction and Afterword. Finally and most important, the book authors have worked creatively and patiently to provide significant and readable chapters.

Foreword

This book deals with what I call a "diamond" type of issue: one that is multifaceted. Although this issue—teaching managerial skill development—has been with us for some time, and has received intensified attention for at least the past 10 years or so, there has as yet been no single volume where its many different aspects have been addressed under "one roof," as it were. Thus, this book helps to fill an important void. It brings together an array of knowledgeable authors to convey and elucidate approaches and insights involved in attempts to meet the challenge of developing and assessing *students'* managerial skills.

There can be little doubt that the challenge is a critical one. Evidence from the corporate world of practice, as reported, for example, in the recently completed study of the American Assembly of Collegiate Schools of Business (AACSB) on the current status and future direction of management education, has identified "people skills" as the weakest area of skills of graduates being turned out by U.S. business schools. Although "people skills" and "management skills" are not totally synonymous, the former is a large component of the latter. It is clear that the AACSB study and other informed observations and commentaries on management education point to an urgent need to see whether it is possible for our institutions of higher education—in particular schools of business and management—to improve the teaching of management and leadership skills. Regardless of whether graduates of these schools spend their careers in business or some other occupation, it is almost certain that most of them will work in some kind of organization and will be confronted with numerous opportunities to use whatever competencies of this type they possess. Therefore, if improvements in the teaching and development of such skills can be accomplished, the larger society, of which we are all part, will benefit.

To help us on the road to doing a better job for our students and for society in this regard, this volume describes—as indicated by its subtitle—"*explorations* in practical knowledge." Explorations always imply the possibility of discovery, and that is a major goal here. However, for those who seek to uncover definitive answers to all of the many questions pertaining to teaching and developing managerial skills, this book will be a disappointment. On the other hand, for those who are willing to delve into the tough intellectual and practical problems inherent in this topic, the book should prove tremendously stimulating. You will be challenged by ideas you have not thought of before, by opinions and views that will elicit a range of agreements and disagreements, and by evidence and examples of methods that have both worked and not worked, but which should, in any event, motivate you and your colleagues to make your own innovative explorations in this area. A good way to approach this book, then, is to have a kind of dialogue with it, to think of it as part of a part of an extended discussion, which includes yourself and many others with a stake in this endeavor.

A book on this kind of topic is really a way point along a long and winding road. It presents some of the best current thinking on the various issues, but it is destined to be superseded by some new volume in coming years that will provide the next way point. In fact, the finest tribute that can be paid to this book is for it to stimulate so much new thinking and so many new advances in teaching and assessing managerial skills that it will become outdated sooner rather than later. In the meantime, however, it should serve to guide and to inspire our best efforts. Though the task is daunting and frequently frustrating, and our attempts to make progress in mastering it often go unappreciated, we need to recall an old Chinese proverb recently called to my attention by my colleague, Judy Rosener: "The person who says it can't be done should not interfere with the person who is doing it."

                                                                    Lyman W. Porter

Introduction

However much thou art read in theory, if thou hast no practice thou art ignorant.

—Sa'di, 1258

This book is about practice—what a person needs to be able to actually *do* to be effective in the world. The type of practice considered in this book is most typically seen in a manager's world. Nonetheless, I think the most powerful way to view this book is in a broader context, as an effort by educators to understand and teach "doing." Consequently, the questions considered in this book will be of interest to any person concerned about effective practice, regardless of the particular practice domain.

What does a person need to know to practice management? How can this knowledge be imparted? These are questions with which colleges of business have been grappling for decades. In recent times there has been a growing dissatisfaction with graduates, stemming from a number of quarters.[1] Apparently the knowledge that college business graduates have been acquiring has not been sufficient to do an entirely satisfactory job.

Habermas (1971) provides a way of thinking about these questions by proposing that there are not one, but three, knowledge domains, deriving from three distinct cognitive interests. He identifies (a) technical knowledge, deriving from the empirical-analytic sciences; (b) practical knowledge, deriving from historical-hermaneutic sciences; and (c) emancipatory knowledge, deriving from critically oriented sciences.

In Habermas's framework, universities have tended to emphasize technical knowledge more and the other two less. This observation is quite consistent with critics, who generally concede that business graduates rate high in their technical abilities. It is also consistent in that they generally rate these same graduates lower in their practical abilities.

This arrangement, in which colleges emphasize technical knowledge, probably worked well in earlier times. Then, higher education was rarer in business. Less-educated people, who had obtained practical knowledge through experience, were in relative abundance. The availability of experienced people, however, has been on the decline as managers are increasingly hired from the ranks of business school graduates. As we are now becoming aware, the technical knowledge of these graduates has been obtained at the expense of their practical knowledge.

Recognition of this problem and attempts to redress it have roots in the 1960s and before. The American Assembly of Collegiate Schools of Business (AACSB) provided a milestone in 1977, when it established a committee to investigate the possibility of using "noncognitive skills" as a part of the accreditation process.[2] The Organizational Behavior Teaching Society provided another milestone in 1983, when it published a special issue of *Exchange* on teaching managerial competencies. Since then a generally acknowledged "skills movement" has been slowly emerging. This movement largely comprises concerned management educators, usually working independently and on their own initiative to introduce practical knowledge into their courses.

More than 13 years have passed since the AACSB began its work, and more than 7 years have passed since the special issue of *Exchange*. Students of large-scale change will not be surprised at the long time periods involved, especially when the possibility of change is raised in universities. What is the current status of the "skills movement"? What have we learned since 1983? The purpose of this book is to address these questions.

The origin of this book was in conversations between myself and Larry Michaelsen, shortly after he assumed editorship of the *Organizational Behavior Teaching Review*. After discussing a number of possibilities, we agreed that it was a good time to again systematically address the question of managerial skills. I sent out a call for papers on managerial action skills to educators affiliated with the Academy of Management and the Organizational Behavior Teaching Society. The result was gratifying, and the chapters of this book were winnowed from the large number of submissions that followed.

In reviewing submissions I was able to identify a number of questions that authors consistently addressed. The most prevalent of these were:

1. What basic issues must be addressed in creating and implementing an effective skills program?
2. How can a skills program be designed so as to be viable in a university setting? What issues must be dealt with in doing so?
3. How can a person's skills be assessed?
4. What are we learning about the nature of skills?

The chapters of this book are divided into four parts, each part focusing somewhat on one of the questions above. I say "somewhat" because most of the authors dealt with more than one of these questions. The four-part division simply represents my judgment as to which of the questions was most significantly dealt with by each of the authors. At the beginning of each section I say more about the contributions of the authors of that section.

I have added an Afterword, where I attempt to pull together some of the learning about managerial skills provided in the chapters and propose an agenda for the action skills movement.

Following the introductory discussion in Part I, the flow of the chapters moves generally from "establishing" to "expanding." That is, earlier chapters describe program and assessment designs that seem to work. Later chapters describe ideas that expand our knowledge of action skills and skill pedagogy. Readers unfamiliar with pedagogies of practical knowledge, therefore, will be particularly interested in Parts II and III. Readers interested in newer insights about practical knowledge will be particularly interested in Part IV and the Afterword.

Enough preamble. The ideas in this book are exciting to me and have significantly changed my ideas about skills and skill pedagogy. I hope you find the book equally significant.

John D. Bigelow

Notes

1. For more detail on the nature of these dissatisfactions, review the chapter introductions.

2. The terms *practical knowledge, noncognitive skills, competencies, action skills,* and the like are considered synonymous.

Part I Issues in Developing Managerial Skills Programs

In 1983 (and again in 1989), Peter Vaill listed eight propositions that he saw underlying the managerial competency movement (CM): for example, that competencies are independent of each other; that manager's jobs have outputs identifiably related to competence; that competence makes a difference to organizational effectiveness; that possessing a competency is to know when and how to use it; and that competencies can be exercised regardless of the morals, motives, and competencies of the other. He argued that these propositions are faulty and that, by implication, the competency movement is faulty. He concluded by stating,

> I think that we have to cling to what it means to be a whole person with purposes in a situation with others who themselves have their purposes. The wholeness of oneself in relation to the wholeness of others is not presently apparent in the CM's approach to management and to its improvement. (p. 54)

I attended an Organizational Behavior Teaching Conference session around 1983 in which Peter and others raised questions of this nature. I remember that in that session I thought the antagonists were perceptive and incisive. The protagonists, however, seemed to say, "I see this approach confirmed in my practice, and I'm too busy trying to make it better to spend time investigating it at that level."

Peter's critique is as pertinent now as it was then. In the interim, however, action skill programs have created a phenomenon that can be examined, thought about, and studied. This, in turn, has stimulated deeper thought in skill educators.

This section focuses on basic issues that must be addressed in implementing an effective skills program. Several authors have touched on such issues as a part of their chapters (most notably Whetten). The chapter by Tim Serey and Kathleen Verderber, however, uniquely addresses this topic and is therefore the only one included in this section. Drawing on their experiences in developing a skills-based program, they discusses a number of educational and philosophical issues that must be resolved in developing a competency-based management education program.

1 Beyond the Wall: Resolving Issues of Educational Philosophy and Pedagogy in the Teaching of Managerial Competencies

Timothy T. Serey

Kathleen S. Verderber

In the concluding chapter of the seminal report, *Management Education and Development: Drift or Thrust Into The 21st Century,* Porter and McKibbin (1988) wrote:

> As has been stressed at several points in this report . . . corporate respondents showed an over-whelming preponderance of opinion that behaviorally oriented subject matter should receive more attention in the curriculum. . . . Perhaps most importantly, the corporate sector gives business school graduates relatively low ratings in terms of the strength (or lack thereof) of their leadership and interpersonal skills.

Referring to these management skills,[1] in 1983 Lyman Porter stated: "Teaching managerial competencies is quite likely to be one of the major issues—perhaps *the* major issue—facing business/management schools in the last half of the 1980's."

Albanese determined that Academy of Management members were generally quite favorably disposed to management competencies (Albanese, Schoenfeldt, Serey, & Whetten, 1987). More than 80% of respondents either agreed or strongly agreed with the statement, "There is a need for more teaching of managerial competencies in management classes." Spurred by the emphasis on skills in the Porter and McKibbin (1988) report, the 1989 Organizational Behavior Teaching Conference (OBTC) ended with the forming of a task force to address the skills issues.

Based on the activity cited above, one might assume that teaching business students behavioral skills has begun to result in widespread acceptance of competency-based educational philosophies. Unfortunately, such is not the case. Rather, to borrow an analogy from the world of marathon running, the integration of managerial skill development into curriculums across the country has "hit the wall." Despite the high expectation held by several experts in Organizational Behavior and Management, skills teaching seems to have met the limits of its endurance. In fact, far from its being seen as "mainstream" or as "the major issue," one leading author recently lamented that many business faculty apparently view competencies as having a "cult-like" following (Cameron, 1989). These views make it clear that the future of the managerial competencies will depend on "breaking through the wall," by adapting current curricula and methodologies to include developing behavioral skill in students. Overcoming the reluctance that some faculty express about teaching competencies will be an important next step remedying the poor performances of business school graduates as reported by Porter and McKibbin (1988).

We believe there are several philosophical and pedagogical issues that may account for the reluctance of some faculty to embrace the task of teaching behaviorally based skills. During the past six years, our experience in teaching management competencies has led us to consider several issues and dilemmas. In many cases we have successfully overcome our own concerns; in other cases we have gained a deeper appreciation of the trade-offs involved.

Based on our experiences, this chapter examines several of the key issues and controversies that must be resolved if the promises of competency-based management education are to be realized. In the remainder of this chapter we address three issues that are central to educational philosophy and four issues critical to pedagogy that must be addressed and resolved if the teaching of managerial competencies in collegiate-level business education is to become commonplace.

Need for and Legitimacy of Skill-Based Education

The shortcomings of the more traditional ways of teaching OB and Management have been known for some time. Ten years ago Filley,

Foster, and Herbert (1979) complained that OB and Management courses emphasized theoretical concepts but were of limited practical value. In 1980 Waters observed that conventional pedagogies tended to emphasize cognitive learning about behavior in organizations. For example, professors lectured on the rationale and principles for providing employees with feedback. Unfortunately, students were left on their own to divine how to actually verbalize and conduct a feedback session. In 1982 Mandt indicted business schools for their failures and called for reforms in an article stingingly titled, "The Failure of Business Education—And What to Do About It." Yet in the 1988 Porter and McKibbin report, business leaders were still critical of the quality of business school graduates' "people skills."

Despite the limits to the current practice of our craft, reluctance to embrace a skills approach remains. We believe that some of this hesitancy is rooted in the philosophical position held by many professors. Some business faculty see competency-based education as mere training sessions. They believe that this feeds the stereotype held by other nonbusiness disciplines that business education is too vocational (i.e., not a "legitimate" scholarly discipline). Some management scholars have also voiced skepticism about the validity of competency education (Vaill, 1983). The AACSB, while ostensibly trying to encourage integration of skills into the business curriculum, may have inadvertently perpetuated the false dichotomy between theory and skill. They differentiated between *cognitive skills* (e.g., analytical skills) and *noncognitive skills* (emphasis added) or management competencies (AACSB Outcome Measurement Project, 1987). In summary, the position held by some business educators is that skill-based learning—while necessary for managerial success—falls outside the purview of the traditional collegiate education.

Yet, emphasis on skill-based education in universities has a long and rich history of preparing students for success in many professions. For example, study in the natural sciences requires that students become adept at using scientific equipment and procedures. The study of any foreign language requires that students engage in activities designed to demonstrate their behavioral competence at speaking and understanding the language. Students of archaeology learn the techniques required for acquiring and preserving artifacts. English majors learn to produce critiques of literature based on the postulates of particular literary theories. Artists in training study the various schools of art and are expected to produce works of artistic merit, using various expressive media. Student musicians are routinely expected to perform at recitals. Even the "hard" sciences expect skill performance. In engineering, students are not only immersed in the theories and mathematics of engineering but are also responsible for completing projects to learn the behaviors required of the practitioner engineer. Similarly, before medical students ever become licensed practitioners, they are require to complete clinical rotations, internships, and residency experiences that are designed to demonstrate behavioral competence.

Thus the integration of competency-based skill development is not outside the mainstream of traditional collegiate education. Rather, the integration of behavioral learning with theoretical learning may be a key characteristic of a mature academic discipline.

We believe that the disciplines of management and organizational behavior have now matured sufficiently in their theoretical development to the point where theory-guided behavioral competencies can be identified and, therefore, taught. Leading management scholars have recognized this for some time and have been urging curriculum reform. For example, in the mid-1970s, Mintzberg articulated the difference between teaching *about management* (which we do) and teaching *how to manage* (which we generally do not do). Continuing, Mintzberg (1975) noted:

> Management schools will begin the serious training of managers when skill training takes a serious place next to cognitive learning. Our management schools need to identify the skills managers use, select students who show potential in these skills, put students into situations where these skills are practiced, and then give them systematic feedback on their performance.

In a similar vein, Katz (1974) complained:

> Programs which concentrate on the mere imparting of information or the cultivation of a specific trait would seem to be largely unproductive in enhancing the administrative skills of candidates . . . The skill conception of administration suggests that we may hope to improve our administrative effectiveness and to develop administrators for the future. This skill conception implies learning by doing.

The significant body of management theory that was developed during the past 30 years enabled several taxonomies of important managerial skills to be developed. Originally begun in 1976, the AACSB-sponsored Outcome Measurement Project (1987) identified six clusters of "skills and personal characteristics" (i.e., competencies) business school graduates should master. The American Management Association identified 18 managerial competencies, which it endorses (Powers, 1983). Arguably the most influential development is the innovative text by Whetten and Cameron (1984), *Developing Management Skills.* This text identifies three intrapersonal (e.g., managing stress, self-awareness) and nine inter-personal skills (e.g., delegating, supportive communication).[2] In sharp conceptual contrast to the microfocus of these management skill approaches, Morgan (1988) emphasizes mastery of macroskills (e.g., empowering employees in self-managing organizations; managing ambiguity and paradox; and reading the environment).

In all cases, these different taxonomies are focused on "real world" management skills and behaviors that Boyatzis (1982) contends are the basis of competency education. They are derived directly from the conceptual and empirical literature. For example, stress management skills include learning to use the Force Field Models of Stress to diagnose sources of stress and identify suitable methods of stress reduction. Skills related to influencing the motivational level in others require that students understand the various theories of motivation to skillfully apply their lessons. To illustrate, to become skillful in motivating others, the student has to be able to define positive reinforcement, recognize examples of it, *and* be able to design and administer an appropriate reinforcement program. Competency-based management education also emphasizes behavioral flexibility and understanding of how situation demands affect enactment of skills. Skill mastery does not consist of rote mastery of a simple list of dos and don'ts, offering prescriptive advice for all situations. On the contrary, competency education is wholly consistent with a contingency view advocated by the theories of OB.

From a theoretical perspective, competency education in general, and Whetten and Cameron's approach in particular, is rooted in Bandura's Social Learning Theory (1977) and in Goldstein and Sorcher's Four Step Learning (1974). The former emphasizes behavior practice and the value of modeling as a key component in the learning process. The latter takes a structured approach to learning skills. Instructors teach underlying principles and theories after which they model or demonstrate examples of effective behaviors. Students complete a learning sequence that includes time for practicing behaviors and receiving feedback based on specific behavioral guidelines.

In summary, as our discipline matures, it is important for the philosophy that guides management education to evolve from imparting of conceptual and theoretical learning to an educational philosophy that includes developing behavioral competence in students. The chorus of critical voices from the AACSB findings and the business community compels us to move toward helping students learn *how* to manage, in addition to learning *about* managing. As professors in a maturing academic discipline, it is our responsibility to incorporate the learning of "how to do" into our curricula.

The Process of Developing
Managerial Competencies

A second educational philosophy concerns how students develop managerial skills. This development is not a discrete or finite process but one that varies, depending on the complexity of the skill and the beginning ability level of the student. Programs whose goals include behavioral skill development must grapple with developing a philosophy toward student learners that acknowledges individual differences while affirming the importance of developing common competencies. Additionally, there must be a willingness to modify or totally redesign the curriculum in order to provide students with sufficient time to acquire complex skills.

Since we began teaching managerial skills we have observed that behavioral skills take more time to master than conceptual material. This is not surprising since the OD literature tells us that effective behavior in organizational settings is complex, and that it takes time to change. Additionally, most skill-oriented courses also teach the theories that underlie competent behavior.

On more than one occasion we have wrestled with this issue by asking ourselves the question, "How much behavioral change is it fair to expect of our students in one semester?" This question is confounded by two realities. First, students clearly bring into a course differing levels of competence. Because their current skill level is the product of their earlier life experiences, formal learning, and prior opportunities for skill development, students sometimes view competency courses as an uneven playing field. Second, individual difference factors also mean that students acquire skills at different learning rates. Because demonstrated mastery of competencies is generally required, students can also experience strong affective reactions (e.g., anxiety, perceived threats to self-presentation).

We have not eliminated these two realities. Instead, we have adopted a philosophy that recognizes individual differences and seeks to create a "safe" learning environment. Managing a supportive learning environment—discussed at some length in a subsequent section—is a requisite characteristic for enhancement of skill acquisition. Nevertheless, our students are expected to display minimum specified levels of skill acquisition at certain points during their course of study. Those who are unable to do this are expected to repeat the material until they can.

Based on our experience in teaching behavioral skills, we are troubled by the misplaced eagerness of some of our colleagues who are "ready for something new . . . want to give this a try," or that they "want to jump on the skills bandwagon, but are not sure where to start." Comments like these were made to one of the authors who took part in a symposium about skills teaching at the Meeting of the Academy of Management in 1987. While we applaud the eagerness to teach managerial competencies, we are also concerned by the naivete about the need to have curricula that are capable of developing *and* sustaining managerial skills in students. After discussions with other professors at several OBTCs, we are convinced that the "let's try it here" approach may be counterproductive. Instead, we assert that schools of business need to develop a "good fit" between the business school curriculum, its objectives, and a skills approach.

In many colleges curriculum revision has traditionally meant adding or deleting one or two courses at a time. It is within this context that many well-intentioned efforts to establish managerial skills (including our first attempts) have occurred. When one finds managerial skill-building occurring as part of a curriculum, it is most frequently done within the context of a single course. These courses become the sole mechanism through which students are expected to achieve competence. Although these courses may result in students' acquiring some additional level of skill, our experience has been that one-shot skill courses are not long enough to result in the "refreezing" of new behaviors necessary for neophyte managers.

If faculty embrace the need for competency goals in the curriculum, then it is important that this be accompanied by the philosophy that each course in the curriculum should contribute to the skill development of students. A move toward managerial competency-based education must necessitate a systematic assessment of the current curriculum, with an eye toward understanding the nature and relationships between various content areas, associated competencies, and the pedagogies used to teach these.

Several years ago our faculty undertook this type of assessment. It began with a process to reach consensus about the theoretical and behavioral learnings we hoped our graduates would achieve. Then we systematically surveyed our current practices in each course. This resulted in an *outcome* × pedagogy × assessment method matrix, which enabled us to identify our curriculum deficiencies.[3] For example, we discovered there was consensus that program graduates should be able to competently present a formal oral presentation, and several courses required students to give such a presentation. Unfortunately, in none of our courses were students instructed on the techniques associated with effective business presentations. Additionally, all oral presentation assignments were done as part of group projects, where the feedback focused on group-centered issues instead of individual presentation critiques. In another area, we discovered that while several courses covered conceptual material associated with work process (i.e., job analysis, management of quality, and so on), in no course were students provided with hands-on skill-building exercises or assessments.

Achieving consensus on our program goals, developing the matrix, and negotiating the changes in our curriculum was hard work. But it resulted in three tangible benefits. First, the redesign of the curriculum was a joint undertaking that began with our agreement on a common educational philosophy. Ownership was spread across our faculty. We did not experience the resistance that is often encountered by some who unilaterally try to move toward a skill-oriented approach. Second, we examined our curriculum in a systematic way, identifying the outcomes we judged to be desirable for our graduates. To do this we set goals that would be realistic in light of the abilities of our students. Third, the process resulted in a curriculum that has a logical progression of skill learning. For example, the development of "people skills" now begins with the requirement for a 200-level course in interpersonal communication skills taught by the speech-communication department on campus. Students then progress to a course titled "Managerial Behavior," which uses the Whetten and Cameron (1984) approach. Upon completion of this course students take a Human Resources (HR) class, which integrates HR theories and research with opportunities to develop the HR skills that line managers need to succeed (such as interviewing, using job analysis to justify position requests, handling complaints about sexual harassment, and conducting performance appraisals). This HR skills focus contrasts sharply with our previous, more conventional approach, which dealt with managing the Personnel function. Other courses teach the theories and skills associated with the management of work processes.

Instead of learning in a piecemeal fashion, our students now experience a continuity of skill development over their entire course of study. We have developed a curriculum consistent with our educational philosophy that sees competency-based learning as a developmental process that must occur over extended lengths of time.

Evaluation and Assessment of Managerial Competence

Most faculty espouse the philosophy that evaluation and assessment of students should be consistent with the learning objectives of a course. However, in courses that have managerial competence goals, this presents a dilemma. Faculty must choose between two philosophical positions regarding what is evaluated.

One position consists of assessing the level of student competency compared to some external goal. This is analogous to the ubiquitous final examination. An individual who scores well on such an evaluation has demonstrated a particular level of competence. Critics of this position suggest that since some students may enter a course with higher levels of skill mastery than others, such evaluations when used for grading purposes are not valid measures of what has been learned.

On the other hand, faculty may choose to adopt a philosophical position that results in focusing their evaluation and grading on skill improvement over the term. This, however, introduces the fairness issue, or the problem of implicitly using a different grading scale for each student. Person "A," for example, may improve more than Person "B," even though B has a more complete mastery of management skills. Either way, OB teachers have to grapple with potential threats to the internal validity of the grading process.

We have no specific solution to this dilemma, but both of us have chosen to base our own evaluation and assessment techniques on the first position. We evaluate the level of competency that our students have achieved compared to a clearly defined standard. In addition to other assessment methods, we use midterm and final behavioral (or oral) exams.

At the beginning of our courses and throughout the term, we note that the classroom is intended to teach the theories about and the behavior expected of people in business. We position the evaluation process as measuring the behaviors business demands of graduates. In this process, students are quick to see the face validity of the skills they are acquiring. While we get our share of positive and negative comments, neither of us has ever had any student challenge or complain about the need to master these key business skills. As one student succinctly put it on a course evaluation, "The skills stuff is where the rubber meets the road."

The decision that we have made to evaluate competency according to a common standard is consistent with the position of the AACSB. Its Outcome Measurement Project (1987) provides business schools with tools for measuring the level of achievement that students have attained with regard to managerial competencies. Deans and faculty can now determine how well they are meeting their educational objectives in the area of acquired personal skills and characteristics, which have been empirically shown to be correlated with management effectiveness.

Issues Related to Pedagogy

In addition to the philosophical issues that must be considered, there is a host of pedagogical issues associated with teaching managerial skills. Pedagogical issues are operationally oriented and include decisions about the personnel assigned to teach behavioral-based courses, methods for structuring a supportive learning environment, methods for evaluating what is learned, and resource demands.

Staffing Competency Classes

We are convinced that the methods utilized in teaching behavioral competencies are among the most demanding we've experienced. In most classes, whether we like it or not, we serve as role models for our students in indirect ways. When teaching managerial competencies, however, there are direct demands placed on the instructor to model effective behavior. This role amplifies the need to ensure that the faculty who teach skills courses have, themselves, developed the competencies they are assigned to teach. Unfortunately, while possessing great conceptual knowledge, some faculty lack adequate interpersonal skills to effectively teach managerial competencies. For example, arrogance, speaking to students in a demeaning tone, losing one's temper, or not being interpersonally self-aware become painfully obvious. When the professor flubs, students see and know it because they have behavioral guidelines—prescriptions about the right way to enact supportive communication, conflict resolution, or other skills—right in front of them. The lost credibility of an instructor or low teacher ratings are not the issues as much as undermining the learning culture of the classroom.

We believe it is important that instructors who teach skills courses "practice what they preach." Otherwise, students may learn from the professor modeling behaviors that are, in fact, inappropriate. Faculty skill development may be enhanced through peer evaluation, behavioral workshops, and "apprenticeship" or co-teaching experiences. What is essential for maintaining the learning culture of the classroom is that instructors possess both the ability and the willingness to take risks openly and be able to openly communicate mistakes for the discussion and learning of all.

Structuring a Supportive Learning Environment

Teaching managerial skills requires that faculty use pedagogies that create a learning climate where students feel safe enough to try new behaviors. But what does this require? How does a professor move beyond the anecdotal folklore and platitudes that surround the teaching of skills courses (e.g., "be open!")?

Based on our experiences we offer these pedagogical guidelines. First, from the beginning of our courses we challenge our class members to become "learners" rather than "students" in the course (Serey & Verderber, 1988). The distinction being made is that class members are expected to take ownership of their skill development and are expected to be actively involved in the skill development of their classmates. This learning-centered culture permeates the entire term. By our establishing a norm for self-management of learning, the responsibility for effectiveness of the classroom activities is distributed among professor and students.

Second, to master management skills, students must be given opportunities to practice. It should be understood that pedagogies permitting active learning (such as role plays) are to be preferred over more passive methods of instruction. These opportunities to practice can be made especially powerful if students are asked to provide scenarios and examples from their own experiences as the stimulus material for practice sessions or assessment exercises. Mastery of managerial skills occurs most readily when students encounter these skills through the lens of their own experiences. It is often useful to have students enact the same scenario with different partners and using different verbal approaches.

One consequence of this learning environment is heightened self-awareness. The comment mentioned most often on our course evaluations is how much students learn about themselves. One student even compared our managerial behavior class to a giant mirror. We've found that structuring time toward the end of class for self-reflection, and for collective reflecting, is helpful. For example, we use a structured group experience (Napier & Gershenfeld, 1981), where team members provide coaching and feedback to one another. Near the midpoint of the term, the larger "organization" (i.e., the class) assesses how we are all doing together. One recent discussion even brought forth several specific ideas about how class members who were more verbally skilled and aggressive could take ownership and help those who were reticent.

Third, an important ingredient in the pedagogy of supportive learning is captured in the phrase "Expect a lot, but be patient." In our skills course, we recast the different roles that managers play (à la Mintzberg) into the professor's roles of expert, assessor, and coach. When most students begin our courses they have usually interacted with faculty only through the first two roles. Yet, coaching may be the most important role that faculty play in skill-oriented courses.

It takes time, patience, skill, and courage to stroke and to confront poor performance. Providing this coaching directly but gently is an absolute necessity if students are to become competent managers. When we provide course feedback and coaching to students in our skills course, we try to balance the need to provide honest feedback with the need to protect the self-image of the student. Candidly, we encounter many reminders about how fragile some of our students' self images are. When we bungle coaching, we feel guilty and are aware of a missed opportunity to help. When coaching students occurs with sensitivity, however, it provides a wonderful source of professional enrichment. A brief anecdote illustrates this point:

> During a recent feedback session with a student, I shared my perception of the student's progress by commenting that the person had started the course somewhat tentatively, but had openly and successfully overcome several skill deficiencies. Surprisingly the student's response was to begin crying uncontrollably. Apologizing for fear that somehow the feedback had been bungled, I found it quite sobering when the student managed to sob "Oh, no . . . you're the first person in my life who has ever made me feel like I was worth anything."

As in any course experience, overall reactions vary. Responses this strong are savored as long-lasting proof that once in a while we really do make a difference. Most reactions to our attempts to create a supportive environment are more ordinary. Though a few people never cope with the anxiety and different pedagogy, generally a stronger bonding between instructor and students does occur.

Methods for Evaluation

Designing evaluation of students' performance for the purposes of assigning a course grade is a complex task. The measurement methods must be congruent with the skills being assessed. Wherever possible, the structure of the evaluation experience should provide students with the opportunity to demonstrate competencies in more realistic settings.

Some skill-based learning can be demonstrated through performances on assignments with which most faculty are familiar. In our managerial behavior class, students complete a write-rewrite memo assignment, which is evaluated on the extent to which it displays the principles of effective business writing. Similarly, students complete an in-class oral presentation, which is assessed according to the principles of effective business communication.

To determine if students have mastered some skills, however, less familiar forms of evaluation must be undertaken. For example, to assess the extent to which our students have mastered behavioral skills, we use oral exams at the midterm and end of our managerial behavior course. For those unfamiliar with this methodology, we recommend Lee, Adler, Hartwick, and Waters (1987-1988) as an excellent overview and discussion of validity issues in the oral exam process. In the Human Resources course that follows, students are assessed as they conduct mock job interviews with fellow students serving as applicants. They are also expected to display skill at screening candidate resumes in an "in basket"-type exercise.

We have found that providing a preview and behavioral model of what will occur in a nontraditional evaluation activity alleviates some of the tension and nervousness students experience. In fact, in our managerial behavior class we stage a "mock exam." After distributing the evaluation form used during the exam to the entire class, we ask for a volunteer to serve as our assessee. We then conduct an abbreviated exam, which serves as an example of what students can expect. The questions we ask are designed to simulate real business situations, in accord with Bigelow (1983). For example, one such question requires the student to respond with appropriate responses (i.e., following behavioral guidelines) to a situation involving a co-worker who habitually drives at excessive speeds in spite of repeated requests by carpoolers to slow down. Of course, our volunteer's grade is not affected by the performance on this practice exam. We also invite the class to use the evaluation form to assess the performance of the volunteer. This process helps build student confidence in the objectivity of the instructor's evaluation. Our grades have always been near the median of student-generated assessments.

The general reactions to oral exams have been mixed. The negative comments from students indicate that, despite our efforts to reduce stress, they still experience oral exams as anxiety-producing events. Given students' concern about grades and the novelty of oral evaluations, perhaps no other outcome should be expected. Our students also report positive comments, similar to those in Lee et al. (1987-1988). They find this nontraditional assessment to be very involving, lifelike, and "just what we really need." And, after all is said and done, a frequent comment made by students is that the exams are not nearly as bad as they had thought they would be. "So it goes with most of life," we reply.

The Resource Requirements of Skills Courses

Teaching skills courses is labor intensive and makes heavy resource demands on the department and on the instructor. Class size impinges on learning effectiveness more in a skills class than in other approaches to teaching OB or Management. Our experience indicates a class size of more than 30 students significantly diminishes course effectiveness. We believe that this is due to the necessity of establishing a coaching relationship with each student. In universities that have significant numbers of graduate teaching assistants (TA), coaching relationships may be developed with a TA in "lab" sections of a larger course. In schools where graduate students are not available, advanced undergraduate students may be used to provide a type of peer coaching. The effectiveness of these approaches is a function of how competent the TAs or peer tutors are at enacting the target skills and at coaching.

Second, skill-oriented classes limit the amount of material that can be covered. This is explained in part by the progression of learning that occurs when a particular content area is to be mastered at a behavioral level. Learning begins by developing an understanding of the relevant theory. This is followed by identification of the behavioral guidelines that stem from the theory. Students are then generally exposed to examples of appropriate and inappropriate behavior. Only then can students be given activities designed to enable them to practice the skill to be acquired. At times, more than one activity must be used to help students become proficient. All of this takes time and can result in the need for additional hours of course work if the curriculum has not been designed to strategically choose which learnings are to be mastered at a behavioral level.

The final resource issue is related to the evaluation process that is used in skill-oriented classes. Oral exams require significant amounts of faculty time to develop, conduct, and evaluate. For example, in our managerial behavior class we spend one hour with each student at midterm and one hour with each student during finals, when we conduct the oral exams. This process is exhausting, and we are limited in the number of sections of the course that we can physically handle.

These and other resource constraints may impede moving to develop a curriculumwide skill orientation. As long as schools of business allow central administrators to view them as the "cash cows" for the university, class sizes will continue to exceed those favorable to encouraging skill acquisition. Curriculum will continue to be condensed and presented in the most quickly transmitted form, and faculty will continue to use primarily evaluation mechanisms that can be electronically graded. While this analysis is grounded in a radical critique, it suggests that there is a significant price that must be paid if graduates of business programs are to enter the work force with the behavioral competencies expected of them by employers.

Conclusion

We began this chapter by suggesting that the movement toward management skills has "hit the wall" and that to break through, faculty needs to confront several issues of educational philosophy and pedagogy. To those who are interested in pursuing skill-based education, we hope that the discussion of these conceptual and operational issues has been helpful.

More important, we're convinced that business schools and our discipline are at a significant choice point. We would paraphrase the Porter and McKibbin title and ask, "What will happen to our nation? Will it be drift or thrust into the next century?" To continue our marathon analogy, the United States is in a very long, competitive global race. The stakes are very high indeed. Evidence is mounting rather rapidly that our discipline and our nation may have "hit the wall." This may be the time in history when we are witnessing a decline of the century of *Pax Americana,* of American hegemony and unprecedented global leadership. The rising ascendancy of a new economic order from across the Pacific (perhaps, *Pax Nipponica*) compels us to question the quality of American management—*and* management education.

We do not pretend for a moment that teaching managerial skills is any sort of panacea to help make business schools be more responsive to the business community, much less to address these fateful issues. We hope that the move to a greater emphasis on teaching skills in business programs can be seen as the logical extension of the maturing business disciplines. We also eagerly hope that by engaging in vigorous discussions about managerial competencies, our discipline will contribute to more effective management of the nation and its organizations.

Management competencies *may* help inspire us to reinvent what will constitute effective management instruction in the next century. The publication of this book and the formation of the Organizational Behavior Teaching Society task force are important first steps.

Notes

1. We use the terms *management skills* and *management competencies* interchangeably.

2. For a complete rationale of the skills chosen for this text, see Whetten and Cameron (1983) and Cameron and Whetten (1984).

3. An abbreviated summary of the outcomes we judged that management majors should master, as well as a brief description of the decision process, is listed in the Appendix.

Appendix: Abbreviate Summary of Curriculum Revision at Northern Kentucky University

The faculty generated lists of outcomes that should be accomplished by management majors. These micro-outcome statements were sorted into the following nine categories:

- Oral Communication Skills
  Formal Presentation Skills
  Interaction Skills
- Written Communication Skills
- Self-Management
  Intrapersonal Skills
  Professional Enhancement Skills
- Managing Others
- Managing Work Processes
- Information-Gathering Skills
- Technical Skills
- Critical Thinking Skills
- Knowledge of Management Theories and Frameworks

We then conducted a round-robin "audit" of the pedagogies and assessment techniques used in our current course work to determine if our present curriculum accomplished the desired outcomes. We share some of the findings here, to illustrate the gaps this systematic assessment revealed.

- Many of our classes require students to present a formal oral assignment, but we rarely "teach" how to do this.
- Interaction skills were taught in only one class.
- Despite the fact that many of our students come from noncollege family backgrounds, we do virtually nothing to socialize them into the world of professionals in business.
- We teach several courses that emphasize work process (i.e., "Management of Quality") but provide almost no opportunity to develop hands-on skill or assessment of performance in this domain.

Part II Approaches to Learning Managerial Skills

In earlier years, those interested in implementing an action skills program had few models to draw on. While skill training was going on in corporations, the corporate model typically required far more capital and personnel resources than are usually available in a university setting. Critics argued that a university was not designed to teach skills and that skills, by their nature, could not be taught in a university setting.

How can a skills program be designed so that it is viable in a university setting? What issues must be dealt with in doing so? This section presents six chapters that address these questions.

Chapters 2, 3, and 4 describe skills programs that have been implemented in universities. Though all are designed to increase participants' skills, they are quite different from one another in design. In Chapter 2, Dave Whetten and his colleagues describe the well-established BA 210 (Introduction to Management) skills course at the University of Illinois-Urbana in the hope that an exemplar will help others adopt such a course on a larger scale. In addition, they discuss the important issue of how to obtain faculty support for a skills program. In Chapter 3, Graham Elkin describes a skills program based on a group wilderness challenge pedagogy. He details the events leading to the program at the Otago University Business School (New Zealand) as well as its goals, current design, advantages, and disadvantages. In Chapter 4, William Ferris describes a humanistic approach to skill learning, involving classical readings, learning logs, and written communications. He describes the MAN 392 course (A Humanistic Approach to Leadership and Management) offered at Western New England College in Springfield, Massachussetts, and relates it to the American Assembly of Collegiate Schools of Business Skills and Personal Characteristics.

A primary issue in developing a skills program concerns pedagogy: What activities lead to increases in skill competence? Probably the most dominant pedagogy currently in use involves a skill-learning sequence something like the one described in Chapter 2: skill preassessment, learning, analysis, practice, and application. Chapters 3 and 4 describe programs that incorporate alternative pedagogies: a group wilderness experience and a more cognitive/holistic approach to skill learning.

Chapters 5 and 6 focus less on programmatic issues and more on alternative pedagogies that can be used in a skills program. In Chapter 5, Vicki Kaman and her colleagues propose that role plays with trained actors are an effective way to learn managerial skills. They describe how they develop such role plays, suggest why they are effective, and provide some guidelines for using "simulated reality" in the classroom. In Chapter 6, Joan Dahl suggests that some managerial skills can be developed using Interactive Personal Computer Cases (IPCCs). She describes her experiences in using IPCCs in a Principles of Management course at California State University-Northridge. In addition, she describes student responses to IPCCs, and the pros and cons of their use in teaching action skills.

A recurrent issue in skill program development concerns the capability of faculty members to teach the course effectively. David Bradford (1983b) pointed out that teaching managerial competencies requires more of the instructor than does a more traditional course and that there may be very few colleagues who have the requisite abilities to teach such a course effectively. In Chapter 7, Richard Boyatzis identifies an important prerequisite to faculty effectiveness: intent. He investigates the relationship between faculty intent and student skill learning, and discusses implications of his findings for the development of skills programs.

2 Bringing Management Skill Education Into the Mainstream

David A. Whetten

Deborah Lundberg Windes

Douglas R. May

Douglas Bookstaver

The diffusion of innovation literature describes several stages in the life cycle of a new idea (Daft, 1978). First, the idea is proposed by a champion. Second, the idea is picked up by a few loyal supporters. Third, the idea is diffused to a broad population of adopters. Fourth, the idea becomes institutionalized as standard practice.

Several individuals in our field have been championing the idea of management skill education for more than a decade. This book, devoted to the topic of management skills, seems an appropriate place in which to assess how far along the diffusion cycle this idea has progressed. It is also useful to assess the obstacles inhibiting broader dissemination of this idea and to examine an exemplar that has overcome many of those obstacles. The purposes of this chapter, then, are: first, take stock of how far the management skill education innovation has progressed; second, examine why MST appears to be stalled at stage two of the diffusion process; and third, describe efforts to institutionalize skills education as "standard practice" in our business school.

Current State of Management Skills Courses

During the Organizational Behavior Teaching Conference at the University of Southern California in 1978, participants were asked to vote on the "teaching philosophy of the future." The choices were: case studies, lecture/discussion, individualized instruction using computer technology, and management skill education. An overwhelming majority predicted that management skill education would become a leading, if not the dominant, form of management instruction during the next decade.

At that time this straw vote appeared to be a bellwether of an emerging revolution in management education. It coincided with an avalanche of scholarly and popular articles criticizing traditional business school education (Livingstone, 1971; Mintzberg, 1973) and the rapid proliferation of skill-based training materials in the corporate training market (Goldstein & Sorcher, 1974; Latham and Saari, 1979).

During the years following the conference, a great deal of attention has focused on adapting the skills approach to the business school classroom. Dozens of seminars have been conducted at various professional meetings and on numerous college campuses; special issues of journals have been devoted to the subject; an informal network of more than 100 faculty interested in this topic has been created; the American Assembly of Collegiate Schools of Business commissioned a large-scale investigation of competency-based instruction (AACSB, 1987); management skill development textbooks have been written (Robbins, 1988; Whetten & Cameron, 1984); research has been conducted on the impact of skill education (Burke & Day, 1986; McEvoy & Cragun, 1986); a variety of pedagogical articles have been written on the "how tos" of skill training (Cameron & Whetten, 1983; Waters, Adler, Poupart, & Hartwick, 1983; Whetten & Cameron, 1983); and the popular press has stressed the need for more relevant management education ("Caught," 1988; Steele, 1987; "The Money Chase," 1981). The continued currency of the skill education concept was demonstrated in the recent Porter and McKibbin study of business school education, commissioned by the AACSB and published in 1988. Based on their year-long investigation involving hundreds of interviews with business executives and business school faculty and administrators, these former business school deans concluded that management education was deficient in developing interpersonal and communication skills (Porter & McKibbin, 1988).

Given this impressive record of course development activity, coupled with an unflagging demand for its implementation, what has been the track record of this innovation thus far? Two sources of information provide a consistent, albeit impressionistic, answer to this question. An interesting pattern emerges from an analysis of the sales of the Whetten and Cameron (1984) textbook. During the 3 1/2-year period from 1986 to mid-1989, the book had been adopted at least once by more than 200 schools; however, only 42 of those adoptions involved orders of more than 100 books a year, and only 69 were in the 50-100 books per year range. Therefore, approximately one half of all the orders were for fewer than 50 copies per year. A representative of our publisher added a not-so-flattering qualitative perspective to these numbers by referring to the text as a "cult book": "It is taught primarily to small groups of students in courses isolated from the mainstream of the curriculum by 'zealots'—loyal converts who must continually defend the legitimacy of the course to the remainder of the traditional faculty."

Second, this assessment is consistent with responses to a brief survey sent to more than 100 faculty who had expressed interest in management skills. They report that the management skills course is typically taught as an advanced elective to a small number of students by a faculty member who feels strongly that this is a superior approach. The course is popular with students but perceived by many colleagues as too "soft." The following quotes support this conclusion: "I am really sold on the skills approach. How do I convince my colleagues?" "My students think the skills class is great. I just wish we could figure out how to expose more students to this experience." "I am having difficulty convincing other faculty that this is a legitimate course. They tend to brand anything that doesn't follow the traditional format as 'soft.' I'm convinced, my students are convinced, but the 'powers that be' aren't convinced. Any suggestions?"

Assuming these observations are reasonably accurate, several concerns bear discussion. First, although schools can point to a "token" skills class as evidence of their responsiveness to external critiques, the bulk of their students are not being impacted by the course. Second, teaching interpersonal skills as an elective generally amounts to "preaching to the converted," in the sense that students enrolling in electives are already sympathetic to the subject and possess above-average proficiency in content mastery. Third, although the merits of skill-oriented education are widely acknowledged, ignorance of its content and suspicion of its method undermine its credibility.

In brief, it appears that the skills approach to teaching management has established a beachhead in many business schools but is having difficulty getting off the beach. Responses to our survey suggest that there are five major obstacles to moving skill education into the mainstream of the management curriculum.

First, it is difficult to teach management skills in large sections, and most introductory Management or Organizational Behavior courses use this format. By definition, a skills course is built around student involvement, which is difficult to manage in a 300-person course.

Second, the course has the reputation of being inherently difficult to teach. This image inhibits acceptance by many faculty who are more comfortable with the traditional lecture/discussion format, which requires fewer personal risks.

Third, there are often conflicts between student expectations regarding appropriate requirements for a required course and the skill development philosophy. Most undergraduates tend to feel uncomfortable in courses that place heavy emphasis on participation, group work, role playing, outside application, self-reflection, and so forth.

Fourth, the course is often viewed as soft on content. It is sometimes confused with the highly experiential "touchy-feely" organizational behavior courses popular during the 1960s. Therefore, OB faculty members who are concerned about potential criticism from "more rigorous" departments may be slow to support a curriculum innovation that might erode their group's political base.

Fifth, there is a great deal of inertia behind the current approaches to teaching management. Irrespective of the merits of older versus newer approaches, older ones tend to persevere due to the institutional support from textbook publishers, course catalogue descriptions, teaching notes, student expectations, and so forth.

Teaching Management Skills as a Required Course

Given this daunting set of obstacles to bringing skill training into the mainstream of the management curriculum, one wonders if it is possible to teach management skills as a required course at a large business school. The primary purpose of this chapter is to share our experience in replacing the required Principles of Management course taught in a very large state university with a management skills course. We have 10 years' experience with this innovation that might be useful to others interested in following a similar path. Obviously, there are some peculiarities to our institution that make direct imitation inappropriate for dissimilar settings. However, even if our design cannot be replicated for a given application, the fact that we have been successful in making the switch may provide the necessary encouragement for other institutions to explore more compatible formats.

Our discussion will focus on course instruction, course design, course requirements, and gaining faculty support for the skills approach.

Course Instruction

Introduction to Management (BA 210) is taught by graduate teaching assistants (TAs) who are supervised by the course coordinator (a faculty member) and an assistant coordinator (an experienced TA). Currently, 750 to 800 students enroll in the course each semester, requiring that 20 sections of 36 to 40 students be scheduled. Ideally, class size would be restricted to 25 students, facilitating discussion and increasing accountability on the part of the students. Unfortunately, current space and budget restrictions necessitate a larger class size. Each section meets twice weekly for 90 minutes over a 16-week period.

A majority of the students enrolled are juniors and seniors majoring in Business Administration, Accounting, Economics, and other business-related fields. The course is required for these students but is also required or recommended for a variety of other majors across campus. The caliber of students is high—entrance into the above programs is highly competitive. The variety of backgrounds and interests, along with the competitiveness of the students, ensures lively class discussions and a high degree of participation.

Teaching assistants are selected from a pool of Organizational Behavior doctoral students and second-year MBA students. Three key characteristics are sought by the coordinator and assistant coordinator as they screen applicants. First, superior interpersonal and communication skills are essential. Because very little lecture takes place in the classroom, TAs must have the ability to lead discussions, direct role plays, facilitate small group exercises, and communicate one-on-one with their students. They must be able to "think on their feet" and respond to feedback from the class. They must be able to demonstrate the very skills that they are teaching, for example, supportive communication, motivation, and conflict resolution.

Second, management-related work experience is a significant asset. This experience serves two functions. First, the TA has experienced many of the hurdles to effective management and can therefore approach the subject as an active participant, rather than merely as an intellectual observer. Second, work experience provides the TA with a wealth of examples that demonstrate the importance of course topics. Our experience has shown that real-life, personal experiences are essential both in establishing the credibility of a TA and in communicating the validity of the course's message.

Third, it is highly desirable that the TA has had courses in Organizational Behavior at the graduate level and is, therefore, familiar with the theories behind effective management skills guidelines.

Successful applicants are hired in the spring before their initial fall semester of teaching. An orientation is held in April, during which they receive class materials and instructions on how to prepare over the summer. These instructions include reading assignments and an outline for the first 2 weeks of class. Because the class format is different from what most have experienced, new teaching assistants are teamed up with experienced TAs and are invited to visit the TA's classroom two or three times before the end of the semester. During at least one of these visits, they are given an opportunity to lead an exercise or discussion in the class. This exposure decreases the uncertainty of what will be expected of them in the fall.

During the week of fall registration, 4 days of teacher training are conducted by the course coordinator, assistant course coordinator, and a representative from a campus teacher training support unit, Instructional Management Services (IMS). After an in-depth discussion of course philosophy and expectations, much of the week is spent in hands-on experience with course material. The instructors are familiarized with the available teaching resources (e.g., videotapes and cases), and then effective classroom discussion, group exercises, and role plays are demonstrated by the training team. Basic teacher training, including classroom discipline, lesson-planning, and exam-writing, is also an important part of the orientation. At the end of the week, instructors participate in a videotaped "microteaching" exercise. They are given 5 minutes to instruct a class of their peers, using one of three exercises. Immediate feedback is given, and the videotape is reviewed at a later date with a representative of IMS.

Although much freedom is given to instructors in their design of lessons, support from, and accountability to, both coordinators and peers is stressed throughout their teaching experience. Meetings are held once a month to discuss classroom problems and successes. Instructors are encouraged to work together in planning discussions, exercises, and tests. Additionally, they are visited in the classroom at least once at the beginning of the term by either the assistant coordinator or an IMS representative and given feedback on their classroom performance. They are also videotaped a few weeks into the term and later observe and discuss this with IMS personnel. If problems occur past a normal adjustment period, additional classroom visits and videotaping are arranged.

Approximately 5 weeks into the term, students are given an opportunity to informally evaluate the course and their instructor. We request information on overall teaching and course experience, as well as on specific instructor strengths and weaknesses. The instructor and the assistant coordinator go over these evaluations, and steps are taken to strengthen weak areas. At the completion of the term, formal evaluations are requested of students, and the results are scored by the IMS office. Students whose scores are in the highest 25% of instructors across campus are rewarded with a published announcement of their accomplishment and letters of commendation, and they are given first choice of teaching times for the following term. The number of instructors from this course receiving this honor has been consistently high.

Over the years, we have developed a support system that involves the following commitment from our university. The course coordinator receives credit for teaching one course each semester for supervising BA 210. The associate course coordinator (an OB Ph.D. student) receives a quarter-time assistantship, and 20 TAs receive a quarter-time assistantship for teaching one section of the course. The campus teacher training support office (IMS) provides staff time for assisting with the initial training, videotaping the TAs, and conducting individual playback sessions. (These activities could be conducted by the course coordinator and assistant coordinator.) The department has purchased two sets of video equipment and has set aside two adjacent classrooms for the course. In addition, it has supported the purchase of several videos. A course development grant from the central university administration was used to fund the production of a series of video cases and several computerized applications.

Design of the Course

The course itself begins with a 2-week introductory period covering the teaching philosophy and an introduction to management skills. During this time, an attempt is made to use students' experiences to delineate important interpersonal skills and demonstrate their relevance for effective management practice. In addition, cases illustrating different, but

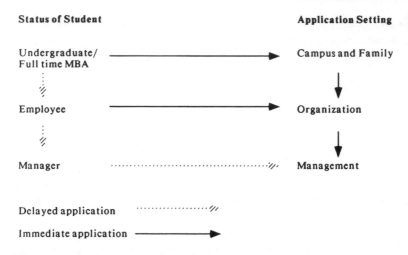

Figure 2.1. Alternative Skill Application "Paths"

equally effective, management styles are used to dispel suspicions that we are simply interested in behavioral mimicry. Also, Will Rogers' observation that "common sense ain't necessarily common practice" is used to stress treating the course as a semester-long management simulation.

Following this introduction, the remainder of the term is spent covering individual skills, with one week devoted to each skill. The textbook, *Developing Management Skills* (Whetten and Cameron, 1984), lays out eight skills deemed essential for effective management. Three weeks are spent covering individual-level topics—self-awareness, stress management, and creativity. An examination of the students' interpersonal orientation, how they manage stress, and their ability to think creatively are seen as essential to the development of effective managerial skills. Not only will these skills assist students in their individual work, but they also provide a baseline for examining students' performance in group and organization level situations. The course then focuses on six group-level topics: supportive communication, power and influence, motivation, delegation, conflict, and group processes.

The textbook approaches each skill area with a five-step learning model. First, a *Skill Preassessment* is given to increase students' awareness of their own skill level in a particular area. This is done in a number of ways, including questionnaires and role plays. Second, students are assigned reading from the *Skill Learning* section, which distills an extensive discussion of relevant theory and research into a set of behavioral guidelines. Third, *Skill Analysis,* through the use of written and videotaped cases

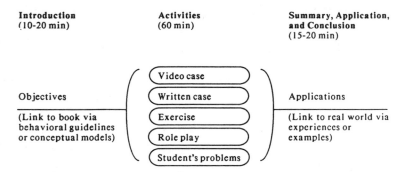

Figure 2.2. Lesson Planning Guide

as well as cases from the students' own experiences, has proven to be an effective way to draw material from the Skill Learning section into the "real world." The fourth step involves *Skill Practice.* In this section, students participate in activities and exercises in the classroom and then discuss how skills might be effectively applied within specific organizational settings. The last step is *Skill Application,* which involves taking what is learned in the classroom and applying it to situations at work or within other groups and organizations in which the student takes part. The purpose of this step is to encourage students to develop proficiency in an interpersonal skill long before they are given the title of manager. The merits of immediately applying skill development learning are shown in Figure 2.1. Students need to understand that just because management examples are used in the course doesn't mean that these interpersonal skills are only appropriate for management activities. The skills are equally applicable in other roles. And the sooner they become part of an individual's behavioral repertoire, the more likely it is that the person will become a manager, and the more effective he or she will perform in that role.

As stated earlier, much freedom is given to instructors as they plan daily activities. Instructors are given an abundance of resources to choose from and are encouraged to seek materials from other sources. Guidelines for the use of these resources are provided in order to maximize the students' learning experience. The outline for a typical class, shown in Figure 2.2, demonstrates this point. Given that two class periods are typically devoted to each skill, the instructor is encouraged to plan multiple learning activities that are complementary and mutually reinforcing.

At the beginning of class, the instructor first sets the stage, in terms of "Where have we been? Where are we going? How are we going to get there?" Second, the instructor focuses students' attention on a few of the behavioral guidelines in the Skill Learning section of the text that the instructor feels are most critical. When the instructor zeroes in on what he or she feels most strongly about, the message comes across as both urgent and relevant. Examples from the instructor's work experience, as well as from experiences students have shared, are integrated into this discussion.

At this point, the instructor moves into the learning activity. Although this can take a number of forms, we stress active student involvement. The following are among the instructor's alternatives:

Video Cases

These include both internally developed cases and those available from external sources. A video case series (Persimmon, Inc.), developed at the University of Illinois, follows the activities of individuals in two firms through their struggles with communication, delegation, motivation, power, and so on. Because it is closely aligned with the textbook, it has been a convenient and useful resource for instructors. Many external resources are also available through film distributors and public television.

Written Cases

There are an abundance of cases available to the instructors from the textbook itself and from magazines and resource books. And when the instructors have the skills, they write brief cases, drawing from their own experiences. We recommend having students read the case prior to class time, breaking them into small groups for discussion, and then bringing them together to compare notes and draw conclusions.

Exercises

These can take a variety of forms. Successful exercises include nego-tiation exercises when discussing power or conflict, "in-basket" problems when discussing decision making, and group development exercises.

Role Playing

This activity is strongly encouraged in this course. The purpose of role playing is to provide a relatively stress-free setting for students to practice newly learned skills. Many students express the opinion that the behav-ioral guidelines are common sense. However, what they quickly learn through role playing is that what may be intuitively obvious is quite often difficult to implement. Role playing provides an opportunity for them to practice supportive communication, conflict resolution, or motivational techniques before they are faced with a "make or break" situation in the workplace.

Role playing can take place either in small groups in the classroom or in front of the class. A typical format involves giving two people different roles to play, with a description of the situation (from the perspective of that role), and the motivations and background of the person each is playing. They are given time to prepare for these roles with the help of other class members. They are then paired with a person playing the opposite role, each being unfamiliar with the role of the other. An example may be a manager and a chronically late employee. The employee has reasons for his or her tardiness, which the manager is unaware of, and it is up to the manager to resolve the problem.

Although students often express some uneasiness with role playing at first, it has proven to be an invaluable learning tool. In a number of cases, students have chosen to have a role-play final exam in lieu of a written test. Former students have commented that what they retained from a role-play experience remained long after the rote knowledge of skill concepts had dissipated.

Students' Problems

An alternative learning activity draws upon the students' own experiences rather than the experiences of others. They are encouraged to relate concerns from their previous or current jobs, or student organizational leadership roles, to skill topics. Breaking up students into small groups and having them consult with one another on these problems brings them one step closer to practicing effective management skills.

When the learning activity is complete, class discussion should focus on the following questions: What have we learned? How does this relate to the key behavioral guidelines discussed at the beginning of class? Which of these were the most difficult to implement? Do we need to consider additional guidelines? How can we continue working toward developing effective management skills in this area? How can we take what we have learned and apply it to our everyday experiences?

Course Requirements and Evaluation Procedures

In Introduction to Management (BA 210), the philosophy underlying the evaluation of students' learning reflects the overall emphasis on the application of course material and behavioral change in students. To achieve these objectives, multiple forms of evaluation are used to test a variety of skills and abilities. All requirements are linked to analogues in real-life organizations. Written criteria are established for each requirement (including classroom participation), and all evaluations are reported, using the stated criteria. Our experience has been that students are much more willing to accept "subjective" ratings (e.g., evaluation of a group presentation) if it is clear that the process was systematic and consistent (i.e., criteria-based).

The requirements of the course involve four facets that help transfer the skills and knowledge involved in management: quizzes and a final exam, Skill Application exercises, classroom participation, and a group project.

Quizzes and Final Exam

Students are required to take four quizzes during the semester, which together account for 30% of the course grade. To maximize the amount of time instructors are able to spend in application-oriented activities in the classroom, students take quizzes over the text material *before* it is discussed in class (two chapters per quiz). While this may seem unusual, the text material is designed to be relatively straightforward. The quizzes then serve both a diagnostic function (identifying material that needs to be clarified in class) and an evaluative function (testing students' knowledge of the material).

The quiz format is also atypical: Quizzes are first taken individually and then in groups. This facilitates both evaluation of individuals' performance and acquainting students with group processes. When quizzes are administered, the quizzes and answer sheets are given to students individually. They are allowed 30 minutes to complete the 25 questions and turn in their individual answer sheets. Quiz groups of about five students each are then formed (either randomly or in advance). Groups are given one answer sheet each and are allowed another 30 minutes to respond to the same quiz questions. At the end of this process, student groups turn in their answer sheets, and the answers to the quiz are then reviewed. Students are given the remainder of the class to write appeals for any of the questions, using their text and a solid, logical argument. These appeals are taken into consideration when grading the quizzes. (For more information on this approach, see Michaelson, 1985).

In addition to the quizzes, a final examination, worth 15% of a student's course grade, is given at the end of the term. This 2-hour exam tests the students' ability to integrate and apply management skills principles to situations or cases. Some instructors choose to use role plays that are graded on criteria established prior to the exam.

Skill Application

The Skill Application exercises are designed to extend the classroom learning experience into real-life situations. To effectively use the skill application approach, instructors make the assignment after the students have covered the relevant reading material on their own and in class. Students acquire a better understanding of the material through the process of integrating it into their own lives.

A sample five-page skill application report might require students to first assess their current level of a management skill and then use this information to analyze how it might impact their effectiveness as a manager. For example, students in the course fill out assessment instruments about their own personal styles of gathering and processing information as well as their interpersonal orientations. Students are then required to analyze these findings with respect to their career goals and plans for future jobs. Through this exercise, students examine the match between their personal characteristics and their chosen career, and how their approach to problems and people might impact their success as managers.

Class Participation

Since this is a highly interactive practicum-style course, class attendance and participation are imperative. Students must be present and actively engaged in classroom activities to maximize their learning. Discussion formats vary from general classroom discussion, to small group activities, to dyadic debates. Class discussion is intended to first establish students' knowledge and comprehension of core ideas, and then proceed to higher levels of understanding involving analysis, synthesis, and application of ideas (Bloom, 1956). Classroom participation and attendance are worth 15% of a student's overall course grade. Classroom participation is evaluated daily, using a three-category system. Students with positive attitudes who contribute significantly to classroom discussion or voluntarily act as group leaders are typically given 2 points; students who attend class and contribute relatively little receive 1 point; those students who do not attend class or are detrimental to class activities receive 0 points. Midsemester feedback meetings are held between the TA and each student to review his or her classroom participation to date. Students are asked to come to the meeting with a self-evaluation of their own participation level.

Group Project

The purpose of the group project is, first, to familiarize students with managers and problems experienced in business organizations and, second, to have students experience and learn about group processes first hand. Since it is common practice in organizations to form work teams based on a specific interest area or expertise, this exercise is designed to facilitate effective group management skills through the tasks involved in the project. Each group in the class is responsible for one of the topics covered in the course and assumes the role of a consulting firm called in to solve a specific problem related to their topic in a real or mythical organization.

Groups are typically composed of four to five students who express interest in the particular subject area. The group uses information gained from required interviews with managers in organizations and from recent business periodicals to formulate their organizational "problem." Thus, the group is responsible for both the creation and solution of a typical problem in contemporary organizations.

Each group is required to make a 30-minute professional classroom presentation, which covers the background of the organization, a description of the problem, a proposed remedy, a proposed implementation plan, and a question and answer period. During the class period prior to their presentation, groups are required to submit a fact sheet, describing their organization and the problem to be addressed. A three- to five-page summary of the group's presentation is turned in the day of the presentation. This summary includes a detailed outline, a description of who performed which project activities, what sources (personal interviews and references) were used for their project, and a paragraph about what the students learned.

The group presentation, summary sheet, and fact sheet are worth 17.5% of a student's course grade. They are graded using criteria that cover both content and presentation style.

Gaining Faculty Support for a Required Skills Course

We are very fortunate to have strong support for the skills orientation at our institution. This is partly due to local history, but it is also to a large extent an outcome of our substantial and consistent efforts to gain legitimacy for the course.

At the time the senior author became interested in experimenting with a skills approach in the Introduction to Management course, there was a great deal of dissatisfaction among the OB faculty with the traditional "principles" approach, for the following reasons. First, there was a feeling that the principles themselves were intellectually flawed. Second, the students felt the highly theoretical orientation of the course was not very relevant or interesting. Third, the management principles textbooks were importing so much OB material that students complained about excessive overlap with the elective OB courses. Fourth, quite frankly, no one was interested in teaching a huge lecture course. Therefore, the proposal to experiment with something new was not opposed.

However, agreement to discontinue current practice does not guarantee acceptance of the proposed alternative. To build political support for the skills approach we have done the following: First, we collected research and anecdotal information about the value of the skills approach. We have found the Accounting faculty particularly supportive because their profession has been criticized by the public accounting firms for turning out technically proficient, but interpersonally deficient, students. We have made sure that interviews with prominent business executives, alumni, and respected faculty, as well as educational research, supporting this position are circulated widely. We also circulate AACSB material supporting competency-based education and make sure the Dean is aware of our efforts to contribute to this important dialogue.

Second, we have stressed the educational, versus training, aspects of the course. We have never used modeling videotapes in the classroom because they create the impression that skill development only involves behavioral mimicry. Instead, we emphasize that the course focuses both on behavioral principles and guidelines that are adapted by the students to their personality and specific organizational circumstances. We also stress that the course is using experiential learning in a deductive, rather than an inductive, mode. That is, rather than have students participate in an exercise and then lead a discussion about what they have learned about leadership or group dynamics, denovo, we tell students that decades of experience and research have demonstrated that certain approaches to interpersonal relations work better than others. Our purpose is to teach "correct principles," to give students ample opportunity to practice them in simulated business settings, then to help them use these principles to solve everyday problems. Our experience is that other faculty are comfortable with a deductive, application-oriented approach to teaching but are highly suspect of experiential activities as the genesis of inductive learning.

Third, we have discussed with colleagues the pedagogical foundations of the skill-development approach, emphasizing its merits. As shown in Table 2.1, the five-step learning model used in our course represents a hybrid of the best features of traditional educational and training approaches (Whetten & Cameron, 1983). The fact that our teaching philosophy and format are conceptually well grounded adds legitimacy and credibility to the course.

Table 2.1
Pedagogical Elements Comprising the Skills Approach to
Management Education

Pedagogical Tradition	Elements Adopted	Elements Discarded
Priniciples of Managment	Teach principles; encourage personalized adaptation.	Traditional list of "principles" which bear little relationship to management practice.
Behaviorial Science	Teach behavioral guidelines grounded in research.	Assumption that valid knowledge can be easily translated into effective practice by learner.
Experiential Learning	Hands-on, practical orientation to learning (learn by doing).	Inductive learning process in which students are asked to "discover" principles.
Behavioral Modeling (Supervisory Training)	Emphasis on practice as the key to behavioral change.	Emphasis on rote memorization and precise modeling of "one right way."

Fourth, we use a text that places a great deal of emphasis on conceptual content. The text provides legitimacy for the course by providing far more than a compilation of exercises and activities. In fact, some colleagues have used the text material (Skill Learning section) to teach complex subjects like motivation and power in a variety of educational settings (e.g., Executive MBA).

Fifth, we use some traditional forms of student evaluation. Although the philosophy of the course is more consistent with nontraditional course requirements (e.g., keeping a diary), our experience is that colleagues and students are more likely to view the course as a legitimate undergraduate educational experience if it utilizes traditional requirements (e.g., tests and papers).

Sixth, we publicize the success of the course by circulating high student ratings, favorable comments from graduates and recruiters, and so on. This is particularly relevant since TAs in general are criticized in the press as being poor teachers. Given that administrators are sensitive to the poor public image of TAs, they are pleased with a TA-taught course that produces consistently high student evaluations.

Seventh, we avoid criticizing other OB courses that use more conventional methods. We do not argue that all OB courses should be skill oriented. Indeed, we see the current curriculum mix as beneficial. We can advise the more theoretically oriented students in BA 210 to take upper-division OB courses, and students in these elective courses are less likely to complain about the discipline's lack of relevance, given their BA 210 experience. An interesting consequence of using the skills approach in the introductory course is that students expect a higher level of classroom involvement in OB electives.

Eighth, we assume responsibility for teaching Ph.D. students how to teach. Our course has evolved into an exemplary teacher development program that provides students with intensive instruction on educational methods, close supervision and support, and an opportunity to gain teaching experience in a course where the content is relatively structured but the teaching process requires them to develop advanced teaching skills. This takes the pressure off other faculty having to supervise TAs in upper-division courses, and it has substantially reduced the complaints from TAs about being put in a "sink or swim" teaching situation.

Finally, we have gained support for our format from departments outside the college. BA 210 is one of the most oversubscribed courses on campus. We like to believe that this is partly due to its good reputation among students, but we also recognize that it has much to do with program requirements in other departments. Many degree programs want students to have some exposure to the management curriculum, so they require the Introduction to Management course. It is very clear that faculty advisers in these user departments are pleased with the hands-on, highly practical approach in our general survey course and thus are strongly supportive of student participation.

Conclusion

We began our discussion by assessing the current status of management skill training as an educational innovation in American business schools. We argued that it is being taught as an elective course in most settings. Although this is obviously the easiest form of the innovation to manage, it is also the least effective, in terms of having a broad-scale impact on the undergraduate business student body. In an effort to understand why more schools have not incorporated the skills approach into their required courses, we examined several obstacles to achieving this level of institutionalization. Then we presented one approach for successfully overcoming those obstacles.

We recognize that it is difficult to generalize from one set of local conditions to another. What has worked for us may not be feasible at another university. Clearly, we were able to capitalize on some favorable circumstances: There were no local champions for the principles approach to teaching management, we had a tradition of using MBAs as TAs, there were instructional support personnel on campus who were experienced in designing teacher training programs. However, we hope that by sharing our "lessons learned" others who are interested in following our lead might benefit from some encouragement as well as practical ideas for removing obstacles in their path.

While it is obvious to all supporters of the skills approach to teaching management that offering it as an elective is superior to not providing the option at all, we hope it is equally obvious that what is good for 30 students is better for 300 (especially if 90% of those 300 will never take another Management/OB course). There are simply too many scholarly articles and research studies challenging the validity of the principles approach and demonstrating the utility of the skills approach to warrant any other conclusion. We are hopeful that our experience will motivate others to aggressively pursue the option of incorporating the skills approach into the mainstream of their management curriculum.

3 Executive Challenge: Using the Outdoors to Develop the Personal Action Skills of MBA Students

Graham Elkin

Organizational Behavior teachers are often concerned to allow students to develop knowledge skills and attitudes toward behavior at work. While OB can be seen as an academic study worthwhile in its own right, many teachers wish to encourage individuals to observe the situations they come across at work more keenly; to understand and explain them; to predict likely behavior; and then behave in such a way as to influence events.

OB courses stress the difficulties of predicting individual behavior in particular situations. However, many students of OB are interested in attempting to predict and influence the behavior of others. This desire is particularly strong in mid-career managers attending MBA programs. Many are strongly motivated by achievement at work and recognize that influencing others is a key determinant of success. One of the most common complaints of MBA students is that the intellectual understanding of theoretical models that partially explain some behavior is insufficient. In order to increase their personal chance of success, the development of personal and portable action skills is needed.

Models of organizational behavior often provide several levels of analysis. A common distinction is between the individual as an individual; the individual interacting with other individuals and small groups; and the whole organizational level of analysis. Robbins (1984) is but one example of this approach.

A process of learning is needed that will allow concrete experience, feedback, reflection, and experimentation if individuals are to develop

41

real world skill beyond mere knowledge and attitudes. Kolb and Fry (1975) popularized this view, variants of which still have great influence.

One process that can offer substantial benefits in managerial skill development in the interpersonal area and makes use of the Kolb model is "Executive Challenge." Executive Challenge is the use of experiential strategies in the outdoors. The experience of the Otago University Business School (New Zealand) suggests that the outdoor Executive Challenge has a useful place in the teaching of organizational behavior based action skills in MBA programs for executives. It has a number of other benefits too.

The Background of the Otago Development

Otago entered the outdoor classroom in 1986. There were two main reasons. First, there was a need to respond to a major learning process problem, which occurred with the entry of students who commenced the MBA program in 1984. Second, there was increasing dissatisfaction from graduates with the small amount their personal management action skills were being developed by the use of academic and technique-oriented learning strategies. Many technical skills and insights were being gained, but when it came to crucial personal skills—the skills for winning in the post-MBA world—many believed little changed as a result of the program.

The Learning Process Problem

A number of factors contributed to the learning process problem. One factor was the success of the program in attracting students who were very able intellectually and had substantial previous management experience. The average age of the 28 students admitted each year was around 34 years and the mean GMAT score 620.

A second factor was the existence of a "we must make it hard for them" view of the faculty. Each year more content was added to the papers, leading to very high volume output expectations.

This view, plus the attempt to complete the content of a 2-year program in 15 months, led to an expectation of very long hours, exhaustion, and social and family disruption. In many cases students could only cope through the rapid and effective development of the study group to which they were assigned. These long-term study groups were constructed by the school to maximize differences in the group in terms of age, national origin, experience, and type of person.

The third factor was the lack of any systematic orientation process or any integrating core courses or material. Many of the papers were taught with little reference to the material covered in the other papers. The synergy and synthesis were believed to come through the study groups.

Pressures grew and, as a result, the director of the program became heavily involved in remedial counseling, peacemaking, and group reconstruction efforts. Even with many hours of facilitation it was an explosive mix: gifted, articulate, and demanding students whose high expectations were not being met; growing demands for output; and no preparation or equipping to cope within the learning groups.

In 1984 an explosion took place. Very severe interpersonal and learning problems manifested themselves. These were both between and within study groups. In addition to this, the whole entry began to be divided by issues that were about individuals and learning processes, although they were sometimes couched in "content" terms.

One study group ceased to operate. It disbanded with great hostility. One member of the group, trained previously in educational psychology, made a number of damaging assertions about individual members of the MBA class and some individual members of the faculty. The claims centered upon the morality of the learning process and a claim that Pascales's (1985) model of socialization was being deliberately followed, including the generation of humiliating and stressful experiences. The student failed two quantitative papers at the height of the problems and began an academic and legal appeal process that led through all levels of university procedures and finally to the Governor General of New Zealand (as the representative of the Queen). He is the final court of appeal as the Visitor of the University.

The stress upon staff and students led to low levels of performance and the resignation of a member of staff from the teaching faculty of the MBA. It proved impossible to recreate any significant level of trust and openness with the particular entry to the program.

Clearly some action needed to be taken to ensure that subsequent groups of students entering the program developed the skills to manage the group-centered learning situation and the pressures within it. The skills required were very similar to the interpersonal and group skills needed to function well under pressure as the leader or a member of a management team in industry.

The Need for Skills

The second area of concern was a growing belief that MBA graduates were leaving with a wealth of knowledge, theoretical models, and techniques but little changed in terms of their personal management action skills. This was despite a 30-hour organizational behavior course being part of the first few months' work. It was a course in which many theoretical models were presented that should have offered explanations of the problems occurring.

A minor issue was the lack of any integrating mechanism to make the parts of the program more than the sum of the parts.

First Steps

A first step was to introduce a 3-day orientation program at the beginning of the MBA. The program covered a certain amount of administrative information. Apart from that information it concentrated on awareness of self and others, sensitivity to group dynamics, and skills in interpersonal communication and relationships. As part of the program, techniques of interaction analysis were introduced from Rackham (1971). Monitoring and feedback skills were practiced. Time was allowed in the first term for groups to examine their processes and way of operating.

The number of unplanned interventions by the director fell below that of the previous 2 years. Some of the planned review meetings with groups were used as OB teaching review sessions.

At the same time a program of physical activity was commenced for one hour per week, started on the whim of the MBA director and a friend in the physical education faculty as a fitness initiative. The one-hour sessions each week allowed students to take controlled risks, see one another in a new light, and struggle together toward real-life skills. Trust grew by experiencing support on a climbing wall or in a trampoline exercise. Fear and overcoming it became a worthwhile endeavor for some.

The overwhelming response from students was to want both the gym and classroom programs to become significant and mandatory parts of the MBA. Members of the faculty became aware that the level of commitment of students to one another and to learning reached a new level as the year proceeded. Although no causal connection could be demonstrated rigorously, enough of the faculty believed there to be a connection to pursue the issues further.

It had also become obvious that the work that had been initiated to help students study under pressure in divergent groups would be useful after completion of the MBA and could go some way toward meeting dissatisfaction with the lack of interpersonal skill development. The 8 hours devoted to the skills in orientation merely scratched the surface.

The First Executive Challenge

In 1986 provision was made for a three-day Executive Challenge program. Two events encouraged us. A member of the faculty had visited Camp Sargent, the Boston facility used for Executive Challenge. At the same time, a program was run with great success for the management team of a New Zealand pasta producer (Rae, Grant, & Pullar, 1984).

Academics in both the Business School and the School of Physical Education were skeptical about the whole development.

Objectives

There was a need both to sell the idea to colleagues and to ensure the participation of students. Time lags in university procedure precluded making participation compulsory, and in New Zealand it was a novel idea. These needs, and the need for the faculty involved to know what they were doing themselves, led to a great deal of discussion about what was desirable and possible in such a program. We had yet to discover the accounts in the literature of similar training events.

Perhaps the most important commitment made was to develop management skills using an outdoor environment and not to try to do a whole range of other things. In particular there was no desire to develop significant skills at outdoor pursuits. The outdoor activity was only as relevant as the building blocks in a classroom tower-building exercise. The important process is the learning about communication, leadership, oneself, and others, rather than developing skills in building towers.

Some of the programs offered aim to "take people to their limits and beyond." The program initiators were sure that was not their intention. Also in the minds of the designers was that the program should not merely be either a break from academic work or a half term break.

The basic desire was to simulate in an inclusive way some of the key skills and processes of management, and to do so in a way that engaged people's minds, bodies, and feelings in experiential learning.

For the first Executive Challenge the stated objectives were:

To develop personal and group awareness skills using a non-traditional environment. Among the areas to be explored are:

1. Coping with ambiguity, new experiences, and risk
2. The development of trust and supportive skills
3. Communication skills (in particular listening, feedback, and persuasive skills)
4. Group leadership and contributing skills
5. Decision making
6. Expressive skills

In many ways such imprecise statements are inadequate as objectives. Ignorance of what could be achieved and of the process meant that only a general idea of intention was possible. In hindsight, there were other unstated objectives. They had to do with developing a high level of cohesion within the class, encouraging identification with the MBA process and with the Otago Business School, and fostering the belief that cooperation was as important as competition.

The six objectives fall reasonably well into the typology of group problem solving, individual challenges requiring team support, and individual stretch management (including risk taking with support networks) that Long (1987) suggests.

Program Design and Content

The design reflected the traditional model of organization behavior, which was being used in the formal paper in that subject. Some exercises were individual and reflective; some focused on one-to-one issues, some on group processes, and others on task issues.

The choice of exercises depended upon a business school academic and a physical education specialist standing in a wet field, discussing what might be attempted to meet the objectives, bearing in mind the environment. Only one outdoor lodge was available, set in a valley between fir-covered slopes, complete with a confidence course and near a river for white water rafting. The activities chosen, together with their purposes, are in Table 3.1. We started with low-key ice-breaking activities and worked toward riding homemade rafts in rough water. Most other programs seem to follow that type of development, with a highlight at the end.

Table 3.1
Executive Challenge 1—Activities

DAY ONE

Afternoon

1. Competitive Group Activity
   — building a bridge over a stream with large poles and rope
   — an immediate activity to begin involvement in a physical task (ice-breaking as well)
   — staff and one member of each group provide some feedback, but willingness to talk the main objective

2. Touching and Trust Activities
   — trust falls, human knots, and people passing
   — becoming used to physical contact and trusting others

3. Group Problem Solving
   — a variety of tasks with 7-meter poles and inner tubes
   — systematic focusing on roles in groups and decisions

Evening.

1. Night Orienteering in Groups Using Compasses
   — communication, problem solving, trust, and support of less agile

2. Self-Awareness and Disclosure
   — indoor exercises involving self and other evaluation; giving and receiving feedback

DAY TWO

All Day

In smaller groups rotating between:

1. Use of Confidence Course
   a. sighted
   b. blindfolded
      — becoming comfortable with risk; fear and the unknown and developing more trust

2. Communication Exercises
   — blind and mute pairs; active listening

3. Problem Solving
   — focusing on decision processes

Evening

1. Values Clarification Exercise

DAY THREE

Building a raft from scrub and inner tubes. Transporting the group two miles through a gorge with some white water.
   — bringing together many of the previous elements in a memorable event to underline learning.

Program Implementation

There was only a very brief introduction to students leaving for the program. At the commencement of the program the facilitators were by no means certain that the students would cooperate, and the briefing was very limited. In the event they did.

It rained the whole time and was bitterly cold, but the program was completed. Physical safety was ensured by the presence of a skilled outdoor expert, and the facilitation was carried out, with some help, by the MBA director.

Results

It is often difficult to provide concrete evidence that management development has been successful. Springett (1987) came close to demonstrating that Executive Challenge programs are worthwhile. He reported that as a result of one program, 73% of sponsoring managers claimed significant achievements had resulted. In another example he quotes, 7 out of 12 members of an in-house program were promoted as a result within 12 months. The normal expectation was for 3 to be promoted.

Using reaction, learning, behavior at work, and organizational benefit as levels of evaluation, there was evidence that the first Otago program was a success.

Reaction was very positive from the participants. Evaluation forms completed 10 days after the event gave high positive feedback in terms of content, method, and usefulness. The opportunity for free-flow comment gave feedback that students were not preoccupied with the outdoor aspect. The chief things they valued were: "getting to know people," "seeing each other in a new light," "seeing everybody's strengths and weakness," and "learning about myself and how I relate to others." The activities chosen seem to have allowed the objectives to be reached.

The criticisms were constructive. There was consensus that the program was too late in the MBA process. It had been held in week 7 of the MBA. The issues needed to be addressed earlier in the course. The inadequate briefing was raised by a number of participants who expressed the view that they did not understand what it was all about before the event. If they had had more information, a number claimed, they would have done some preparatory self-evaluation before the program. More time was requested for unstructured reflection and also more facilitation throughout the challenge program.

Table 3.2
Unplanned Interventions in Support of Group Learning Process

Year	Number of Hours Intervention	Comment
1984	Very many	severe problems
1985	15	First orientation
1986	10	Exec.Chall. week 7
1987	4	Exec.Chall. week 3
1988	Insignificant	

At the level of learning, the only evidence are the remarks of the participants, the observations of faculty, and the improvements in task and group maintenance behaviors during the MBA program.

Better evidence is available concerning the transfer to the work situation and the benefits to the organization. During the year the number of times interventions were necessary by the MBA director fell again. Only two interventions were required after the Executive Challenge program. Both of these were in the study group where two members did not take part. Only 4 hours of intervention were required. Another 6 hours had been necessary prior to the challenge program, making 10 or so for the year. The previous year more than 15 hours were required. The year before more than 100 hours failed to achieve successful learning groups. In the following year (1987) the need for interventions fell again and in 1988 became insignificant. Table 3.2 shows the reduction.

Quality of learning was enhanced. Students achieved higher grades, and more MBAs with Distinction were awarded. The whole level of commitment seems to have been raised. The MBA director who ran the challenge program was also the Organization Behavior teacher. He reported a quantum leap in the perceived relevance of his classes and the application of theory to real life.

The Subsequent Executive Challenge Programs

The following years (1987 and 1988) saw a number of changes as a result of the experience of the first program: more structured preparation for students, further instruments for structuring feedback, and much more immediate facilitation during the program—after every exercise. Participants are also provided with formats to reflect on the experience before, during, and after the event.

The MBA program now begins the development of the skills in the orientation week and continues with one session per week and the Executive Challenge in week 3 or 4.

The level of commitment and effectiveness in group learning and whole class learning has remained high with no significant personal or process problems. In 1989 a new-style program was introduced with an integrating core of papers and personal development. Executive Challenge remains a significant part of that process and the development of action skills.

Advantages and Disadvantages of the Executive Challenge Approach

While it would be rash to suggest that cause and effect can be established between the introduction of Executive Challenge and the improvement in learning and reduction in process problems, the Otago experience encourages the view that the method has substantial advantages.

Advantages

1. It is real.

Perhaps the most significant advantage of Executive Challenge is that managers find it real. Cresswick (1979) finds:

> Managing an outdoor situation is like managing life. It is full of unpredictable events and people; a result has to be achieved and there are limited resources and time available . . . because the tasks are so different to normal work the underlying processes are laid bare.

2. It can turn theory into practice.

Mid-career students found the outdoor situation of the Otago experience real. The theoretical models from organization behavior were reinforced and made part of real life. This provides a challenge to the OB teacher when the models are questioned, and the difficulty of individual prediction is made real as well.

3. It is experiential.

Executive Challenge allows organizational behavior to be encountered with the whole person, mind, body, and emotions. The meaning of good communication, trust, leadership, and group dynamics is more fully experienced. The learning has a clear element of discovery by the individual.

4. It is leveling.

Everybody is placed on the same footing, and previous experience is unlikely to be helpful. All participants are faced with a challenge that cannot be ignored. They are forced to be vulnerable and open to others for support. Shared inadequacy overcome is a powerful producer of cohesiveness.

5. It builds transferable skills.

Skills can be built and not merely understanding, because experimentation, feedback, and practice are present. When the tasks are well selected, management skills can be practiced and developed that have good transferability to the workplace. Some of these skills are clearly not developed by traditional classroom methods.

Bhogal (1988) suggests that the key skill developed is a habit of analyzing experiences and self, which is a powerful assistance to exercising leadership at work.

6. It enhances the ability to learn.

Executive Challenge does not only allow personal management skills to be developed. The groups involved learn how to learn as a group. If groups are continuing as students they are able to learn together better. Obviously, in the organizational behavior field there are direct spin-offs in terms of content, but learning improves in other areas of subject matter.

Disadvantages

There are a number of disadvantages with Executive Challenge.

1. It may be misunderstood.

Using the outdoors for management teaching is often misunderstood. It can be seen either as forcing individuals to their limits in physical activity or as a Boy Scout activity.

2. It involves high risk.

It is a risky activity for both the facilitator and the participant. The risk ought not to lie in the physical environment, which can be safeguarded to a large extent. The risk lies in the vulnerability required by participants and in the unpredictability of people. The uncertain outcomes with exercises and programs lead to a high possibility of failure.

3. Failure can be very costly.

Failure can lead to the destruction of individual self-esteem, damage to the working groups involved, and even loss of life. Gahin (1988) records that from its beginning, outdoor training has been hampered by fatalities, injuries, illnesses, and dropout. He cites a wilderness expedition sponsored by a school in Oregon in 1987 in which 9 of the 11 participants were killed, and the other 2 severely injured; he also cites the death of five advertising executives rafting in British Columbia. Even with the mild, cautious programs run at Otago, two participants have broken ribs and one has broken a nose.

4. High-order skills are required.

The facilitation skills that are required are of a high order. Reacting to the unexpected and making learning out of the unforeseen in which individuals integrate theory and gain skills is a rare skill. The process of acquiring the skills in this environment takes time and great sensitivity.

5. Some programs can discriminate.

Programs that rely upon physical strength and fitness sometimes discriminate against women and those who are older.

Conclusion: Key Considerations

A number of things need to be considered in the use of the outdoors for teaching management skills either as part of an OB program or as an activity in its own right.

The *objectives* that are to be achieved need to be clear and related to the particular situation and not just the adoption of a standard package. The strategy of integrating the learning into the overall program and for encouraging transfer needs to be considered.

Facilitation is a key activity. Preparation by participants, reflection during the program, and facilitator inputs need to be well designed and concentrated on confidence building. Gall (1987) contends that facilitators must be skilled in organizational development, team building, organizational communication and dynamics, change management, and leadership development. The Otago experience suggests that such people are few and far between.

The *choice of physical activities* needs to be varied and appropriate. They need to be graphic, demonstrating cause and effect; unfamiliar, with no one an expert; fun, so that laughing together occurs; and involving some touching, which lowers barriers. Activities need to be flexible, allowing changes in the program to meet needs that arise during the process. They must also have a perception of risk and be achievable, resulting in success, not failure.

Safety needs to be a consideration—physical as well as psychological safety. Growth requires vulnerability, but challenges must allow growth, not demand quantum changes in people.

The experience at Otago suggests that the teaching of OB can be enhanced by the use of the outdoors. The teaching in areas such as learning and skill development, using a nonexperiential methodology, tends to make the content less believable. Executive Challenge has the characteristic of allowing OB and management skills to developed in an environment where the methodology enhances understanding by its nature. This account has been largely descriptive, and much more could be done to explore the ideas.

4 A Humanistic Approach to Leadership Skill-Building

William P. Ferris

In the past few years, much attention has been paid to the need for business schools to modify both their curricular and pedagogical approaches. We have not been educating our students with enough regard to competencies, self-image, skills, and personal characteristics (Boyatzis, 1982; Porter & McKibbin, 1988). We have failed to focus enough on ethics. We have lived in a domestic cocoon in the midst of a global environment. We have not sufficiently connected our theories with the real world—that is, engaged our students in applications, internships, and experiential learning. And according to our deans, our corporate friends and foes, and our colleagues, we have not integrated very well what we have attempted to teach. It is all well detailed in the Porter and McKibbin report (1988), and if you missed it there, you can read about it in any recent sampling of *The Wall Street Journal, Business Week,* or *Fortune.*

It should come, then, as no surprise that many, if not most, of us are in the midst of rethinking our curricula and how we deliver it. While no single course can remedy all wrongs, this chapter is written to report on a new course that tries to strike out in a somewhat different direction to supply at least a small part of what has been missing. It is called "A Humanistic Approach to Leadership and Management," and it has been taught on both the undergraduate and MBA levels for two years now.

The essential premise of the course is this: While the traditional management curriculum defines planning, organizing, motivating, and controlling in a series of chapters that turn into courses that refine those definitions, this course instead asks students how they would (should)

54

behave when placed in a variety of everyday leadership and management situations, calling for difficult decision making in front of and beside many impressionable and inquiring minds—those of their subordinates and their superiors. It uses a mix of three-fourths literature and one-fourth management theory readings as well as some film clips to provide guidance and stimulate reflection and discussion. (See Syllabus in the Appendix).

The Criticism

Before introducing the elements of the course, however, a brief review of the points from the Porter and McKibbin report that are salient to the current discussion is in order. In researching where American business school education is succeeding and failing, Porter and McKibbin surveyed and/or interviewed a sample of all the deans, placement directors, provosts, and other administrators of all 620 U.S. member schools of the AACSB, 10% of those schools' faculty members (approximately 2,800 faculty members contacted), and students and alumni of both BBA and MBA programs at the schools. More than 8,700 questionnaires alone were returned. Interviews were conducted at 50 different colleges and universities. Additionally, 1,692 executives from 958 *Fortune* companies and 281 non-*Fortune* companies were returned. One of the most dramatic findings among the results of this survey was that, with the exception of the faculty members, all groups feel decisively and overwhelmingly that we are emphasizing the quantitative side of our curricula far too much. Executives were especially staunch on this point. On the other hand, all groups, including the faculty, feel even more decisively that we are emphasizing the behavioral side far too little. For example, 66% to 72% of executives felt we are emphasizing the behavioral side too little, while only 4% to 9% felt we are emphasizing it too much. For purposes of this course, then, we are especially concerned with focusing on the particular areas of skills and personal characteristics (SAPC) requiring emphasis within the behavioral side.

The nine SAPCs appearing in the research are:

1. Analytical
2. Computer
3. Decision making
4. Initiative

5. Leadership/interpersonal
6. Oral communication
7. Planning/organizing
8. Risk taking
9. Written communication

Of these, all groups surveyed generally felt that B-schools are coming the closest to the proper emphasis on the analytical and computer SAPCs, while they are doing the most poorly in the other seven areas. The corporate view, represented only by vice presidents of human resources and managers of small businesses due to a need to keep the surveys short for other corporate groups, suggests that B-schools should spend more time on all nine of these SAPCs, but the most time on leadership/interpersonal skills, oral communication, and written communication, in that order. Interestingly, deans and faculty members agree that written and oral communication should be rated at the top, and they include analytical skills in the group, too. *But they have yet to understand the urgency of the business world's needs in the leadership/interpersonal skills area.* For deans, leadership/interpersonal skills are (a close) fourth, and for faculty members, a distant tie for fifth. This latter finding suggests that *faculty members, who are least likely to find themselves in a leadership position, have the least regard for the need for such skills and are the most out of touch with what the corporate world says it needs the most.*

The traditional academic research done by Boyatzis and his McBer associates found 19 types of competencies related to high performance (at various levels) among more than 2,000 managers studied in 41 different management jobs in 12 organizations (Boyatzis, 1982). These competencies break down into five clusters: Goal and Action Management, Leadership, Human Resource Management, Directing Subordinates, and Focus on Others. All five of these clusters contain elements of essentially the same characteristics that were of such concern to the respondents in Porter and McKibbin's report.

Clearly, we must begin to focus on these competencies, skills, and personal characteristics in a more direct and effective way at both the BBA and MBA level. We hope that a course such as "A Humanistic Approach to Leadership and Management" does exactly that.

A Cornucopia of Literature and Theory

Course readings are carefully integrated to cover leadership/management issues through dramatic or literary examples of such issues, followed by a management theory piece that relates directly to the issue(s) revealed. For example, Sophocles's *Antigone* is followed by Kelley's (1989) "In Praise of Followers" and Kouzes's (1989) "When Leadership Collides with Loyalty." Selections from Willa Cather's *O Pioneers!* and Golda Meir's *My Story* are followed by Virginia Schein's (1989) "Would Women Lead Differently?" Other works that have been read in their entirety in the course include Golding's *Lord of the Flies*, Wouk's *The Caine Mutiny*, Styron's *The Confessions of Nat Turner*, and the novel that culminates and integrates the whole undertaking, Adams's *Watership Down*. Selections are read from Melville's *Moby Dick*, Hemingway's *For Whom The Bell Tolls*, Marquand's *Point of No Return*, White's *View from the Fortieth Floor*, among many others. Historical and nonfiction accounts of leaders as varied as Pericles, Cochise, Churchill, General Patton, Mahatma Ghandi, Lyndon Johnson, Robert Moses, Martin Luther King, and many others are read. Management theory pieces read include articles and chapters by Bennis and Nanus (1985), Bradford and Cohen (1984), Conger and Kanungo (1987, 1988b), Reich (1984), Yukl (1989), and Zaleznik (1989a, 1989b), among others.

All the fictional readings are selected to reveal something about leadership and management. Some works of literature commonly associated with business courses—for example, Lewis's *Babbitt*, Vonnegut's *Player Piano*, and Miller's *Death of a Salesman*,—are not read because they shed little light, except perhaps in a very oblique way (e.g., the scene in which Howard fires Willie in *Death of a Salesman*), on the main focus of this particular course, which is not business in literature, but rather what it takes to be a humanistic leader and manager. Of course, what it may take is always the subject of much debate, but in the interests of getting started, the course focuses on the very skills and personal characteristics identified by the AACSB (1987), highlighted in the Porter and McKibbin report and largely derived from Boyatzis's research on the competent manager that have been previously mentioned. At the same time, it uses Bradford and Cohen's concept of the "post-heroic" developmental manager for a philosophical underpinning.

Learning Logs and Scenarios in the Service of Skill-Building

The course uses some variations on the journal and the oral presentation to help students approach skill-building. For example, instead of defining *proactivity* and exhorting students to be proactive rather than reactive in their future management styles, this course requires them to write out in their "learning logs" exactly which initiatives they would expect them-selves to take in given situations. These logs are kept for the purpose of allowing students to reflect on their possible alternative courses of action in various difficult management situations. Situations described can be imminent and real or they can be imagined as realistic future possibilities. Regardless, students are expected to develop a "canon" of principles to follow, deriving from their best consideration of these alternatives. The hope is that such an exercise helps them consider the proper course for an imminent situation or prepares them so that when they are later unexpect-edly thrust into some of the very situations they are writing about, they will have less chance of doing something precipitous that they might later regret. They will have already considered whether they should lie to their subordinates, for example, or under what conditions, if any, "omitting the truth," would be acceptable. Or, in a more sophisticated vein, they will have a clearer idea of how to approach such seldom-discussed issues as what kinds of rules and policies they should avoid making for their subordinates, or what is the difference between inconsistency and intelli-gent reversal of the rules. This kind of analysis precipitates discussion of effective decision making and risk taking as well.

Another example may make the point. Classes often become obsessed with such question as: Can a manager maintain the same kind of friendship with his or her "best friend" if that best friend has just become his or her subordinate? In what ways does the new work relationship necessarily affect the friendship, if at all? Should the manager ever confide in any subordinate? Should managers allow a subordinate to confide in them? And if so, what kind of information would be an acceptable confidence? Discussions can rage over such questions, questions students don't usually consider, even in Organizational Behavior courses. In this course, they must write out answers and scenarios as to how they will behave in their learning logs as well as in papers that make reference to their readings. Part-time graduate students may get an opportunity to act out their scenarios for real at their full-time jobs, while full-time undergraduates may have the opportunity to do so in their part-time jobs. After a little encouragement, both are happy to report to the class on their results. The subject has been inspired by their class reading of a novelette by Joseph Conrad titled *The Secret Sharer*. Later, the class gets into the deeper subject of that work: In what ways must one know oneself to take command?

Creative oral presentations offer students another avenue for approach-ing the business of learning how to behave as effective managers. The presentations require them to script and act out "management dilemma" scenarios suggested in fictional and biographical works taken from a reading list rich with examples of failed or successful leadership. Students are provided with a guide to effective presentations in advance and are required to lead a short discussion of the major leadership questions they think they have raised following their presentations. This course assignment requires definite risk taking from normally reserved graduate students. Undergraduates have fewer inhibitions but still see themselves as being in a clearly risk-taking mode. The benefits are large, though: that students will actually practice thinking out some initiatives that they could see themselves undertaking and, in the presentations, actually take some of these initiatives in a "pretend" or "laboratory" setting. Then, when a similar scenario occurs in their postgraduate (or present) managerial lives, they will have already considered the possible responses; they will start from a much broader understanding of possible implications than one might normally expect from a B-school graduate. The whole approach represents a small insurance policy against every manager's biggest fear—surprise.

Now it might be of value to describe some recent examples of the highly creative scenarios of which students are capable. In one presentation, two students read Tip O'Neill's recent book, *Man of the House*. One took the role of Tip, complete with powdered hair, cigar, and a pillow under his disheveled suit, while the other brought the props to play several roles in rapid-fire succession—Presidents Kennedy and Johnson, Congressman Edward Boland, author-collaborator William Novak, and wife Millie O'Neill. Their 30-minute skit divided into eight vignettes, in which they were able to make eight separate points about the nature of effective leadership. Shirtboards with the points succinctly summarized in marking pen appeared on the chalk rail as each skit ended. The presentation culminated with an overhead projection of some further points. Following the presentation, students ran a discussion on points raised. In another presentation, Winston Churchill, complete with cane, tailcoat, and top hat, was interviewed on "television" by a "BBC reporter," who affected a brash reportorial tone of voice and a strong British accent from beginning to end. The Larry King format was used, with viewers calling in with tough questions for Winston (read from cards held in the reporter's hand). One volume of Martin Gilbert's biography of Churchill was brought to life in a very unusual way. We have also had "Donahue," "Oprah Winfrey," and several original skits which sought only to replicate the concepts from books read, rather than the actual material in the books themselves. The students who put on these presentations and run the discussions after them demonstrate great initiative and risk taking in doing so. And they gain self-confidence from their successes. In one oral presentation, which they will remember long after they graduate from their programs, they have discovered that initiative and risk taking pay off. We have covered three of the SAPCs directly in a new way.

It certainly is not to be assumed, though, that we feel that we need do nothing more in this regard to help develop these SAPCs. While no other oral presentations are required in the course, students will continue to mull over initiative and risk taking as they read about countless literary and historical figures who have taken some dramatic initiatives and risks. Additionally, they will see and discuss films and film clips that portray such leaders, for example, the CBS film clip containing biographical information and the "I have a dream" speech of Martin Luther King or clips from such movies as *Stand and Deliver, Moby Dick,* and *The Caine Mutiny.* Finally, we will read topical theoretical material, such as some of the articles contained in Conger and Kanungo (1988a) on characteristics of charismatic leadership.

At this point, a word on preparation may well be in order. Students do have an opportunity to practice oral expression skills prior to engaging in their scenarios. Much classwork involves small groups dealing with difficult questions concerning the readings and then reporting the results to the group. Some examples are: "What key leadership behavior omissions prevented Ralph from becoming an effective leader in *Lord of the Flies*?" or "Construct some present-day managerial analogies to Ahab's dismissal of the captain of the *Rachel*'s request for help in favor of continuing his pursuit of Moby Dick," or "In what ways does Alexandra Bergson's leadership style in *O Pioneers!* suggest dilemmas of leadership still present for women leaders in American business today?" Considered responses to these questions must be presented by groups to the class as a whole following small group discussions and considerations of the relevant issue. These responses both stimulate large group discussion and constitute the first practice to the oral presentations of the second half of the semester. A formal midsemester participation evaluation is also in place to help students with oral communication skills.

Additional Skill Building in Written Communication

In addition to the learning logs required of each student in this course, written communication includes a weekly quiz, consisting of one comprehensive short essay question, as well as three papers handed in during the semester. The goal of the essay question quiz is twofold: to require students to demonstrate that they have done the reading and to compel them to associate some key issue relevant to leadership to that reading. Sample quiz questions include: "Provide specific examples of how Creon made it difficult to be a good follower in his kingdom" (after reading *Antigone* and Kelley's "In Praise of Followers"). "Compare the leadership skills of Pericles and Churchill" (after selections from Thucydides and Gilbert). "Discuss charismatic characteristics of Captain Ahab" (after selections from *Moby Dick* and an article by Conger and Kanungo (1987) on behavioral aspects of charisma). Topics chosen by students for their papers have included: "How the American Indian Chiefs used Bennis' Four Leadership Strategies" (after reading selections from Dee Brown's *Bury My Heart at Wounded Knee* and Bennis and Nanus); "Why Vision is Not Enough" (after reading Styron's *Confessions of Nat Turner*); "Ralph and Jack—A Comparison of Leadership Failures" (after reading Golding's *Lord of the Flies*). Papers are saved to diskettes, and rewriting is encouraged where necessary; formal written communication is a skill easily studied in the course.

Answering the Criticism Through a Humanistic Approach

It has already been suggested how some of the SAPCs are encouraged in the course—how leadership, initiative, and risk taking are studied in literature and encouraged in oral presentations and how written communication is practiced through the papers and essay quizzes. But what exactly is it that makes this approach to skill-building a *humanistic* one?

It may have been noticed that nowhere so far in this description of the course has mention been made of contingency leadership, situational leadership, task and relationship orientations, managerial grid, and so on. The course does not take a traditional or historical social science approach to the subject. Certainly, important terms such as *Theory X/Theory Y* or *initiating structure* and *consideration behavior* come up in discussion or readings, but they are not studied per se. Instead, the course tries to focus on the situations and dilemmas attendant to the task of being an effective leader and manager by using a deductive approach. What has worked in novels? What has worked in history? What has failed, and why? Can we find some management theory that will confirm or enhance our understanding of the answers to these questions? It is concerned with leadership and management on a very basic level—what is power, why do I need it, how do I get it, how do I maintain it, and how do I use it for good (the inevitable ethical perspective)? It begins on a microscopic level, but it moves to a macroscopic one in a vicariously experiential way. We read about successful and failed leadership, and we identify with the leaders and managers or with the followers. Either way, this identification helps us develop our SAPCs in a manner unavailable in courses using more traditional techniques.

The course, then, is *humanistic* in that it uses fiction, biography, drama, film, and even current events to examine the subject of leadership in human groups. It is eclectic in its perspective, hoping to recall the humanism of the Renaissance in spirit. It is a humanities-oriented approach, using readings from the arts as a centerpiece, readings from the social sciences for refocus and direction.

Some valuable by-products result from the use of such an approach. While the study of ethics in business is not expressly covered in the course, the subject comes up every day in connection with the discussion of effective leaders whose goals are/were destructive, of "negative" charisma, and of the "right" course to chart out of any of hundreds of managerial dilemmas. It is a major interest of the learning logs. Another valuable by-product comes in students' new appreciation of the value of the liberal arts, specifically drama and literature, in helping one become a better businessperson. Students who never understood the relevance of Greek drama, for example, want to argue endlessly over where loyalty should stop and disobedience begin in Creon's kingdom, a subject continued rather neatly in their reading about Captain Queeg and his concept of "constructive loyalty" in *The Caine Mutiny*. Thus, the course becomes humanistic in one more way. Students learn the value of approaching leadership with due respect for man's humanity to man; consideration behavior can become instilled at the emotional level that made great literature great in the first place.

Finally, the course helps students integrate concepts learned in management classes not just with the rest of the business curriculum, as the Porter and McKibbin report calls for, but also with their readings from their English, history, psychology, sociology, and anthropology classes. It is a kind of integration that may go beyond what we have envisioned for our curricula in the past, but not beyond what our colleagues in the school of arts and science and in the upper levels of corporate America have envisioned. It says that taking arts and sciences courses in the first 2 years of college and business courses in the second 2 is not good enough by itself to make certain our education is complete. The two curricula should meet in ways that prove they are really parts of the same educational purpose—preparing us for life after the university. This course is one such meeting ground.

Student Response to the Course

But deans will say: "Who on my faculty can teach such a course? You have to have a degree in English or the humanities." *The people who can teach such a course are any of those from the business faculty who have the interest.* We management faculty have never had trouble reading extensive cases featuring difficult problems in organizational behavior and presenting them to students for analysis. The idea in this course has never been to approach the literary works from the point of view of style or literary history. Any literary techniques or devices that can be pointed out may be a bonus to the students but are in no way required for purposes of the types of analysis being done in the management classroom. In fact, it may well be that *only* management professors, who are trained in identifying, understanding, and presenting the management theory that goes with the reading of the artistic and historic literature of this course, could effectively discuss the scenes, actions, and behaviors depicted in the books read and films watched in connection with that professional literature.

Finally, what do students say? So far, I have presented this course twice to undergraduates and once to graduate students. It has scored in the high 90th percentiles on the majority of categories of the Student Instructional Report, notably the following:

- overall value of this course to me
- my interest in the subject area has been stimulated
- overall value of class discussions
- overall rating of the course readings
- challenging questions or problems were raised for discussion

One fascinating descriptive statistic is that half the students who took the undergraduate courses self-reported GPAs of between 2.0 and 2.5, which would put them in the bottom third of their college class. One might wait a long time to see such students sign up for an upperclass elective requiring readings by Sophocles, Thucydides, Melville, Conrad, among others, in more traditional courses.

Written "general comments" were entirely laudatory, with many undergraduates saying it should be required of all business majors: "It teaches the student to think more creatively and more freely," "More courses of this format are needed here," "This class taught me a different way to think and look at things I've read and learn from them," "I have learned a great deal about how to 'see' the alternatives to a situation, from both the leaders' and subordinates' points of view. I think this should be a required course for all management majors," "I enjoyed this course more than any other of my college courses. I would like to see more of these types of courses, especially in the field of management," "This course examines management in a more real-world sense than all my previous management classes," "Helped me to open my mind and analyze different situations and prepare myself on how I would handle them in the future," "The way all of the readings related to leadership gives a whole new outlook on fiction," and "I took this class because I thought it would help me with management skills. It did just that."

Graduate student comments have been in much the same vein: "Has heightened my interest in reading," "Has made me more aware of my work environment," "At first I felt intimidated by the readings but now I enjoy them," and "*Very* stimulating—will help in my dealings with other employees and as a manager." The only negative comments have concerned the amount of reading—150 to 200 pages per week.

Conclusion

For management professors who like to read eclectically and see connections from what they read to their professional interests, this approach to management curriculum and pedagogy will reinvigorate their teaching. For corporate and academic followers of the Porter and McKibbin report and other treatises either directly or indirectly arguing for the necessity of a management action skills approach, it covers some of the bases they feel are left untouched. For students, it seems to fill a void identified in our curriculum and bring a subject formerly resident mostly in some rather dry textbooks out into each student's own special spotlight for examination. In fact, the introduction that students get to some excellent primary management theory sources in their reading from professional journals and monographs in this course should help them bridge the gap from assigned textbook reading to finding their own counsel in primary professional sources as they travel through the business world.

Nevertheless, the single greatest benefit may well remain students' discovery of new perspectives in connecting great literature to the specific behaviors they will contemplate and undertake in their professional lives. It is both instructive and gratifying to see them anxiously racing through our great books, some of them over 600 pages long, in search of help with their questions on how to manage better. After all, fiction, nonfiction, and film are much more likely than our textbooks to be their curriculum after college. If they have identified and practiced the concepts and skills of leadership and management revealed in that curriculum in college, then they are much more likely to make the connection to effective demonstration of such skills in their careers.

Appendix: Syllabus—Undergraduate Course

MAN 392—A Humanistic Approach
to Leadership and Management

This course uses literature and film to arrive at a better understanding of how effective leadership and management occur. We will read mainly fiction and nonfiction examples of both effective and ineffective leadership in action to help us form a clear idea of the elements crucial to success, not only in the initiation of good leadership, but also in maintaining the organization or organizational unit following the leader's tenure. Our readings will also include some management theory selections as background. All readings will be available through the college duplicating service or in paperback. Leadership style self-surveys taken at the beginning and end of the course will seek to measure any changes in students' understanding and attitudes in attempting leadership and management initiatives of their own.

Objectives

1. To introduce students to the value of literature—especially fiction, critical biography, and autobiography—in helping them to be better managers and leaders.
2. To assist students to the realization that management and leadership situations occur both within and outside a business context and that the same principles of good practice apply in all such situations.
3. To encourage students to connect management and leadership theories to their own lives, using examples from literature as an intermediary step.

The course divides into five sections:

I.   Introduction and Definitions (Weeks 1-2)
II.   Attaining the Power to Lead (Weeks 3-8)
III. Maintaining Power (Weeks 8-9)
IV.   Managing for Achievement (Weeks 10-12)
V.   Assuring Organizational Continuity (Weeks 13-15)

Fiction and nonfiction readings, usually book excerpts, will be assigned weekly for each subtopic. Management readings and film excerpts will be interspersed as well. Quizzes, "learning logs," 3 short papers, and a short presentation with a classmate will form the basis for grading. Classes will be held seminar style.

I. Introduction and Definitions

Week 1: Introduction; The American Manager: the Popular View; The American Manager as Hero
Assignment: Yukl, Ch. 4; Bradford and Cohen, Ch. 3; Begin *Lord of the Flies*; *Contemporary Issues in Leadership* (Part 1 sel.)
Week 2: The Developmental Manager
To Be Discussed: *Lord of the Flies*; Yukl; Bradford and Cohen; *I Heard the Owl Call My Name* sel.

II. Attaining Power

Week 3: Position Power; Formal and Informal Power Compared
To Be Discussed: *The Secret Sharer*; Yukl, Ch. 2
Week 4: Referent Power ("charisma")
To Be Discussed: *Lord of the Flies*; *Confessions of Nat Turner* sel.; *Moby Dick* sel.; Yukl, Ch. 10; *Bury My Heart at Wounded Knee* sel.; *CIL* (Part 2)
Week 5: The Importance of Vision
To Be Discussed: Bennis sel.; *View from the Fortieth Floor* sel.; *O Pioneers!* sel.; *CIL* Article 12 and Part 4 sel.
Week 6: Expert Power
To Be Discussed: *For Whom the Bell Tolls* sel.; *War as I Knew It* (Patton) sel.; *Power Broker* sel.
Week 7: Other Types of Power: Coercive, Association, Informational, and others. "Manipulation"
To Be Discussed: *The Years of Lyndon Johnson: The Path to Power* sel.; *The Caine Mutiny* sel.; *Point of No Return* sel.
Week 8: Other Types of Power (cont.)
To Be Discussed: *Antigone*; *Single Pebble* sel.

III. Maintaining Power

Week 9: Communicator of Meaning; Persuader
To Be Discussed: *Complete Writings of Thucydides* sel.; Bennis; Gilbert and Manchester sel. from Winston Churchill biog.

IV. Managing for Achievement

Week 10: Motivator
To Be Discussed: *Moby Dick* sel.; Begin *Watership Down*; Bradford and Cohen, Ch. 5 (opt.).

Week 11: Organizer
  To Be Discussed: *Watership Down*; *My Life* (Golda Meir); Bradford and
  Cohen, Ch. 7.
Week 12: Teambuilder
  To Be Discussed: *Watership Down*; Bradford and Cohen; Reich article,
  "Entrepreneurship Reconsidered: The Team as Hero"

V. Assuring Continuity

Week 13: Empowerer
  To Be Discussed: *Watership Down*; article on empowerment: Conger and
  Kanungo, "The Empowerment Process: Integrating Theory and Practice"
Week 14: Guardian, Transformer, and Translator of the Organizational Culture
  To Be Discussed: *Watership Down*; Peters or Deal and Kennedy; *Something
  Happened* sel.
Week 15: Tying It All Together
  To Be Discussed: Yukl, ch. 12; *CIL* sel.; entire reading list

Notes: Weekly quizzes will be given. One may be missed due to absence,
or the lowest grade dropped at student's discretion. There will be no
make-ups. The first paper will be due the 5th week, the second will be due
the 10th week, and the third will be due the last week. Papers will be typed
and will not be expected to exceed five pages. Students will sign up for
presentations during the first three classes. Presentations will be given at
the rate of no more than one per week and will last no more than 25
minutes, including 15-minute class discussion of points raised. The
instructor will clarify the format of papers, learning logs, and presentations in advance and will supply a reading list from which presentation
books may be chosen. Perfect attendance will be worth 20 points, with 5
points off for each class missed. Coming in late or leaving early will result
in partial credit. There will be no exams.

Personal Grade Record—MAN 392

Name			Semester		Date	
		Max	Me		**Grade**	**Schedule**
I. Three Short Papers					A :	>280
					A–	270
	paper 1 **(10/5)**	30				
					B+:	260
	paper 2 **(11/2)**	30			B :	250
					B–:	240
	paper 3 **(11/30)**	30				
					C+:	230
II. Oral Project		40			C :	220
					C–:	210
III. Essay Quizzes (<1 page)						
					D+:	200
Quiz	1	5			D :	180
	2	5				
	3	5			F :	<180
	4	5				
	5	5				
	6	5			**Notes**	
	7	5				
	8	5				
	9	5				
	10	5				
	11	5				
	12	5				
	13	5				
	14	5				
IV. Learning Logs						
	Week 4 **(9/28)**	25				
	Week 14 **(12/14)**	30				
V. Participation						
	Week 7	15				
	Week 14	15				
VI. Attendance		20				
Total		300				

Learning Logs

What is a Learning Log? Have you ever kept a journal or a diary about your personal life? If you did, you may remember jotting down entries any time of day, as the mood struck you or you just felt moved by an insight or a memory or an idea. You really didn't care if the words written were grammatically correct or spelled properly. The main idea was to feel free to write down an idea or a thought.

Learning Logs operate in much the same way as diaries or journals, except they try to capture your ideas or insights on a particular topic and then put them into a particular format. The ideas as the author develops them become a little more refined and developed.

Your topic for this course's Learning Logs is:

What questions can I raise about good/effective leadership and management? What leadership dilemmas can I foresee before they might happen to me? In other words, can I visualize myself caught in the same kind of crises as some of the fictional (and real) leaders and managers? If so, how should I act now that I have the benefit of foresight? Given the time to ponder the best responses to such difficult situations, what do I think would be the best course of action?

In this course, you will read about leaders who rose to extraordinary heights of leadership and some who fell flat on their faces. What can you do to make sure your chances are best for rising rather than falling?

I would suggest topic headings like the following for parts of your log:

- Moral Dilemmas of Leadership (e.g., should you ever violate the confidence of a subordinate? If so, when?)
- Analogues (e.g., The situation of X in command of his ship is analogous to me as chairman of the such and such committee, or to that of my father as patriarch of the family.)
- Leadership Behavior Questions (e.g., Question: Is it okay to try to pursue friendship with a subordinate to as complete a degree as you might pursue friendship with a "peer"? Answer: X's attempt to do this ruined him. I can't think of anything he could have done differently. Maybe the highest form of friendship is not possible with a subordinate. Therefore, maybe I should consider trying to cultivate my very best friends away from work.)

You will pass in your Learning Logs twice during the semester, as noted. They should contain references from all nontheory readings. Their length is up to you. Don't worry about grammar.

5 Creating Realistic Interactions Using Actor-Enhanced Role Plays

Vicki S. Kaman

Cynthia Bentson

Waldo R. Jones

Training of managerial action skills must be based on an understanding of what managers *do*. Managers make requests to their superiors, diagnose problems with employees, talk to difficult and important customers, negotiate with groups of workers, and explain discrepancies to regulatory agencies. Managers must be able to come across to others as assertive, understanding, confident, calm, enthusiastic, receptive, quick, thoughtful . . . and so on during the continuous, planned and unplanned, long and short, face-to-face interactions that they experience during a typical working day. Operating managers, as well as management students, recognize the importance of "people skills" to management competence and are asking that their education and training include more practice in these skills (Porter & McKibbin, 1988).

Role-playing techniques are often used to diagnose interactive skills, to provide models and practice, and to motivate individuals to pay more attention to their interpersonal impact (Milroy, 1982; Wexley & Latham, 1981; Wohlking, 1976). Some limitations of role-playing as an attitude and behavior change technique have been discussed (Kidron, 1977), but the technique is popular and is widely used by teachers and trainers in both academia and industry. Although the effectiveness of more complex behavior modeling techniques using role-playing has been researched

71

(Wexley & Latham, 1981), there is a lack of new suggestions on how to enhance role-playing itself. We are convinced that an interdisciplinary approach to role-playing, which includes involvement of trained actors, is one way to both enhance and better understand the effectiveness of certain role-playing applications.

Actor-Enhanced Role Plays

During several years of work with role-play simulations in assessment centers (Bentson & Kaman, 1989; Kaman & Bentson, 1988), we have learned that there are logical reasons derived from learning principles, research on role-playing, and acting theory to support the employment of trained actors in creating realistic and engaging role-play situations. When assessing candidate skills for the job of a city personnel director, for example, two trained actors, contacted through the local professional theater group, played the roles of two informal employee representatives who were threatening to unionize labor-trades employees. Candidates, who had been given the chance to prepare a negotiation strategy, were brought face-to-face with the actor-employees, who not only skillfully attempted to manipulate the candidate-personnel directors but also argued with each other. Other roles for which we have employed trained actors include those of opinionated supervisors who will not cooperate with colleagues, distressed police officers who inappropriately handle volatile citizens (also actors), and valuable employees who are unhappy with their jobs. Participants in these actor-enhanced role-play situations have found them to be so real and engaging that we have named the role plays "Simulated Realities" (Bentson & Kaman, 1989).

Recently, we recognized the potential for creating similar realistic situations for management training or, in select situations, for the college classroom. In the first author's graduate Organization Development (OD) class, for example, it was desirable to give students some realistic practice interviewing managers before sending them out to test their skills with local business people. The instructor worked with the actor to create the role of a manager who wanted help, but who was defensive; alluded to problems, but who then claimed they had been solved; believed in modern management principles, but who did not basically value his employees. The actor-manager came to the class fully prepared to discuss his business and realistically communicated his desire to obtain some quick suggestions on how to boost productivity. Three teams of three to four students interviewed the manager in order to conduct a preliminary diagnosis of management issues and recommend whether OD strategies could be useful. The next class session was spent diagnosing the manager and organization and discussing how to improve OD interviewing skills.

During a third class period, half the class wrote their versions of how the "manager" would give feedback to his employees, while the other half wrote dialogue for their feedback to the manager. This process, adapted from Argyris (1982), revealed that the students' feedback to the manager was parental, self-serving, did not communicate real understanding, and was likely to elicit defensiveness. The students' approach to giving feedback was, to everyone's amazement, very similar to the approach they felt would be used by the "Theory X" manager they had interviewed. It then also became evident to the class that they had not communicated understanding and had elicited defensiveness from the "real" manager during their interviews. The entire process provided a relatively safe but very dramatic demonstration of how even those of us who know better often interact in ineffective ways. Subsequent discussions dealt with the difficulties and skills involved with effective interactions and regularly referenced specific parts of the meeting with the actor-manager to illustrate important points.

How Actor-Enhanced Role Plays Are Developed

1. A Relevant Situation Is Defined

Actor-enhanced role plays should represent the critical, relevant, and complex aspects of situations that are likely to be faced by the managers or managers-to-be. In academic settings (e.g., a graduate program in business), ideas might come from case studies that are normally used in class, the instructor's insights into management work, students' observations and work experiences, or lists of competencies that serve as course objectives (Bigelow, 1983). In a corporate training situation, a critical-incident-based task analysis (Wexley & Latham, 1981) of management jobs is used to determine both the skills to be elicited in the role play and the critical attributes of the situation in which that skill must be performed (Kaman & Bentson, 1988).

2. Background Material Is Written

A trained actor aiming to create a complete, live character for an enhanced role play will need more than the usual couple of paragraphs of background information given in most role-play exercises. Our background materials look more like novelettes than exercise instructions and include information such as where and when the characters were born, where they went to school, what their family and work history has been, whom they like and dislike, as well as the standard information on how they got to the situation to be role-played. Writing out this information helps us, the creators and users of the role-play exercise, to clarify what our training objectives are as we not only think through the questions and reactions that our participants are likely to have but also anticipate what behaviors they will have the opportunity to demonstrate.

While detailed information must be provided to the actors, the background information given the student or trainee varies, depending on the exercise. Some exercises require the ability to incorporate detailed information (a strategic planning meeting, for example), whereas others (e.g., dealing with a customer in the participant's own company) would be handled with very little preparation in real life. The aim of these enhanced role plays is to have the participant play him or herself so that, once the situation is defined, the participant draws from his or her own experience and skills during the interaction.

3. Actor and Creator Work Together

An effective actor will need some time to flesh out the character in his or her own mind and rehearse the character to develop a consistent presentation of the character's desired attributes. At the very least, actors need to "talk through" the scenario with the exercise developer. A full-blown rehearsal, with a couple of "trial" participants going through the exercise, is extremely helpful with more complex scenarios.

These dry runs help clarify what is expected from both actor and participant. First, the actor must understand what the objectives of the exercise are. A proficient improvisational actor will create opportunities for all participants to demonstrate the target knowledge or skills. If sensitivity to a subtle employee problem is appropriate, for example, the actor may give several cues to his situation when the participant does not pick up on the first one. The rehearsal allows the actor to develop several scripted lines, which are inserted appropriately each time the scene is played. It also allows the actor to assess how far to push a participant and to anticipate possible participant responses. In a negotiation role play, for example, the actor may be asked to give in on some points if the participant genuinely listens and considers the actor's point of view.

Why Actor-Enhanced Role Plays Are Effective

1. They Are Realistic and Involving

It is easy to understand why role plays, despite their requirements for active participation, often elicit only limited involvement (Kidron, 1977). Class participants are asked to interact with colleagues, who, they know, have been given limited information on the background of a situation and, possibly, are playing someone very different from themselves. Participants playing managers know that they must limit their actions and questions to issues contained in the predefined situation. A student role-playing a manager in class, for example, knows that the role-played employee will have trouble answering questions about years of experience with the company or plans for the future when this information has not been given in advance.

Trained actors, however, know how to take their own experiences, regardless of whether these experiences are directly related to the scenario at hand, and draw from them to create a real person who matches the role-play scenario but with significantly more depth and breadth than a set of role-play instructions can provide. The depth comes from the actor's ability to create a real character, using his or her own real experiences and real emotions. Actors are trained to tap their inner resources to create a character who is different from their everyday selves and, yet, who is genuine (Bates, 1987; Carnovsky & Sander, 1984). The actor's ability to interact as a genuine person, along with the capability of improvising within the defined parameters of the role play, engages participants so that the self-conscious, artificial behaviors we often see in role plays are replaced by involved, genuine behaviors by the participant.

We have also found that most trained actors are very capable of quickly generating "factual" material that they may need during a role-play situation. They can either provide credible information based on their own experiences and preparation or quickly change the focus of the situation from the unknown facts to something more relevant. We have seen actors, for example, quickly generate the name and job title of hypothetical employees or offer to bring budgetary figures to a manager later in the day.

2. Actors Provide Immediate Feedback

Feedback is an essential component of any well-designed training program (Wexley & Latham, 1981). Role-play exercises typically provide summary feedback for the trainee or student via observations by class-mates or instructors, which are given after the situation has been played to completion (Wohlking, 1976). Trained actors provide feedback throughout the exercise, which is immediate and which the participant is highly motivated to attend to, since it provides clues about how to behave in the here and now. An actor selects and experiences those emotions that are appropriate for the character and the situation. Since the actor's emotional responses are real, the character's verbal and nonverbal behavior come across as real (Bates, 1987). Although these reactions cannot be specifically scripted, an effective actor portrays a real person and behaves consistently as that character. If the "manager" behaves in a way that would be calming to a distressed employee, the actor will be visibly calmer than before the calming management behavior. If the participant-manager behaves in a way that would anger the actor-employee, the trained actor will give clues reflecting the anger he feels, while maintaining the behavior of a realistic employee, who is afraid to express anger directly at the "boss." This immediate, realistic feedback can inspire participants to try out new behavior during the exercise and receive additional feedback on their success.

To be successful, actors develop a heightened sensitivity to both their own and others' reactions and feelings. We have found that trained actors provide very useful feedback to participants after a role-play exercise because they can clearly describe how specific participant behavior affected them. Actors may point out, for example, that a participant's tone of voice made them feel intimidated, or that they did not believe that their "manager" would follow through with a commitment. The actor's feedback can add an important new dimension to the feedback based on observations of the instructor and classmates.

3. Actors Provide Consistency for Practice

Trained actors working on the development of a role-play exercise will ask a lot of questions about the individual they are about to "play." They want not only to establish the background facts about the situation and character but also to understand who the person is and how he or she is likely to behave in any situation. Consistency in a trained actor's role play comes from the fact that the actor becomes a genuine person and no longer needs a script to know how that person will think, feel, and act. This consistency is essential if role plays are to be used for skill practice. Ideally, participants will have the opportunity to consider their performance feedback and then manage the role-play situation again, with increased competence. A trained improvisational actor will change responses to match the participant's increased competency.

4. Perceptions of Game-Playing Are Minimized

One explanation for the underutilization of simulations is that participation seems more like playing than work, and the training process seems trivial (Jacobs & Baum, 1987). Participation in many role-play exercises does seem like a game when an individual steps in and out of a role or "burlesques" a role (Wohlking, 1976). The game-playing quality of many exercises can serve as a protective mechanism for the participant, the trainer, and any amateur role players who act to create a scenario. Students or trainees can see the exercise as a game that does not reflect their true abilities. Administrators and role players respect the "right" of the participant not to have to reveal his/her inner self and to be protected from a potentially threatening situation.

The actor's training, however, emphasizes control (Bates, 1987; Carnovsky & Sander, 1984), and a trained actor can push a participant enough to force real involvement and real reactions without overly damaging the participant's self-esteem and motivation to continue skill improvement. For example, a trained actor can play a difficult person subtly (e.g., by being sarcastic or by using nonverbal signs of arrogance), which allows the participant a choice in deciding which aspects of the situation to deal with. The actor's control, however, does not allow the difficult aspects to go away, and an effective actor can persist until the participant feels ready to confront the anxiety-producing difficulties. A trained actor can actively push the participant "manager" by behavior such as arguing, screaming, and being very assertive, but will know when the participant has reached a level of discomfort beyond which pushing will suppress, rather than elicit, appropriate behavior. Effective improvisational acting includes knowing when to end or change a situation if it is not progressing. Of course, a class climate conducive to trust, adequate preparation, and use of constructive feedback by the class and instructor will still be important to the ethics and success of role-play-based training (Wohlking, 1976).

5. Participants Have the Opportunity to Improvise

While effective role plays must not stray far from the training objectives (Wohlking, 1976), attitude and behavior changes resulting from role plays are more likely if participants become involved, can genuinely consider the issues involved in the situation (Kidron, 1977), and have the opportunity to improvise, based on their own choices to participate in the exercise (Goldstein & Sorcher, 1974; Kidron, 1977). It is difficult to improvise and use varied behavior when you must accommodate the limited capabilities of a role-playing classmate. When role-play participants are fully involved in a realistic situation with a trained actor, they have no choice other than to behave genuinely themselves and must improvise, using their own knowledge and skills, to handle an immediate situation that has fully engaged their attention.

Using Simulated Realities in the Classroom

Working with and watching trained actors can be a tremendous amount of fun, but there are some important issues to consider, both philosophical and practical, before implementing actor-enhanced role plays in the classroom.

1. Select Appropriate Applications

These role-play simulations require more effort and usually cost more than less sophisticated techniques and are not an appropriate choice for every learning situation calling for a role-play exercise. For our most recent OD class role play, the instructor spent about three hours developing the character with the actor and arranged for an honorarium of $75 for the 1 hour and 15 minute class appearance. When a role play is used to stimulate discussion or to clarify issues (Milroy, 1982), using student role players seems perfectly appropriate. Similarly, most students have enough information and experience to serve as the basis for an exercise designed to demonstrate and allow practice of a specific skill, such as active listening. (See, for example, Lau and Shani's [1988] coaching and goal-setting exercise, #27, p. 323).

Actor-enhanced role plays are most effective when individuals are learning to deal with complex situations, which, like the realities of management life, require that a variety of management skills be effectively integrated and applied at the same time (Bigelow, 1983). In the OD class exercise involving interviews of an actor-manager described above, for example, the trained actor was able to realistically portray much of the typically experienced verbal and nonverbal defensive managerial behavior in a more engaging way than a student role player would have done, and in a shorter time period than the experience with a real manager would have required. Employment of the actor also allowed the class to practice interviewing skills with much less risk of embarrassment (for both the students and the business college) than if a real manager had been invited to class.

2. Consider the Ethics of Deception

In a teaching or training situation, it is possible to successfully convince participants that they are interacting with an individual who really is the person being portrayed by the actor. In the OD simulation described above, for example, graduate management students were told that a manager was coming to visit with the class, and they believed throughout the role-play exercise that the stranger in the class was really a manager and company owner. While student motivation to meet with the manager was very high, debriefing was particularly important, especially since students had concerns about their ability to help someone who had spent time talking with them. We believe that a temporary deception is okay, if justified by the learning opportunity and if students are properly debriefed. We suggest both debriefing as soon as possible after the role play and discussing the benefits of using trained actors. In our experience, students were relieved to find out that they had been practicing in a "safe" situation and appreciated the realism of the simulation.

3. Obtain Resources Creatively

Most business colleges probably don't have funds specified in the budget for actors—yet. Some department chairs and deans might find actors' fees to be an unconventional classroom expense. A rationale that may work is to consider whether funds are used for expenses such as videotape rental, speakers, or field trips. The learning opportunity offered by a trained actor who is effectively used is certainly as great as that offered by the other resources. Many trained actors welcome the opportunity to do improvisational performing and, while effective acting is work deserving compensation, the opportunity offered the actor can be part of the compensation package.

Regardless of whether funds are available, there is always a possibility for collegial reciprocity. Most universities have theater departments that may appreciate the opportunity for their students to learn about applications of their skills in the business world. Community theater groups are another good resource. Often, trained actors in these groups have jobs outside the theater and many experiences that can help them portray realistic business interactions. The opportunity to combine their acting skills with their other job experiences can be very appealing. An additional suggestion is to find out whether anyone within your class or among your faculty has acting skills and to ask whether he or she would like to work with you to create a simulation. Another alternative is for you or a department resource person to obtain some training so that your classes can benefit from some more engaging role-play scenarios.

4. Make the Most of Each Simulated Reality

Since much effort must go into the planning of the scenarios we call Simulated Realities, it makes sense to reuse successful scenes and make the most of any enacted situation. Actors are trained to be consistent as they replay the same character, so they will not mind repeating the same scenario with several students or for several class sessions. Since the scenarios are complex and realistic, situations do not lose their impact when students who have observed others have an opportunity to interact with the actor. Trained improvisational actors are also able to continue portraying the same real person through a sequence of related events while different students take over a managerial role, for example. Videotaping capabilities further enhance the usefulness of a simulation. The videotape can be shown to participants when discussing their performance, so that they see and hear their behavior, rather than rely on faulty or biased memories. Videotapes can also be used to illustrate effective and ineffective approaches to subsequent classes who do not have the opportunity to role play themselves.

Conclusion

Actor-enhanced role plays offer the opportunity to create very realistic, engaging, standardized situations so that students can experience organizational realities and practice management skills within the relatively safe confines of the classroom. Those who implement these exercises in their classes can expect to gain a thorough understanding of their own teaching objectives and of management interactions as they both work closely with trained actors to define their expectations and work with students to analyze the events that unfold. They can expect to obtain a different perspective on human behavior, as they have the opportunity to predict what will happen in a structured, yet natural, interpersonal situation. And they can expect to gain a new appreciation for the acting discipline and perhaps even consider the possibility that acting skills might be useful for managers themselves.

Student participants typically are impressed with the actor's ability to elicit real reactions and real involvement from them but can also be disappointed with their performance in complex interactions. It is important that they be given both the opportunity to discuss simulated events and the opportunity to improve and feel competent. Ideally, they will be able to replay their interactions more effectively or, at least, they will be able to discuss how to improve and practice new skills. Students who observe their peers interacting with trained actors will be attentive and can learn much about observation and feedback skills. Providing guidance and coaching observers is an important role for the teacher or facilitator.

Teachers, students, and actors have the opportunity to learn more about themselves and the nature of human interaction at work. As with most learning, not all that we find out is fun. Students may find that they are not as competent as they want to be, teachers may find that they can't handle every interaction effectively themselves, and actors may find that improvisational acting is tough work. The costs and risks of simulated realities indicate that they should be used sparingly and only when there is enough time and energy for adequate preparation, analysis, and debriefing. A manager's interpersonal skills, however, are an essential aspect of his or her effectiveness. Realistic opportunities to diagnose and practice these skills are valuable tools for developing needed competencies.

6 The Application of Interactive Personal Computer Cases to Teaching Managerial Action Skills

Joan G. Dahl

We are currently in the midst of the age of the personal computer (PC). PCs have caused a revolution in management education across the country. PC labs are now a common fixture of the business school environment. Course outlines, homework assignments, and entire curricula have been affected by PCs (Render, 1985). Initially, PCs were used extensively in quantitatively oriented courses such as statistics, operations research, and accounting (Render, 1985). Courses in Management and Organizational Behavior have used a variety of PC-based computer applications. Bigelow (1986) reports PC programs used in OB classes as personal assessment tools to determine stress levels or personal learning style. He also discusses what was, in 1986, a promising new development in personal computer applications for the management classroom, interactive personal computer cases (IPCCs).

Interactive personal computer cases seek to develop diagnostic and application skills, action skills that are essential to effective management. Boyatzis (1982) demonstrated the importance of diagnostic and application skills in a study involving more than 2,000 managers from both public and private organizations. He identified "Diagnostic Use of Concepts" as an action skill that is significantly related to effective managerial performance and serves to distinguish superior performers from poor performers. The Diagnostic Use of Concepts skill involves the diagnosis of a situation to enable an effective response through the application of appropriate theories or models. The opportunity to sharpen this skill is, in essence, what IPPCs are designed to do. They provide the student with the experience of having to "live with" the managerial decisions they make. The cases themselves rest on a series of decision points, with each decision changing the subsequent situations or alternatives given to the student. Students must diagnose the needs of the situation and apply course material to arrive at a solution. Diagnostic and application skills are sharpened through coaching provided by the computer whenever the response given is suboptimal. Unlike the conventional cases that are often used in management and organizational behavior courses, interactive personal computer cases provide students with direct and instant feedback as to how well they diagnosed and dealt with the situations presented.

Interactive personal computer cases have been available commercially since 1988. To date, little has been written about the use of this type of case in management and organizational behavior courses. This chapter reports my experience with IPCCs in Principles of Management courses. First, student responses to IPPCs are examined. Then, the advantages and limitations of using IPCCs in teaching diagnostic and application skills are discussed.

Student Responses to Interactive Computer Cases

A total of 61 college business students enrolled in an upper-division Principles of Management course completed interactive personal computer cases as a class requirement. They worked on the IPCCs outside of class, either in one of the university's personal computer labs or on their own personal computers at home. The interactive personal computer cases chosen for the course required dealing with situations covering a variety of topics, such as planning, motivation, and group dynamics. Successful resolution of a case depended upon the student's diagnostic and application skills. At the end of the term, with the professor absent, students completed an anonymous questionnaire in which they were asked to assess their overall experience using the IPCCs and the extent to which they felt the cases provided a valuable learning experience. Completion of the questionnaire was strictly voluntary.

Questionnaire Measures

On 5-point Likert scales, students rated several different aspects of their interactive personal computer case experience over the term. The first measure asked to what extent they felt the cases provided a challenge to apply the material they had learned in the course. Next they assessed the extent to which they found the IPCCs to be a valuable learning experience, as compared to the rest of their learning experience in the course. To obtain a measure of the extent to which they found working on the IPCCs an enjoyable experience, the students were asked to rate how much "fun" the cases were (assuming any homework assignments could be considered fun). Two measures assessed frustration in completing the computer assignments. The first dealt with frustration arising from disagreement with what the computer gave as an optimal answer. This was used to indicate the extent to which creativity in applying course material was felt to be thwarted by the computer's supplying an "optimal" answer. The second assessment of "frustration" sought to determine the extent to which equipment failure or technical problems were encountered in running the IPCCs on the computer.

Results and Commentary

Means, standard deviations, and frequency distributions were computed for all the questionnaire variables. Intercorrelations were calculated to determine the relationships among the questionnaire variables. The results reveal an overall student reaction to the interactive personal computer cases that was quite positive in nature. Students found the cases to be an interesting and involving experience. The data indicate few problems were encountered in the mechanics of running the cases on the computer. Frequency distributions show the extent to which students found the cases to be a valuable experience. Means, standard deviations, and highlights from the frequency distributions for the variables are presented in Table 6.1. Intercorrelations are given in Table 6.2. The results are discussed below.

Means, Standard Deviations, and Frequencies

The mean for the first measure, the extent to which the cases were a challenge to apply course material, was 3.43 with a standard deviation of .98. This is interpreted to mean that to some extent the cases required the use of application skills. It is interesting to note that 47.5% of the students felt the cases required the use of application skills to a great extent or a very great extent. Only 14.8% of the respondents overall felt the cases provided little challenge to utilize their application skills. This response

Table 6.1
Means, Standard Deviations, and Frequency Distribution Highlights

	Mean	*SD*	*% ≥ 4*
Application Challenge	3.43	.98	47.5
IPCCs A Valuable Learning Experience	3.73	.94	60.6
IPCCs Were Fun	3.43	1.05	49.2
Frustrating, Didn't Agree w/IPCCs	2.40	.98	11.4
Frustrating, Problems w/Running IPCCs	1.60	.85	3.3

Scale: 1 = to no extent; 2 = to little extent; 3 = to some extent; 4 = to a great extent; 5 = to a very great extent.

could perhaps be attributable to a belief that the cases were not reflective of course materials, thus required little use of application skills. As this was an introductory course, an alternate explanation may be that these students' diagnostic and application skills were insufficient to allow them to see the relevance of the cases to the course materials.

The IPCCs were felt to be to a valuable learning experience by the majority of the students. Nearly 61% reported ratings of 4 or higher, indicating "a learning experience to a great or very great extent." The mean for this variable was 3.73 with a standard deviation of .94. Conversations with students indicated they gained new insights and felt their diagnostic skills were sharpened through the use of the interactive personal computer cases. The immediate feedback helped them to identify weaknesses in their application skills and conceptual areas where additional study was warranted. Fully 82% of the students reported having fun to some extent with the cases. Nearly half of the respondents (49.2%) rated the cases as fun "to a great or very great extent." The mean for this variable was 3.43. As an aside, while it is not necessary that students have any fun when learning diagnostic skills, application skills, or any skills (for that matter), a strong case could be made linking greater enjoyment of an activity with greater motivation. For the professor, greater motivation on the part of the students often results in the class being more enjoyable to teach.

Students, on the whole, didn't seem to feel stifled by the computer's supplying the "optimal" answer to each of the situations presented in the case. The mean for this variable (frustration because of nonagreement with the computer) was only 2.4. Only 11.4% of the respondents reported frustration to a great or very great extent. Apparently, the students did not find the learning experience diminished by being provided with a "right" answer, even if they did not agree that it was correct. However, it should be noted that this finding could be due in part to the introductory nature of the course.

One possible problem of any skill-teaching method that is equipment dependent is obviously tied to equipment failure. The final measure of the questionnaire sought to determine the extent to which equipment failure or technical problems running the IPPCs detracted from the overall experience. Students were asked to rate the extent to which they were frustrated due to computer problems. This was of special concern since several of the students completed the IPCCs on their own computers at home, as opposed to the supervised personal computer labs on campus where trained technicians were readily available. Only 3.3% of the students reported great or very great frustration in using the computer cases. The mean (1.6) for this variable indicates few problems were encountered by the students. The results for this variable could be attributable to a combination of factors. The university's personal computer labs are staffed with highly trained technicians who are extremely competent in a variety of different software applications. Additionally, the students in the Principles of Management and Organizational Behavior courses tend to be a computer-literate group due to prerequisite courses involving computer work that they encounter early in their university careers.

Intercorrelations

Not too surprisingly, some of the variables were significantly intercorrelated. Students who felt the IPCCs provided a challenge to utilize their application skills also felt the cases provided a valuable learning experience ($r = .66$, $p < .001$). From this we can conclude that students value the individualized opportunity to sharpen their application and diagnostic skills that the interactive personal computer cases provide. It could readily have been predicted that feeling the cases were "fun" would be significantly correlated with several variables. The correlation between "fun" and "application challenge" was .51 ($p < .001$). Between "fun" and "valuable learning experience," the correlation was even higher ($r = .60$, $p < .001$). "Fun" and "frustration with running the IPCCs" were negatively correlated ($r = -.23$, $p < .05$). Thus being challenged and having a valuable learning experience is considered enjoyable, while frustration over trying to run an uncooperative computer program is not enjoyable. There was a significant correlation between frustration in running the IPCCs and

Table 6.2
Intercorrelations

	Application Challenge	Valuable Experience	Fun	Frust. Didn't Agree	Frust. Running IPCCs
Application Challenge					
Valuable Experience	.66***				
Fun	.51***	.60***			
Frustrating—Didn't Agree	.06	−.06	−.11		
Frustrating—Running IPCCs	−.05	−.01	−.23*	.29*	

* $p < .05$
*** $p < .001$

frustration over not agreeing with the computer's "optimal" answer ($r = .29$, $p < .05$). This can perhaps best be explained by one frustrating experience begetting another.

Advantages and Limitations of IPCCs

Bigelow (1986) raises the question of what kind of learning is accomplished when computer applications are used in management education. Interactive personal computer cases, such as those used in the present investigation, tend to excel in giving students practice and drill in developing diagnostic and application skills. These programs require the student to diagnose situations and apply the concepts that are pertinent to resolve the problems presented. Additionally, Bigelow questions whether computer methodologies allow the student to learn to interact effectively with complex situations. IPCCs are much more reflective of the complexity of human interaction than are more traditional case materials. With the traditional case materials, students deal with the case situation as a whole, rather than as a set of interrelated incidents that are unfolding before their eyes. This serial aspect of the interactive personal computer case forces the student to take responsibility for the decisions he or she makes, because he or she has to deal with the consequences of those decisions in later situations. Traditional case materials often do not have this serial option. The student using an IPCC has the advantage of frequent feedback and reinforcement for his or her work. Often with more traditional methods of skill acquisition, individual reinforcement is not so immediate.

The feedback and reinforcement characteristics of interactive personal computer cases serve as both an advantage and a limitation in the teaching of managerial action skills. An IPCC is, after all, only a computer program. While it is more reflective of human interaction than traditional case materials, it cannot possibly replace human interaction in refining managerial action skills. The way in which the IPCCs used in this study were constructed was such that every situation had one optimal answer. While this doubtless provides an excellent tool for feedback and drill, it might also have the side effect of inhibiting growth in skill development. Once the student has learned some basic techniques for diagnosing situations, discerning possible underlying causes, and applying a variety of conceptual tools to various situations, an IPCC that provides one "optimal" answer might give the student the mistaken impression that all situations are solvable "by formula." This naive approach to human interaction could have an adverse effect on future skill refinement or additional skill acquisition. To avoid the possibility of students learning "human interaction by formula," two elements seem necessary. First, IPCCs that allow for multiple solutions should be developed. Second, IPCCs should be followed by skill practice exercises involving interaction with others.

Interactive personal computer cases provide a psychologically "safe" environment for skill acquisition. Students are free to test a multiplicity of behavioral responses with no fear of reprisals. After all, negative feedback from a computer is nowhere near as potentially threatening as negative feedback from a professor or colleague. For this reason, IPCCs should be used for the acquisition and refinement of basic skill levels, with human interaction taking place after the student has acquired some level of competence and confidence with the skills being taught. IPCCs as a pedagogy could be applied to learning a variety of essential skills such as decision making, controlling, planning, and organizing (Sherman, 1988).

Conclusion

Interactive personal computer cases have both advantages and limitations in the teaching of action skills. They provide a very efficient way for students to gain feedback regarding their own skill levels. Students seem to enjoy using the cases, and there is a chance that this enthusiasm will be carried over into other aspects of their studies. The cases seem to be particularly well suited to introductory courses, where practice and drill of newly acquired skills in a well-controlled environment is especially important. However "single optimal answer" IPCCs as a pedagogy for the advanced student may have a possible "stunting" effect on skill refinement. Additionally, IPCCs are limited in that the situations presented occur in the rather sterile, controlled environment of the computer.

To use IPCCs most effectively, a 3-phase intervention seems optimal. First, students could be introduced to the action skill through classroom presentation of the concepts underlying the skill. Second, IPCCs could be used for skill acquisition, drill, and refinement. When computer feedback indicates an acceptable level of competence and the student feels reasonably comfortable in his or her ability to demonstrate the skill, a third phase would be implemented. Students would participate in a specially designed in-class experiential exercise that would require them to demonstrate their skills in a "live," less-controlled setting. This three-pronged approach would allow students to practice and refine their newly acquired action skills in a variety of settings. IPCCs can provide drill and practice with a skill, but they are not sufficient by themselves for teaching action skills. At the very least, IPCCs should be combined with class discussion to introduce the student to the additional complexities of human nature not addressed in the computer case.

Interactive personal computer cases are a relatively new and promising method for action skill-building in Management and Organizational Behavior courses. As with any new methodology, there are flaws that have yet to be corrected. IPCCs will most certainly never be able to replace human interaction in the acquisition of action skills for managers. The challenge to Management and Organizational Behavior professors is to determine if interactive personal computer cases are a methodology they could utilize to enhance the skill learning of their students, and if so, how it might best be applied.

7 Faculty Intent and Student Outcome in Graduate Management Education

Richard E. Boyatzis

Just as other areas of both undergraduate and graduate education are being called to account, schools of management have been called upon to account for the effect of their MBA programs. Students, parents, and prospective employers are asking management schools to show results on their unique "bottom line"—what are the retained learnings? The lack of agreement as to the goals of management education (Duncan, 1983) often leads the discussion of accountability to faculty effectiveness.

Faculty in graduate schools are the first gatekeepers of entrance into the occupations and professions they represent. Accrediting and licensing bodies and professional associations can be viewed as the second and third gatekeepers. Knowledge, appropriate norms of conduct, and values are transmitted to graduate students as they are socialized into a field or profession. Faculty are not the only sources of impact on students in graduate school. Exposure to other students, internships, projects, clubs, professional associations, and community activities also have an impact, but none commands more attention, time, or engagement than faculty. Therefore, examining the effectiveness of professional education on its two main objectives of adding value to students and evaluating their competence to enter a profession can be turned into an examination of the effectiveness of faculty.

AUTHOR'S NOTE: The author wishes to thank John Aram, David Bowers, David Kolb, Eric Neilsen, Jack Ruhl, Tojo Thachankery, and Xiaoping Tian for assisting in the collection and analysis of the information reported in this study, and to Anne Renio and Lorraine Thompson for assistance in data analysis.

Before faculty effectiveness can be assessed, the overall impact of MBA programs on students must be documented. Although a number of studies (Boyatzis & Renio, 1989; Boyatzis, Renio, & Thompson, 1991; Porter & McKibbin, 1988) have found that MBA programs have a positive impact on students, there is still confusion concerning the nature and degree of this impact. Outcome studies conducted to assess the added value of programs to students' abilities (i.e., comparing graduating students to entering students) have shown statistically significant positive increases on various abilities from five MBA programs (Boyatzis & Renio, 1989; Boyatzis, Renio, & Thompson, 1991; Boyatzis & Sokol, 1982; Development Dimensions International [DDI], 1985). These studies focused on abilities because prior discussion as to the effectiveness of professional education has typically focused on knowledge. While effective transmission of knowledge by faculty in schools of management has been assumed (Keys & Wolfe, 1988), the discussions have often resulted in debates as to the relevance of various bodies of knowledge. The traditionally exclusive focus of the discussion of faculty effectiveness on knowledge has often resulted in ignoring the impact of faculty and graduate programs on students' abilities. The latter have been shown to have greater impact on performance than only possession of knowledge in various professions (McClelland, 1973) and management (Crooks, Campbell, & Rock, 1979).

Even with regard to abilities, the relevance and appropriateness of what is taught must be examined prior to assessing the effectiveness of the teaching. Employers and faculty should be studied to determine what abilities graduates will need to perform effectively in management or other related jobs. Part of the question can be answered by surveys of employers and studies of effective and less-effective managers, effective and less-effective financial analysts, salespeople, and so forth, regarding each of the occupations MBA graduates enter. Various studies have been conducted in this manner (Boyatzis, 1982; Campbell, Dunnette, Lawler, & Weick, 1970; Howard & Bray, 1988; Kotter, 1988).

Similarly, faculty can be surveyed as to what they believe to be the relevant and appropriate abilities. Porter and McKibbin (1988) collected information from various stakeholders regarding their views of the impact of MBA programs. The study included interviews and questionnaires of 2,055 faculty and 1,835 MBA students from the 620 schools in the American Assembly of Collegiate Schools of Business (AACSB) regarding skills and personal characteristics. They found that faculty and students agreed as to where the current emphasis was placed in MBA programs. Analytical and decision-making skills were seen as being "emphasized very much" by more than half of the students and more than one third of the faculty. With the exception of computer skills, the order of the skills on the basis of the percentage of responses saying it was "emphasized very much" is identical. Both students and faculty felt that the order of emphasis was: analytical (62% and 38%, respectively); decision making (51% and 32%); planning and organizing (51% and 18%); written communication (42% and 15%); oral communication (28% and 14%); leadership and interpersonal (26% and 14%); initiative (21% and 11%); and risk-taking skills (8% and 5%). Computer skills ranked eighth in the view of students and fourth in the view of faculty (14% and 15%). In summary, the faculty's and students' view of MBA programs' emphasis on particular abilities appears consistent with employer observations that students with MBA degrees enter the work force with a great deal of analytic and quantitative ability and less interpersonal, communications, and entrepreneurial ability than desired (Byrne, Norman, & Miles, 1988; Porter & McKibbin, 1988).

While providing a great deal of useful information, Porter and McKibbin's (1988) survey asked faculty and students for their overall view of program emphasis. This type of inquiry may have suffered from distortion because faculty's and students' generalized views as to what occurs may have been different from what does occur (Argyris, 1985). A study focused on the classroom behavior and outcome would provide further information relevant to the assessment of faculty effectiveness.

The effectiveness of faculty, therefore, can be assessed through a comparison of the faculty *intent* and student *outcome*. The intentions of faculty include their learning objectives, determination of relevant topics, and organization of material in the design and delivery of their courses. It reflects how faculty assess and guide themselves during the delivery of a course. Student outcome is the progress, or change, shown in students between entering and graduating from a program. The present study attempted to compare faculty intent and student outcome on various abilities related to effectiveness in management and occupations of graduating MBAs.

Methods Used in the Study

In the spring and summer of 1988, faculty at the Weatherhead School of Management were interviewed by a special senior faculty committee about specific courses each had recently taught in the MBA program. Forty-two of the 47 full-time faculty who taught in the MBA program during the prior year were interviewed. Twenty-nine faculty were interviewed regarding the required courses. At least two faculty were interviewed regarding each of the 13 required courses. Of the 38 elective courses taught during the same year, 21 faculty were interviewed regarding 29 (76%) of the elective courses. Some faculty were interviewed about required and elective courses, but in such cases the interview protocol was completed concerning each course separately.

The interview involved three questions and administration of one instrument. Questions were asked about each specific course: (a) In general, what are you trying to teach in this course? What are your overall objectives?; (b) What topics do you see as important to cover in the course?; and (c) What other objectives, besides course topics, are you trying to cover in this course? Following the second question, the syllabus was reviewed and discussed.

Following the answers to these questions, the faculty member was asked to repeat the answer to the third question in a way that could assist analysis across courses by means of an adaptation of the Executive Skills Profile (ESP). The ESP is a card-sort instrument in which a person is asked to describe his or her skills and the demands of his or her job by sorting 72 cards with statements of specific skills or activities. The cards are placed into stacks, up to a maximum of seven, reflecting various levels of the skill. The scales have been shown to be reliable and valid measures of skills in a number of studies (Boyatzis & Kolb, in press). In this case, the instructions were modified and the faculty member was asked to describe the specific course being discussed by placing each of the 72 cards into one of the following five categories: (a) Skills that are of primary importance to me in designing and conducting my class; (b) Skills that are important but not primary in designing and conducting my class; (c) Skills that are less clearly addressed or "implicit" in designing and conducting my class; (d) Skills that are mentioned or addressed only once or twice in designing and conducting my class; and (e) Skills that are not addressed and/or are not applicable in designing and conducting my class. The faculty member was then asked to review each stack to ensure appropriate placement of the cards.

The numeric value assigned to each statement (i.e., each card) corresponded to the number of the stack into which the faculty member placed the card. Scale scores were computed as a total of the items in each scale.

The full response of each faculty member to all questions for each course was written and reviewed with the faculty members, including a list of all of the ESP items he/she listed as a level "5" for the course. Any changes desired by the faculty members were made, and the resulting written documents and the complete ESP scores were used in the analysis. Only the analysis regarding the abilities assessed with the ESP are reported in this study. For each course in which several faculty provided information, an average score per item in the ESP was calculated. The resulting scores for the 42 courses (i.e., 13 required and 29 elective courses) were used for the analysis.

Student outcome data were used from the first year of a multiyear study of the impact of the MBA program at the Weatherhead School of Management (Boyatzis & Renio, 1989). The study assessed a random sample of 26 entering part-time students (10% of the population), 72 of the entering full-time students during the orientation program (72%), a random sample of 27 graduating full-time students (44%), and a random sample of 23 graduating part-time students (51%). The ESP was one of the instruments used in the study.

Results of the Study

Analysis of ESP scores for all courses indicated that faculty intent was to emphasize Adapting Skills above all, then Planning Skills, followed by Information Analysis Skills, Entrepreneurship Skills, Setting and Managing to Goals Skills, Quantitative Analysis Skills, and Information Gathering Skills, as shown in Table 7.1. Other skills were relatively less important in terms of faculty intent. They were, in order of decreasing importance: Technology Management Skills, Leadership Skills, Taking Action Skills, Relationship Skills, and Helping and Delegating Skills.

Comparison of the graduating and entering students' scores on the ESP are summarized in Table 7.1. The mean difference is reported with the associated significance level from analyses of variance (Boyatzis & Renio, 1989). Examination of the skills on which significant change occurred reveals that they tended to be the skills emphasized by the faculty in their courses. A visual comparison of the entering students' scores, the graduating students' scores, and the faculty's intent scores are shown in Figure 7.1. Graphically, it appears that the students increase on a skill during their MBA program when their level at point of entry into the program is lower than the level of faculty intent, or desired impact on the skill.

Table 7.1

Comparison of Faculty Intent and Student Change

	Faculty Intent, N = 42 Courses	Student Change: Graduates (N = 50) as Compared to Entering Student (N = 98)
Adapting	23.40	1.6!
Planning	22.55	4.1***
Information Analysis	22.00	4.2***
Entrepreneurial	19.52	2.1*
Setting/Managing to Goals	19.19	1.1
Quantitative Analysis	19.10	6.1***
Information Gathering	18.62	1.2
Technology Management	15.98	3.3**
Leadership	15.67	0.9
Taking Action	15.42	2.2**
Relationship	15.33	0.7
Helping & Delegating	12.83	0.6

$!p < .10$; $*p < .05$; $**p < .01$; $***p < .001$
SOURCE: From Boyatzis and Renio (1989)

To help understand the faculty intent, the six items with the highest mean score and the six items with the lowest mean score are shown in Table 7.2. The items with the highest overall mean score, showing that they were considered "primary" and "important but not primary" in the design and conducting of courses, concerned conceptual, analytic, and planning skills. Meanwhile, the items with the lowest mean score, showing that they were "not addressed at all," "implicit," or "mentioned only once or twice," concerned managing people, interpersonal relationships, and self-awareness.

A transformation of the ESP data was required to compare faculty intent and student outcome in more detail. The percentage of each scale score to the total score of all scales was computed to adjust for the difference between a 7-point and a 5-point scale. The adjusted score indicates relative emphasis of a skill within each set of data.

A comparison of the entering MBA students' skills versus the faculty emphasis using the adjusted scores is shown in Table 7.3. The entering students had significantly greater relative strength on Leadership Skills, Relationship Skills, Helping and Delegating Skills, Taking Action Skills, and Entrepreneurship Skills than the faculty relative emphasis in their courses. The faculty had significantly more relative emphasis on Adapting Skills, Information Analysis Skills, Planning Skills, Quantitative Analysis

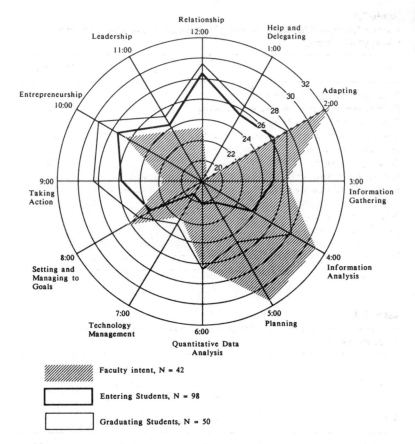

Figure 7.1. Profile Comparison of Faculty Intent, Entering, and Graduating MBA Students on the ESP Scales*

Skills, and near significant Technology Management Skills than the relative strength of the entering students on these skills.

A summary of the comparisons is shown in Table 7.4. The graduates improved, as compared to entering students, on all four skills for which the relative emphasis of faculty was significantly greater than entering students' relative abilities. These were: Adapting Skills, Information Analysis Skills, Planning Skills, and Quantitative Analysis Skills. On the

Table 7.2
Faculty Intent on ESP Items Showing Highest and Lowest Mean Scores
Over All 42 Courses

Item	Mean Score
Identifying and defining problems	4.62
Building conceptual models/conceptual thinking	4.48
Seeing how things fit in the big picture	4.38
Making decisions under conditions of risk and uncertainty	4.17
Innovating/developing new solutions to problems	4.10
Adapting to changing circumstances	4.07
Establishing trusting, dependable relationships with co-workers	2.14
Establishing relationships with co-workers in which honest feedback is given and received	2.07
Helping others gain opportunities to develop their abilities	2.07
Directing and supervising the work of others	2.05
Understanding and being influenced by the feelings of others—empathy	2.05
Being aware of and understanding yourself, assessing yourself accurately	2.02

Table 7.3
A Comparison of the Relative Priority of Faculty Intent and Entering
Students' Skills

	Percentage of Total Skills Score		
	Entering Students	Faculty Intent	
Skill	N = 98	N = 42	t
Leadership	8.30	7.04	4.00***
Relationship	9.79	6.87	7.76***
Helping and Delegating	8.80	5.70	7.69***
Adapting	9.03	10.80	−5.46***
Information Gathering	8.63	8.40	1.04
Information Analysis	8.21	10.16	−5.43***
Planning	7.04	10.44	−10.03***
Quantitative Analysis	6.98	8.86	−3.32**
Technology Management	6.63	7.35	−1.76!
Setting/Managing to Goals	8.18	8.68	−1.63!
Taking Action	8.91	6.86	7.75***
Entrepreneurship	9.51	8.86	2.30*

!$p < .10$; *$p < .05$; **$p < .01$; ***$p < .001$

Table 7.4
Summary Comparison of Faculty Intent and Entering Students' Skills
With Outcome

Skill	*Faculty Intent* *vs. Entering MBA*	*Student* *Outcome*
Adapting	Faculty >> Students	Grads > Entering
Information Analysis	Faculty >> Students	Grads >> Entering
Planning	Faculty >> Students	Grads >> Entering
Quantitative Analysis	Faculty >> Students	Grads >> Entering
Technology Management	Faculty >> Students	Grads >> Entering
Setting/Managing to Goals	Faculty >> Students	ns
Information Gathering	ns	ns
Leadership	Students >> Faculty	ns
Relationship	Students >> Faculty	ns
Helping and Delegating	Students >> Faculty	ns
Taking Action	Students >> Faculty	Grads >> Entering
Entrepreneurship	Students >> Faculty	Grads >> Entering

">" means near significant, $p < .10$; ">>" means significant, $p < .05$

two skills where faculty emphasis was greater than entering students'
relative abilities at a near significant level, there was significant change
on Technology Management Skills but no change on Setting and Managing to Goals Skills. On four of the six skills on which either there was no
difference between faculty emphasis and entering students' relative abilities or the entering students had relatively more ability than the faculty
emphasis, there was no improvement in students between entering and
graduating from the MBA program. They were: Information Gathering
Skills, Leadership Skills, Relationship Skills, and Helping and Delegating
Skills. On Taking Action Skills and Entrepreneurial Skills, entering students had relatively more ability than faculty emphasis, and yet graduates
improved as compared to entering students.

How Does Faculty Intent Impact on Students?

The way the faculty design and conduct their classes has a significant
impact on how students change during an MBA program. Students
increase on seven skills and remain about the same on five skills, and it
appears that faculty drive the change in the direction they desire. In those
areas where faculty intention is high, improvement of students is seen,

specifically on Information Analysis Skills, Planning Skills, Quantitative Analysis Skills, Entrepreneurial Skills, and Adapting Skills. In those areas where faculty intention is low, little change occurs in students, specifically on Information Gathering Skills, Leadership Skills, Relationship Skills, and Helping and Delegating Skills. There is one exception: A relatively high faculty intention does not appear to affect student change on Setting and Managing to Goals Skills.

At the same time, it can be noted that although faculty had relatively low intentions regarding certain skills, students do significantly improve on Technology Management Skills and Taking Action Skills. The positive impact could be attributed to effects of the school, program, faculty contact outside of courses, or community activities. Using a median to split the scales into High Faculty Intent and Low Faculty Intent, it appears that students improve, significantly or near significantly, on five of the High Faculty Intent scales (83%) and do not improve or change on four of the Low Faculty Intent scales (67%).

The pattern of student change showed further support a year later in another study of the impact of this program. A sample of 106 MBA students was selected in the same manner (Boyatzis, Renio, & Thompson, 1991). This sample included a very small Intent and Outcome longitudinal sample of nine students from the first-year study. Both the sample from the second study and the small longitudinal sample showed significant improvement in students' Information Analysis, Planning, and Quantitative Analysis skills. The small longitudinal sample also showed a significant increase on the Technology Management skill.

The number of items in each scale for which students showed significant or near significant improvement further illustrated the impact of faculty intent. The number of items on which students showed improvement for the five scales on which faculty intent was greater than entering students skills was 4.0 per scale (see Table 7.3). For the two scales on which faculty intent and entering students showed no or near significant differences, the number of items that showed improvement was 1.0 per scale. For the five scales on which entering students were significantly greater than faculty intent, the number of items that showed improvement was 1.4 per scale.

An alternative explanation would be that students compensate for their skill levels at point of entry into the MBA program. They might seek to improve on their relatively weak skills and not pay attention to their relatively strong skills. This effect should work regardless of faculty intent. The concept of compensating development worked on 7 of the 12 skill areas. A median split on entering students' skill levels revealed that students improved on four of the six skills with which they entered the program relatively low (67%), and showed little or no change on three of the skills with which they entered the program relatively high (50%). Four of the five skills on which the student-change data did not confirm the compensating effect are involved in implementation and are the most action-oriented skills assessed in the ESP. It appears that students change the most on those abilities on which they are relatively weak and do not change much on those abilities on which they are relatively strong.

Despite the impact of the compensating development effect on students' learning, it appears that faculty intentions have a profound effect on students' learning. The good news is: When faculty intend a change, the students improve. The bad news is: When faculty do not intend a change, the students do not improve.

Although this study provides a more rigorous assessment of faculty intentions than Porter and McKibbin (1988), both studies show strong faculty emphasis on similar skills, with the exception of this program's significant impact on Taking Action Skills, Entrepreneurial Skills, and Technology Management Skills. Does this suggest that much of the relationship between faculty intentions and student outcome found in this study would also be characteristic of other management programs? Until MBA programs assess this relationship, it will be difficult to determine how similar or dissimilar these findings are to other programs' faculty intentions and student changes.

It is also possible that the relationship found in this program is similar to the impact of graduate professional education in other fields. A number of studies of alumni of graduate engineering and social work programs showed increased Information Analysis, Information Gathering, Planning, and Quantitative Analysis Skills attributed to their graduate education. In a similar vein, Friedman (1989) reported that female, middle-level managers with Master's degrees had significantly higher levels of the Information Analysis, Planning, and Quantitative Analysis Skills than their less-educated colleagues. The intentions of the faculty in those graduate programs was not known, so it is difficult to conclude that student change was a function of an emphasis on similar abilities from the faculty of the various graduate programs.

These findings suggest that regarding impact on students' abilities, graduate professional education increases abilities in the areas of information collection and analysis, planning, and quantitative analysis. Likewise, it appears that interpersonal and self-awareness abilities are not

affected. It seems likely, therefore, that the positive impact of this particular program on Technology Management, Taking Action, and Entrepreneurial Skills is related to either its specific program or characteristics of
the field of management. The faculty views of relative emphasis of MBA
education reported in Porter and McKibbin (1988) suggest that there is
relatively low emphasis on these skills in most programs.

It could be argued that the faculty intent shown here and in other
graduate professional education programs is, in part, a result of the student
impact. That is, over the years, faculty come to realize that students only
improve, or add value, on these information collection and analysis
abilities. Therefore, the faculty focus their intent only on those abilities
they believe can be changed during graduate education.

While the influence of past impact on students cannot be eliminated as
a contributor to socialization of faculty, thereby affecting their expectations and intent, there seems to be literature suggesting that faculty seek
to have impact on students in broader arenas. Some faculty have expressed
doubt in faculty meetings about the efficacy of influencing a person's
interpersonal ability, ability to work with others in groups, or action and
implementation abilities. At the same time, there seem to be far more
faculty who feel that they have a positive impact on a student's maturation
and improvement on a broad range of skills. Literature in the field
contends that faculty in schools of management should have even greater
impact than we have had in many of these other areas (Porter & McKibbin,
1988).

The desirability of influencing many of a student's abilities is neither a
new phenomenon nor an archaic one. The apprenticeship and tutorial
aspects of advanced, professional education, first popularized by Socra-
tes, Plato, and Aristotle, continue to have advocates in John Dewey,
Malcolm Knowles, David Kolb, and many others for engaging the whole
student. The "affective education" movement of the 1960s, the "experiential learning" movement of the 1970s, the "competency-based education" movement of the 1980s, and the efforts of professional schools to
become closely connected to the settings and expectations in which their
graduates work share the intent to develop the "whole" student. They want
to help students develop any and all knowledge and abilities related to the
practice of their profession and improvement of that practice. Within this
context, it is difficult to embrace the notion that faculty have limited their
intent to only those information collection and analytic abilities on which
students have been shown to change in the past.

Conclusion

Faculty intent appears to affect the degree of graduate student learning in terms of abilities. Other aspects of the program assessed may also have a positive impact on students in facilitating change; but on the whole, if faculty do not view a skill as a key item on which to focus, the students will not change during their graduate program. Student outcomes indicate that faculty are effective in their teaching of abilities.

Unfortunately, the abilities on which faculty focus may be too limited for the intended and desired occupations of their graduates. If the criticisms reported in Porter and McKibbin (1988) and gaps in substantive progress in terms of innovation in management education (Keys & Wolfe, 1988) are taken seriously, then faculty must choose to either change their focus within courses, and/or to change the focus of the graduate program through other aspects of the program. Faculty could change their focus on skills without changing the content of their courses by changing the way in which they are taught, the type of assignments, and the type of interaction expected from students. Other program elements can also be introduced into a curriculum, such as learning teams (Caie, 1987; Prideaux & Ford, 1988), to bolster attention on those skill areas not thoroughly addressed in courses.

Whether the desire for curriculum change and change of the impact on students comes from employers, students, parents, or administrators, the faculty must be directly involved. They already have intentions, in terms of learning objectives, selection of topics, the design, and the delivery of their courses. These intentions address content topics and abilities. To stimulate a change effort, the faculty must "buy into" the effort.

Once a deficiency in a curriculum is noted, the standard academic response is to add a course on the topic. The findings of this study suggest that merely adding another course in the curriculum would not have the desired effect. For example, adding a course on leadership or a course on ethics will not significantly alter the overall impact of the courses and program on a student as to leadership abilities or ethical behavior. The time and experiences to which he/she is exposed in one course are miniscule compared to the combined effect of all courses, faculty, and the entire program. The results of this study suggest that expansion of faculty focus on abilities will, most likely, result in more impact on students, more added value, and greater retained learnings than are currently experienced. While a sense of purpose and focus shared by the faculty maybe difficult to achieve, it is an essential first step in the direction of increased positive impact on students' abilities.

Part III Assessing Managerial Skills

A skills course differs from many university courses in that it sets out to accomplish a radically different type of learning objective. Whereas a more traditional management course might have objectives of "introducing students to management concepts," or "enabling students to apply management models," or "to develop a critical approach to management problems," a skills course will aim to improve actual student skills.

This means that current methods by which learning accomplishment is assessed become suspect. In fact it appears that such methods as multiple choice, essay, paper assignments, and the like are designed to measure more cognitive-type learning goals. They provide little evidence concerning a person's skill development.

How can a person's skills be assessed? The four chapters of this section address this question. At this point two basic methods have emerged for assessing a person's skill accomplishment in a university setting. The first is an "assessment center" approach, which involves establishing a center that exists apart from particular courses. Students in skills courses are sent to the center to undergo assessment activities and receive feedback on their skill development. In Chapter 8, Renee McConnell and John Seybolt describe one such center, which was established at the University of Utah. They discuss skill assessment at the undergraduate, MBA, and Executive MBA levels, responses of assessees, and the lessons they learned from conducting the center.

One attraction of an assessment center is that it can provide pre- and post-measures for different courses, making possible the comparison of the effects of different course pedagogies. In Chapter 9, Ralph Mullin and his colleagues do just this, by describing an assessment center established at Central Missouri State University. They describe a pedagogy for teaching management skills and inquire into its effectiveness by analyzing pre- and post-test results of students who have engaged in the pedagogy.

A second method for assessing skill accomplishment is the "action exam." In this approach the course instructor sets up individual interviews with students during the course. During these interviews students demonstrate skills in role-play situations (alternatively, this information may be provided through videotaped role plays). Skill competence is scored using a checklist. In Chapter 10, I describe what I have learned in the course of giving more than 1,000 action exams. I describe details of how I currently structure an exam, discuss a number of student tactics and how I respond, and consider how action exams have impacted the course and my role. In Chapter 11, Glenn McEvoy compares action exam scores with other indications of skill development. His findings are rich with implications for skill testing.

8 Assessment Center Technology: One Approach for Integrating and Assessing Management Skills in the Business School Curriculum

Renee V. McConnell

John W. Seybolt

Surveys of business school students, graduates, and faculty members, as well as employers have resulted in remarkable agreement on the following points: (a) the management curriculum represents an opportunity for students to gain skills in technical competence as well as skills for more effective management of people; (b) students expect to acquire "real-world" skills; and (c) prospective employers place high importance on students' acquiring management, leadership, and other interpersonal skills (Benson, 1983; Porter & McKibbin, 1988; Whetten & Cameron, 1983). Yet, as described by Porter and McKibbin, the management curriculum often falls short in providing these skills, particularly in the balance between technical and behavioral skills. In fact, one of the conclusions of this chapter is that we pay insufficient attention to the actual processes of managing people and the development of leadership skills. An implication is that there can be some question as to the relevance of the training our business schools offer their students in terms of the specific managerial work that they will perform in the decades ahead (O'Malley, 1989).

Most business school programs attempt to "teach" students to improve their management skills. Most often, however, this teaching appears almost exclusively as information about these skills. In general, professors use selected readings, class discussions, group projects, and written exams, but they frequently do not distinguish between knowing the content (the "what") and the process (the "how") of management. This means that most business schools have not adequately emphasized the individual "output" aspects of learning relevant skills. Management curricula have too often avoided the demonstration and evaluation of specific management skills through structured activities that could reveal behaviorally observable, value-added components. What has been especially absent, even in the experiential focus of many organizational behavior classes, has been evaluations of students as they demonstrate these skills and feedback regarding their developmental needs.

The purpose of this chapter is to present examples of one approach to assessing management behavior in business schools, discussing three different ways for integrating action skills at the undergraduate, MBA, and Executive MBA levels. To address the critical issue of modes for evaluating individuals' demonstrations of these skills, each of these applications offers specific feedback regarding demonstrated strengths and weaknesses, as well as recommendations for further skill development. Management faculty members wanting to emphasize the development of management action skills can integrate a skills track in some part of their curricular offerings by applying these three options or variations of them.

The Underlying Model: Assessment Center Technology

A large body of literature addresses how to assess managerial skills and talents (Dunnette, 1971; Grant, Katkovsky & Bray, 1967; Hinrichs, 1969; Taft, 1959). Much of this literature focuses on the development and testing of the managerial assessment center technology, where individuals are assessed by various methods for their level of skills in numerous managerial situations (Bray & Grant, 1966; Finkle, 1976; Jaffee & Frank, 1978; Moses & Byham, 1977; Wollowick & McNamara, 1969). While this technology has been quite well documented as an effective method not only for assessing skill level, but also for enhancing the performance of both those who are assessed and those who are assessors, there has been limited crossover and use of this assessment center technology in business schools (Moses & Byham, 1977). One notable exception is a required course in Management Assessment/Development at the Weatherhead School of Management at Case Western Reserve University, which serves as the basis for developing competency-based educational plans for incoming MBA students (Roman, 1989). Yet this is truly the exception, and most business schools have not adopted competency-based learning approaches.

One reason for this absence may be the extremely high labor intensity and associated labor costs that assessment center technology requires (Cohen, 1980; Howard, 1974). Typical classroom situations make it extremely difficult to incorporate this technology since it requires a high level of individualized observation and consultation. In addition, since assessment center technology was developed in industry and the world of training and development, some may see it as more of a training activity than an educational activity, and consequently somewhat outside the domain of more traditional business school curricula (Byham, 1982; Hart & Thompson, 1979). Nonetheless, the assessment center model can be particularly effective in assessing action skills in today's business school environment.

This chapter will discuss examples of such use: (a) an undergraduate leadership course focusing on teaching leadership skills and models through lectures, readings, and assessment simulations; (b) a pilot communication competence program using an assessment center model to preassess, train, and postassess MBA students on skills in the areas of oral, interpersonal, and written communication; and (c) an Executive MBA skill assessment with students participating in a traditional one-day assessment center.

Assessing Action-Skill Learning at the Undergraduate Level

A quarter-long undergraduate course in leadership focused on learning leadership skills through participation in assessment exercises. The instructor spent 2 of the 4 hours each week discussing leadership theories, models, and applications. During this time, the instructor would define behavior that signifies high levels of effectiveness in relation to the particular skill. Ten managerial action skills were singled out for inclusion in this assessment program. Those 10 skills were: planning, analysis, decision making, influence, verbal communication, sensitivity, organizing, delegation, management control, and written communication. For each skill, operational definitions were developed, upon which assessments of the students' skills could then be based. For example, the skill decision making was operationally defined as: coming to decisions systematically by clearly defining a problem, exploring alternative solutions, choosing the best alternative, and making a definite and specific choice as to which course of action to take. This dimension focuses on the processes used to make decisions, as well as the judgment employed in choosing one alternative over another. A person demonstrating this skill will have enacted the following behavior:

- Clearly stated what the problem is
- Described "what is happening now" and "what should be happening" when discussing the problem
- Avoided quick or impulsive decisions
- Suggested that criteria be established for making the decision
- Chosen the most logical solution based on the facts suggested
- Stated the solutions chosen in definite terms
- Explained the rationale behind the solution he or she supported

From these operationalizations of the specific managerial skills, checklists were developed which could then be used to observe and document the students' behavior.

Class discussions included real-world examples at both supervisory and nonsupervisory levels, illustrating the difference between effective and ineffective managerial behavior and the consequences of each. In addition, leadership theories were discussed to illustrate why the skill dimensions that had been selected were relevant. The other weekly 2-hour class was spent in typical assessment exercises that were designed to elicit the 10 targeted skills. These exercises were adapted from assessment center exercises developed for managers in several work organizations in both the public and private sectors. The assessment activities included: a problem-solving task force, a meeting with a problem subordinate, conflict with a superior, an in-basket, a leaderless group discussion, and a presentation to the board. Each exercise was conducted on a different week of the quarter, enabling students to demonstrate improvement in the various skills that were assessed during each of the exercises.

Individual assessment and written feedback regarding skill level were provided by the instructor and the three Ph.D. student assessors who had been previously trained in the assessment center process. Information regarding the presence or absence of certain behavior as well overall patterns of recurring behavior were noted. Students were rated on a 5-point scale (1 = needing much development; 5 = exceptional skills). Comparisons were made between assessment ratings received early in the quarter and those in the final weeks of the course. Student self-reports at the conclusion of the course indicated a high level of both learning and satisfaction. Not only did the undergraduates have the input of leadership theory, but they could also demonstrate a high level of output, as evidenced in the assessment exercises.

Assessing Action-Skill Learning at the MBA Level

A communication skills program for MBA students was developed outside the regular course curriculum to address the development of skills in three areas of communication: interpersonal, oral, and written. Experiences designed for these three areas were spread over two quarters and scheduled in 3-hour segments. Eighteen students participated in the program.

Like the undergraduate leadership class, this program used assessment center technology. Three instructors designed experiences assessing these communication skills. Operational definitions of the concepts guided the assessment activities. For example, interpersonal communication competence was defined as skill in active listening, feedback and "I messages," congruent nonverbal behavior, problem-solving skills, and behavioral flexibility. The operational definition of written communication competence included such skills as reader analysis, message formats, organization, tone and style, and mechanics of writing. The operational definition of oral communication competence included verbal and nonverbal delivery skills, audience analysis, organization, reasoning, and choice of language. Research suggests that these skills are valued by both prospective employers and students who have recently graduated from business schools (Andrews & Sigband, 1984; Curtis, Winsor & Stephens, 1989).

Each of these skills was broken down into observable behavior which, when demonstrated with frequency and effectiveness, was construed as evidence of competence. For example, a person demonstrating the skill of appropriate nonverbal behavior would have enacted the following specific behavior in oral delivery: used appropriate pace, used appropriate volume level, demonstrated conviction through vocal enthusiasm, established eye contact, and used natural gestures.

Once the nature of the communication skills was determined, the instructors developed the three learning modules. Commonality among the three modules included: 15 to 18 hours of skill-learning time, microlectures, skill-oriented reading packets, videotaped or computer-recorded assessment activities, instructor modeling of appropriate behavior, and one-on-one developmental feedback regarding competence in assessment activities.

Preassessment and postassessment exercises were designed to assess the value-added impact of learning in the interpersonal, oral, and written communication modules. Using a 4-point scale (1 = needs much development; 4 = superior), the students were rated on how well they communicated in a videotaped interaction between a manager and his or her subordinate, a videotaped oral presentation, and a computer-developed memo. Parallel exercises were used for the purposes of pre- and posttraining ratings. Mean instructor ratings of these students were:

interpersonal communication: pre = 1.30, post = 3.05;
oral presentations: pre = 1.59, post = 3.08;
written communication: pre = 2.74, post = 3.53.

Although these instructor ratings appear somewhat global, they were drawn from specific behavioral assessor rating forms. These forms listed well-defined types of behavior targeted for identification, similar to the nonverbal behavior described earlier. These forms also enhanced student and teacher awareness of skill deficiency. With these forms in hand, one-on-one feedback was given to review the assessment activity, that is, the videotaped interpersonal and oral communication exercises and the written communication memo—prior to each communication module. This suggested to the students where they should concentrate their efforts in making certain behavioral changes. Learning of the action skills was further facilitated during the modules by frequent reference to "doing" or "showing" the skills as they were defined behaviorally on the rating forms. Finally, the rating forms became a springboard for reviewing strategies for further development of communication skills, particularly for those types of behavior in which postassessment ratings were weak.

Student responses to this extracurricular communication program were positive. On an 8-point rating scale (1 = poor; 8 = excellent) mean student ratings were 7.4. Some illustrative student comments were: "It was super to have such intensive, one-on-one help, teaching and feedback," "I liked the informal atmosphere where participation was encouraged," and "The instructors really seemed to care, making it an enjoyable, nonthreatening experience, unlike most other MBA courses." These students also described the content of the communication program as relevant and the targeted performance achievable, for example, "I have never learned this type of material before and it is relevant to all aspects of life," "Actually practicing the skills was the best aspect of the program," and "This program is so important to our career success that it should be required of all MBA students." The program appeared relevant to traditional American students, as well as to international students. One of the two foreign students in the program stated, "I've appreciated this chance to improve my communication skills and to understand American culture better. Thank you very much."

Based on these very limited data, it would appear that the students found the communication skills relevant and that the program met their needs as they moved from the content ("knowing what") to the process ("knowing how").

Assessing Action-Skill Learning at the Executive MBA Level

A one-day assessment center was developed for 35 Executive MBA (EMBA) students to assess their competence in the same 10 management action skills previously listed. These students had completed readings on uses of assessment center technology and had also had discussions and readings concerning leadership effectiveness. Twenty students were selected to participate as assessees while the remainder of the class was assigned to be assessors. Three "expert" assessors were assigned to be assessor facilitators for the project. Those selected as assessors had either prior assessment center experience or had had some form of fairly similar management-development experience. This assessment experience was strictly developmental; no letter grade was attached to either the role of assessee or assessor.

EMBA assessors participated in one day of intensive training prior to the scheduled assessment center, designed to help them learn to recognize behaviors that represent each management skill, practice differentiating between behavior and inferences, review rating errors and how to avoid them, and categorize and record types of management behavior. At the conclusion of the training, assessors reported a substantial gain, not only in behavioral observation and assessment skills, but also in their awareness of the nature of critical management skills. This gain in awareness was further supported by participation in the actual assessment exercises. A center administrator with previous assessment experience was designated to oversee procedures during the assessment experience. This administrator explained to the participants issues such as professionalism, confidentiality, stress, reading the assessment schedule, and so forth. Five experienced assessors were assigned as "team facilitators" to provide additional professionalism and experience to the assessor teams. Finally, the importance of professional career development was highlighted by collecting career-related information, as well as self-perceptions of the participants, both prior to and after the assessment experience.

The assessment procedure included four of the assessment exercises discussed above: a problem-solving task force, two role plays—a counseling interview and a meeting with a vice president, a problem analysis, and, as an extension of the problem analysis, an oral presentation. These exercises focused on executive management actions and provided multiple opportunities for candidates to demonstrate competence in each management skill. Each individual was assessed during different exercises and simulations by four assessors. Although these exercises were designed to be fairly stressful, the schedule included time for individuals to assemble for a closing discussion and evaluation of the assessment experience.

Seven-hour consensus discussions followed the assessment exercises. During these discussions each assessor described both positive and negative behavior observed during the assessment process, with assessors reporting observations for each of the assessees in a different exercise. As a team, the assessors evaluated the participant's performance on each exercise and reached consensus on a rating for each management skill. In addition, assessors described positive and negative behavior demonstrated by the participant, with suggestions for improvement. Finally, one of the "expert" assessment facilitators wrote an elaborate feedback report for each individual assessed, using the input derived from the consensus discussions among the four assessors who had observed the individual being assessed.

To provide feedback and discuss written evaluations, one member of the assessment team met with each assessee individually. Each assessee received an overall assessment rating, an overview of individual strengths and weaknesses in the various management skills, a graphic representation of the skill ratings, and written documentation of behavior observed in each of the assessed skills. Additionally, each candidate and the member of the assessment team discussed strategies for further development, such as books to read or recommended course work. Although no follow-up activities were required, the connection between the recommended strategy and future career opportunities was an integral part of the discussion.

Both assessees and assessors rated as "positive" the value of participating in the assessment process. Although admittedly anxious at the outset, the assessees left the assessment experience with not only clear documentation of their strengths in targeted management skills but also with a strategy for future growth. This was particularly helpful for those individuals in the mid-stages of their careers. Their comments supported the developmental value of the assessment process: "This is the most extensive feedback I've ever received," "There are no excuses now. This feedback will be the catalyst for me to develop my skills in communication, problem solving, and delegation," "Overall, extremely useful information," and "If I get a promotion, you can take the credit!" Assessors were equally supportive of the value of the assessment process. They noted, "This has strengthened my observational skills," "I now have a better framework for mentoring others in specific behavior," "My rating skills are definitely sharper," and "Even documenting and writing meaningful feedback should be easier."

Lessons Learned

Based on the three experiences described here, the advantages of teaching action skills clearly outweigh some of the admittedly obvious disadvantages of such assessment techniques, for example, high investment of time, difficulty in securing trained assessors, design of meaningful exercises, coordination of complex assessment activities, preparation of detailed feedback reports, integration of program in the curriculum, and so on. To help avoid some of these problems in teaching action skills, the experiences in using assessment center technology described here suggest attention to certain issues are critical, regardless of the approach chosen. The following guidelines have evolved over the past 3 years and, while not exhaustive, reflect some important lessons:

1. Enlist the interest and support of faculty members, cross-departmentally, in an action-skill focus. While OB/HRM, or even more broadly, the management faculty may be the primary supporters of such a focus, it is necessary to have input from marketing, finance, and accounting in implementing a program that is relevant to the entire business curriculum.

2. Network with others in the business community who are using assessment activities as part of employee selection or development programs. These individuals will be helpful in start-up and maintenance activities, such as determining relevant skills, developing exercises to reveal relevant skills, and participating as assessors.

3. Train a group of interested students in behavioral observation. A large pool of individuals from which to draw for assessor teams is needed.

4. Define the nature of managerial skills as the "basics." While it might be interesting to examine various facets and nuances of skills, there is not enough time to assess accurately and teach more than 10 or 12 skills in the kinds of experiences described above, given the time constraints of quarter and semester systems.

5. Use existing exercises and role plays as prototypes for drawing out the skills that have been targeted. After experiencing some success with these, they can be varied according to different industries and sectors (e.g., health care, mining, manufacturing, retail sales, and so on).

6. Integrate the microcomputer into the assessment process. This is certainly feasible and desirable for activities such as an in-basket or a problem analysis.

7. Use videotape to record all interpersonal interactions. This allows the scheduling of activities through an instructional media lab, where instructors, assessors, and assessees can review the tape and assess the behavior at convenient times. This tape can also be given to other assessors for their review and feedback. The most potent feedback is the visual feedback of specific behavior.

8. Draw on the mentoring skills of former business graduates who are perceived as effective managers. These individuals can work one-on-one with students who are weak in certain skills.

9. Provide the students with documentation of the "value added" by their participation in a skill-assessment learning experience.

10. Seek opportunities to share with business school constituents what is happening with this approach to management action skills. Faculty, students, prospective employers, and the business community should be aware of how the assessment process can be a vital link between "the university on the hill" and the "real world."

11. Work with the dean and department chairs to build a reward system so that there will be a payoff for faculty members to engage in action-skill teaching. The labor intensity of the program must be somehow balanced by an incentive system seen as equitable to the faculty members involved.

12. Actively seek private funding to provide opportunities for expanding both the depth and breadth of the action-skill focus.

Conclusion: The Challenge for the 1990s

If business schools are to respond to the needs of the management world in the decade ahead, more emphasis on the actual attainment of managerial skills must become a part of the curriculum. Applying the assessment center technology to the business curriculum offers one method of ensuring not only that business students are exposed to relevant managerial skills, but also that they are apprised of their competence in those skills, trained to enhance those skills, and then reassessed to ascertain progress in those skills. This technology also offers a way to establish an approach oriented toward ensuring that business students are prepared for the complexity of the managerial tasks that they will face in the "real world."

Such an approach to skill assessment and development can be accomplished at each of the various levels of the business school curricula. The three approaches described here illustrate how different student "clients" can be offered exposure to the assessment technology both within and outside their business school curriculum. The lessons that were learned from these three experiences certainly suggest that the process is not a panacea. Yet, it is clear that an action-skill focus is well worth the investment of time, energy, and money required. Through a skill focus such as this, business schools can and will provide a strong link between the input and output of management education. This approach not only offers a way to address some of the undernourished curricular areas noted by Porter and McKibbin (1988) but also offers a way to address their concern with the lack of sufficient integration across disciplines. The use of the assessment technology offers one of the best mechanisms to allow the student/participant to practice the integration of several managerial skills and analytical techniques learned from the broad business school educational process.

9 A Study of the Assessment Center Method of Teaching Basic Management Skills

Ralph F. Mullin

Paul L. Shaffer

Michael J. Grelle

Phase I: A Pretest-Posttest of Assessment Center Impact

Thirty years ago, Gordon and Howell (1959, pp. 44, 81, 104-105) identified four basic sets of skills purported to make up business competence. They found these skills, necessary for success in business, were clearly not being developed by business schools.

> Neither their published statements, their educational programs, nor our conversations with deans and faculties in all parts of the country revealed a clear awareness of what these skills are or how they may best be developed (p. 45).

In 1983 Cameron and Whetten (1983) reviewed a decade of criticism of business school curricula and concluded that management skills were

AUTHORS' NOTES: Ralph F. Mullin and Paul L. Shaffer wrote Phase I of this chapter; Michael J. Grelle joined them in the writing of Phase II.
We gratefully acknowledge support for this research from Central Missouri State University, which funded the project ($75,000) to provide a research grounded basis for development of a model of learning and assessment that will focus on explicit performance-based student outcomes.

still not being taught—at best, students are taught about management (content knowledge) rather than how to manage. The American Assembly of Collegiate Schools of Business (AACSB) Outcome Measurement Project Report explicitly recognizes that basic management skills are "seldom systematically addressed by curricula" (1987, p. 2). Porter and McKibbin's (1988, pp. 71-72) findings continue to confirm the rather large gap between the current reality and what "should" be in terms of behavioral emphasis in business school curricula. The "Big 8" accounting firms' *Perspectives on Education* (Accounting Education Change Commission, 1989) states:

> There must be a focus on the broader skills. . . . Without a clear set of capabilities to use as objectives in the curriculum design process, it is unlikely that changes in the current content or teaching methods will be responsive to the needs of the profession. . . . Basing pre-entry education (university) on capabilities will mean fundamental changes in the curriculum. (p. 5)

In spite of the evidence that basic management skills are not being systematically integrated into B-school curricula, they are frequently a topic at professional conferences.

What are these basic management skills? The AACSB Outcome Measurement Project (1987) identifies and defines both academic subject knowledge (seven content areas) and skills and personal characteristics (SAPCs). Development Dimensions International (DDI), in the skills diagnostic program (SDP) designed for AACSB, elaborates nine dimensions of management skills and personal characteristics (SAPCs). Importantly, DDI has developed operational definitions and a set of assessment center type exercises and evaluation procedures to measure these skills. While there are numerous taxonomies of the basic skills essential to successful practice, the degree of commonality is indeed striking. Table 9.1 displays the similarities of a few of these.

How can these skills best be developed? Cameron and Whetten (1983) emphasize that achieving change in student management skill behaviors requires a different type of learning than does the acquisition of content knowledge. The chief executive officers of the "Big 8," in *Perspectives on Education,* suggest new methods are demanded.

> The current textbook-based, rule-intensive, lecture/problem style should not survive as the primary means of presentation. New methods, both those used in other disciplines and those that are totally new to university education, must be explored. (1989, p. 11)

Table 9.1
Taxonomies of Basic Management Skills

1959 Gordon & Howell	1988 Porter & McKibbin	1988 Development Dimensions Inc.	1984 Cameron & Whetten	1989 Big Eight Accounting Firms	1989 Albanese
PROBLEM-SOLVING	ANALYTICAL	ANALYSIS	CREATIVE PROBLEM-SOLVING	INTELLECTUAL Problem-solving	Decision-making
Decision-making	DECISION MAKING	JUDGMENT	GROUP DECISION-MAKING	Creative Unstructured Problem anticipation Inductive thought	Creative Problem Solving
Analysis	RISK TAKING			Judgment	
Judgment			SELF AWARENESS Ethical issues	Value-based reasoning	Developing Self-Awareness
ORGANIZATIONAL	PLANNING/ ORGANIZING	PLANNING & ORGANIZING	IMPROVING EMPLOYEE PERFORMRANCE	Organization of work to meet priorities	Goal setting & planning Organizing Delegating Controlling Conducting Group Meetings Managing Time
Information flow Division of labor Plan, Delegate Coordinate		DELEGATION CONTROL	DELEGATION & JOINT D-M		

INTERPERSONAL RELATIONS	LEADERSHIP Individual Group Disposition to lead*	MANAGING CONFLICT MANAGING PERSONAL STRESS GAINING POWER & INFLUENCE	INTERPERSONAL Influence Delegation Motivation Conflict resolution	Leading Acquiring Power & Influence Managing Conflict Motivating Employee Performance Managing Group Processes Developing Subordinates Appraising Employee Performance
Strong personal motivation*				
LEADERSHIP/ Interpersonal	COMMUNICATION Oral: Communication Presentation Written	ESTABLISHING SUPPORTIVE COMMUNICATION	COMMUNICATION Presentation formal/informal oral/written	Communicating: Oral
Initiative*				Communicating: Written
COMMUNICATION Oral Written			Listening Obtain & organize information	Active listening
COMPUTER SKILLS				
COMMUNICATION Oral & nonverbal Verbal, numerical Idea formulation Generating/transmitting/receiving /interpreting nonquantitative & quantitative information & data				

*Attitude that contributes indirectly to skills

Gordon and Howell (1959) suggest three emphases in teaching business courses—descriptive, analytical, and managerial-clinical. They repeatedly stress "managerial-clinical teaching" as particularly well suited for teaching managerial skills (pp. 109, 135, 136, 360). Porter & McKibbin repeat the emphasis on the "clinical approach" (1988, p. 342). The assessment center method is one operationalization of the clinical method, as it entails one-on-one expert observation of the learner's practice performance with developmental feedback artd repeated performance for improvement. Alverno College's application of the assessment center method to student learning, called assessment-as-learning, is based on the principle that students will learn developmentally by continuous assessment of performance plus feedback (Marchese, 1987). This performance-based learning process is explained by Bandura's social learning theory (1977). Table 9.2 extends Cameron and Whetten's (1983) model to more completely operationalize Bandura's theory.

A number of business schools have experimented with teaching management skills. These include Alverno College, Boise State University, Brigham Young University, The University of Illinois, University of Pittsburgh, Utah State University, and Detroit University. This study is, therefore, viewed as an extension of this earlier work and as a pilot study preliminarily testing the effectiveness of the assessment center method for student learning of the set of management skills identified by AACSB and operationalized by DDI. Ed Pavur of DDI (1988) comments on the uniqueness of the study: "While SDP assessments have been conducted in schools across the country since 1983, your use of the program is unique. No other application has the set of characteristics which you are employing."

Methodology

The general hypothesis is: Students who participate in the experimental course will demonstrate significantly higher levels of competency on a set of basic management skills as measured by equivalent DDI pre- and postassessment exercises.

Sample

Thirty-five junior, senior, and graduate business students registered in a course titled Business Administration Practicum, offered as an elective in the fall of 1988. Although subjects self-selected into the sample, an

Table 9.2

Generalized Learning Model: Managerial Skills Assessment & Development

COMPONENTS	CONTENTS	OBJECTIVES
Skill Preassessment	*Battery of assessment exercises (6)*	*Assess current level of skill competence*

Skill Learning:

Feedback	Feedback of results of preassessment	Raise self-awareness of skill level—specific B
Specific behavioral guidelines (what)	Behavioral guidelines Video tape examples: Correct & Incorrect	Learn specific principles Specific what to do Specific what not to do
Skill analysis (examples)	Assess pretest tapes: Teammate's exercise Group discussion Assess own exercise	Demonstration of principles Learn assessment of skills Focus on key behaviors Learn self-objectivity
Skill understanding (why)	Behavioral theory Read/lecture/discuss Team discussion	Learn rationale for (why) behaviorial guidelines Understand & internalize rationale & guidelines
Skill Practice	Practice exercises perforamnce feedback Assess exercises	Practice behaviors Adjust performance Internalize guidelines Develop self assessment skill
Skill Goals & Plans	Development of self-learning goals	Motivation to learn Direction of effort
Skill Application	Action assignments Journal keeping Progress charting	Transfer learning to real-life situations (on-job) Continue skill practice
Goal Plan Finalization	Adjust & complete student 1/5 yr. plan	Establish discipline of skill practice & assessment
Skill Postassessment	Parallel assessment exercises	Assess new level of competence—value added

SOURCE: Adaptation and extension of Cameron & Whetten (1983)
A Model for Teaching Management Skills, *The Organizational Behavior Teaching Journal, III,* 2.

Table 9.3
Comparison of Sample Characteristics

Characteristic	Course	College	University
Number of students	35	2,500	10,104
Sex: Male	51%	49.76%	48.4%
Female	49%	50.24%	51.6%
Age	23.5	22.93	21.7
Race: Majority	94%	83%	89%
Minority	6%	17%	11%
High School Rank	78%	76%	63%
Undergraduate GPA	2.95	2.90	2.86
Self-report	2.83		
ACT Score	20	20	17.2
Nelson-Denny	13	13.5	n/a

* Asian students in the MBA program are included in this figure

examination of Table 9.3 indicates they did not differ significantly on variables related to the research.

Research Design

The basic research design was a one-group, before-after (Pretest-Posttest, O1 X O2).

Measures

The pretest (O1) of student skill levels was the set of six assessment exercises developed by DDI to operationalize the skills and personal characteristics (SAPCs) defined by the AACSB Outcome Measurement Project Skills Diagnostic Program (1987). An explicit assumption is that the DDI measures and exercises are reasonably content- and construct-valid operationalizations of the basic management skills in the literature. These exercises, described in Table 9.4, were administered (13 hours of assessment) in the first 2 weeks of the course. DDI provided expert evaluation and scoring. Data on the reliability and validity of these exercises are reported in AACSB (1987). The posttest (O2) measured the 35 students on eight of the original nine dimensions, using DDI parallel exercises. The posttest instruments and external scoring were also provided by DDI.

> The post-training simulations can be considered parallel to the pre-training simulations because of overlap in the key behaviors and dimensions which the simulations elicit. Specifically, 92% of the key behaviors and 100% of the dimensions are targeted for observation in both of the in-basket simulations; 100% of the key behaviors and 100% of the dimensions are targeted for observation in both of the interview simulations. . . . the two sets of exercises represent parallel versions and should meet your needs for equivalent materials. (Pavur, 1988)

In addition to the DDI skill performance measures, two questionnaires were administered to the 35 students—at the first and last sessions of the course. These covered demographics on school grade level (GLVL) and grades (GPA), parental occupation (POCC) and education (PED), work experiences (EXP), plus students' self-report perceptions of course importance (CIMP), course relevance (CREL), commitment to study (COMS), and level of performance (PERF) for each of the skill dimensions (beginning and ending).

The Learning Intervention

The learning intervention (X) consisted of: individualized conferences for feedback of pretest results and initial goal planning; ten 3-hour learning modules emphasizing team and individual experiences in practicing and assessing management skill exercises; and evolution of each student's goals and development plan. Table 9.5 outlines the course content and schedule. Resources were provided by the university and the participating telecommunications firm.

Methods of Analysis

To test the general hypothesis, both MANOVA and *t*-tests were performed to determine if there was a significant difference between pretest and posttest scores on measures of the eight dimensions. The MANOVA analysis of the pre- and posttreatment results was approached as a 2×8 within-subjects design.

Table 9.4
Measures: DDI Set of Assessment Instruments

1. In-Basket Exercise
    Role: Middle-level manager, manufacturing
    Task: Managing a budget, directing subordinates, and carrying out project planning,
       managing labor, public & government relations
    Presentation: Response in writing to the in-basket items
    Dimensions: Planning & organizing, Judgment, Problem analysis, Delegation, Control,
       Written communication
    Time: 3 hours, 15 minutes

2. Analysis/Oral Presentation Exercise
    Role: manager
    Task: Make recommendations to senior management re. expansion of production
       capacity, financing, product mix
    Presentation: Written report & brief oral presentation—videotaped.
    Dimensions: Judgment, Problem analysis, Oral presentation, Written communication
    Time: 3 hours, 15 minutes

3. Planning Exercise
    Role: Manager, company finance division
    Task: Plan start-up of a word-processing unit
    Presentation: Written planning document
    Dimensions Assessed: Planning and organizing, Written communication
    Time: 2 hours

4. Group Discussion Exercise
    Role: Middle-level manager, large organization
    Task: Represent department and candidate for share of $8,000 salary increase funds
       (discretionary)
    Objective: Secure maximum share for candidate and complete group task quickly
       and fairly
    Presentation: Group discussion and data videotaped.
    Dimensions: Oral communication, Group leadership, Oral presentation
    Time: 2 hours

5. Interview Simulation
    Role: Manager, Thrift Program Management section of a large bank
    Task: Business development and administration of thrift savings programs which
       corporations offer to employees as part of a benefits package
    Objective: Meet with employee whose performance has slumped recently and help
       him/her solve problems and improve performance
    Presentation: Videotaped interaction with trained role player
    Dimensions: Control, Oral communication, Individual leadership
    Time: 1 hour

6. Self-Report Inventories
    Instrument: Two self-report inventories
    Dimension: Disposition to lead
    Time: Administration is untimed, but should require no more than 1 hour and 30 minutes

Table 9.5

Managerial Skills Assessment and Development: Course Format and Schedule

Module* # Date	Activity & Method	Dimension/Exercise	Assignment
1. 8/24- 9/3	PRETEST 13 hours of assessment exercises	All six DDD Exercises Eleven Dimensions	None
2. 10/3 10/4	Feedback DDI Results Team Assignments Assess Performance Assess Improving Perf	All All Interview: 3 L,OC,C Interview: " "	Self-assess Interview Ex Video tape
3. 10/10 10/11	Discuss Course Plan Rate 2 training Videos Improving Work Habits Delegating Resp. Group Discussion	FB on Dimensions Interview Delegating " "	Work pp 193-202 Module III Phase I
4. 10/17	Leadership Concepts Values Clarification Goal-setting/Planning	Self-analysis Quest Values Exercise Goal-setting Ex.	Do Module 1 parts 1-4 Meet w Mullin
5. 10/24 10/35	Goal-setting Time Management Decision-making	Finish Goals Draft 7 Day Time Analysis Exercise, p.263	Mod. I Part 4 Mod. I Part 6 Mod III Part 5
6. 10/31 11.1	Review Interview Ex. Interview Exercise Team Evaluation of Ex.	Leadership/Control /Oral communication	Review Interview Exercise Guide
7. 11/7 11/8	Complete In-basket Exercise (Woodlands)	In-basket, 6 Dmns 3 hour exercise	Review of In- basket Guide
8. 11/14 11/15	Assess In-basket Ex. Terry Butler (Union 152-4)	Planning/organizaing Judgment, analysis Control, Delegation	Self-assess DDI In-basket
9. 11/21 11/22	Assess In-basket Exer. (Union 152-154	Laura Marquart, UTS Malloy Gould, CMSU	Complete UTS In-basket Ex.
10. 11/28 11/29	POST-TEST DDI Interview Exercise	Three Dimensions	Review videos
11. 12/5 12/6	DDI In-basket Exercise (Union 152-154)	Six Dimensions	Review: 3 In- baskets + notes
12. 12/9 F 4-6PM	Focus Groups	Course Evaluation Term Paper due	Review notes Complete Goals

* Three-hour class except for the 13 hours of pretesting

Table 9.6
Test of General Hypothesis

Learning Effects (Difference)

MANOVA (2×8)	Canonical Cor.	p-value
Pre-Post Difference	.97	0.000
Interaction: Pre-Post (2) with Dimensions (8)	.82	0.001

t-tests: Difference (Posttest—Pretest) on Individual Dimensions

Dimension	t-value	p-value
1. Leadership	1.43	0.16
2. Oral Comm.	−0.48	0.63
3. Written Comm.	−0.30	0.77
4. Planning & Org.	0.91	0.37
5. Analysis	1.77	0.08
6. Judgment	3.33	0.002 *
7. Delegation	6.35	0.000 *
8. Control	−0.15	0.88

NOTE: In addition to tests of the general hypothesis, several analyses were performed to identify independent variables that predicted performance for pretest (PRET), posttest (POST), and gain (GAIN) scores. A series of regression analyses (including stepwise) were used to determine the significance and magnitude of these effects. Considering the small sample size, a priori statistical significance was set at a p-value of 0.05.

Results

The general hypothesis was supported. Both a t-test on total gain scores for all eight dimensions ($p = .0001$) and the MANOVA 2×8 (Canonical Correlation $= 0.968$, $p = .0001$) provide statistically significant evidence that learning from the pretest and treatment was effective in increasing overall student performance on the target set of basic skills as measured by the pretest-posttest difference (GAIN).

It was not hypothesized that the students would show statistically significant ($p = 0.05$ or less) gain scores on the eight individual skill dimensions; however, gains in two of the eight dimensions—judgment and delegation—were significant. Additionally, the analysis dimension approached significance (Table 9.6).

Discussion

The results provide evidence that students can learn basic management skills in an academic setting using an assessment center method that combines skill practice with assessment and feedback. The one-group pre-post research design, though commonly used in educational research, is weak from a research perspective. This design has several obvious inadequacies, for example, measurement, maturation, history, and regression effects. The most serious of these, in terms of affecting dependent variables, is measurement effect. In this case, the pretest measure is highly reactive—13 hours of assessment exercises. Used in this manner the pretest is an important and integral part of the learning treatment itself. Measurement of the independent learning effects of the pretest and intervention will require a stronger research design.

Adoption of the assessment center method for management skill assessment and development by business schools will require convincing evidence that the assessment center method and specific operationalizations produce significantly greater learning outcomes than traditional methods. Thus, a study using a stronger research design and longitudinal tests should be conducted.

A more difficult question for research is whether these skills are learned more effectively within specially designed courses focused on these skills or by systematic integration of skill learning and practice across the curriculum. For example, testing the comparative effectiveness of the University of Illinois program, where basic skills are taught in a dedicated Principles of Management course, and Alverno College's program, where skill assessment and learning are integrated throughout the curriculum.

Conclusion

The literature suggests that the need for business schools to teach basic management skills has been evident for 30 years. Business schools as a group have, consciously or unconsciously, failed to make a well-defined response. Results of the preliminary study support the proposition that basic management skills, as defined, can be learned in an academic setting, using the assessment center method. The assessment center method may provide business school faculty and administrators a credible means for response. Further study, however, is needed to determine the differential effects of alternative methods.

Phase II: A Solomon Four Design Test of Methods

This section extends the study described previously, which provided evidence that students can learn a well-defined set of basic management skills in a traditional undergraduate academic setting, using the assessment center method that combines skill practice with assessment and feedback. The preliminary study's limited one-group pre-post research design, however, provided no evidence as to the comparative effectiveness of this method.

Since adoption of the assessment center method for management skill learning by business schools will require more convincing evidence, one purpose of this Part 2 study was to test the effectiveness of the assessment center method against a more traditional textbook/lecture-intensive method, using a stronger research design. Additional research questions included: Can learning of basic management skills be achieved without a commensurate loss of content knowledge learning? Will faculty using the assessment center method receive lower student course evaluations? Can basic management skills be adequately learned within a single course (e.g., Whetten [19XX], University of Illinois), or does skill acquisition require student learning and assessment developmentally across the curriculum (e.g., Alverno College's ability-based learning program)? The following hypotheses were developed to test all but the last question:

H1: Students who participate in experimental, assessment-center method classes (X1) will demonstrate higher levels of competence on a target set of basic management skills, measured by equivalent DDI preassessments (O1) and postassessments (O2), than students in traditional classes (X2);

H2: Students who take the DDI skills preassessment (O1) will perform higher on the parallel postassessments (O2) than students not given the extensive preassessment exercises (O2 only);

H3: Despite experimental classes (X1) devoting up to 40% less class time to content knowledge acquisition than traditional classes (X2), no statistically significant difference is expected between classes on content knowledge acquisition as measured by four objective tests;

H4: No significant difference is expected in instructor ratings, as measured by the Educational Testing Service's (ETS) Student Instructional Rating (SIR), regardless of the method used (X1 or X2).

The Literature

Gordon and Howell (1959) identified the need for business schools to develop in students a set of basic managerial skills. Thirty years of study and applied experimentation have provided considerable knowledge about what these abilities are (definitions and taxonomies) and about how to facilitate student learning of them (AACSB, 1987; Cameron & Whetten, 1983; Mintzberg, 1973; Porter & McKibben, 1988). In summary, the literature suggests:

1. Although different labels are used, for example, basic management skills, competencies, capabilities, skills and personal characteristics (SAPCs), or abilities, they appear to be describing the same or quite similar basic construct namely, what the students can actually do as a result of learning (AACSB, 1987; Accounting Education Change Commission, 1989; Boyatzis, 1982; Gordon & Howell, 1959).
2. Similarly, much commonality exists between the variety of definitions and taxonomies that have been developed (Table 9.1).
3. A variety of experiential methods have demonstrated effectiveness as means of facilitating student learning of these abilities in academic settings (Bigelow, 1988; Cameron & Whetten, 1983; Henderson, 1981; McEvoy, 1989; see also Chapters 5 and 11 of this volume).
4. Management faculty generally believe competency-based management education (CBME) is possible and desirable, further definition of competencies should be achieved, and the philosophical arguments used to oppose CBME are logically inadequate and unsupported by theory and research (Albanese, 1989).
5. The management skills development movement is stalled (Whetten, Windes, May, & Bookstaver, Chapter 2 of this volume). Continued faculty resistance on philosophical, methodological, logistical, personal interests, and negative sanctions, both institutional and professional, may explain this lack of progress.

Methodology

Random assignment of students to sections of the Principles of Management course proved not to be feasible; thus, students were allowed to enroll freely in any of eight sections paired by time period (to control for class time period differences). To establish comparability of groups, simple (one-way) analyses of variance tests were performed on the grade point averages of the students from the eight sections of Principles of Management (MGT 3310). No significant differences were found ($F = 1.65, p > .10$), suggesting that the groups were equivalent prior to the start of the experiment.

Research Design

The design was a special type of 2×2 factorial, called a Solomon Four Group. The factors were Pretest (Yes/No), and Instruction (Experimental/Traditional). The design was chosen because it allows for the measurement of Pretest effects alone, Instruction effects with and without the effects of Pretest, and the assessment of the interaction between Pretest and Instruction.

To control for differences attributable to teaching effectiveness, two instructors were chosen by the researchers and the department chair on the basis of equivalent experience, comparable student ratings, qualifications, sex, and age. Each instructor was assigned to four equivalent sections of MGT 3310, representing each of the four design conditions.

Measures

Measures included (a) parallel assessment exercises (pretest-posttest measures), (b) four traditional objective tests of content knowledge, and (c) student course evaluations.

1. Assessment Exercises

The pre- and postassessments of student management skills were equivalent sets of three assessment exercises developed by Development Dimensions International (DDI) to operationalize 14 skills and personal characteristics (SAPCs) defined by the Skills Diagnostic Program (SDP) of the Outcome Measurement Project (AACSB, 1987). Table 9.7 describes the assessment exercises and the skill dimensions measured. DDI provided expert evaluation and scoring. Data on the reliability and validity of the pretest exercises are reported in AACSB (1987). The parallel postassessment exercises were newly developed by DDI specifically for this project, and no reliability or validity data were available at the time of the study.

Table 9.7
Measures: DDI Set of Assessment Instruments

---

1. IN-BASKET EXERCISE
   Role: Middle-level manager, manufacturing
   Task: Managing a budget, directing subordinates, and carrying out project planning,
      managing labor, public & government relations
   Presentation: Response in writing to the in-basket items
   Skill Dimensions: Planning & organizing, Judgment, Problem analysis, Delegation,
      Control, Written communication
   Time: 3 hours, 15 minutes

2. MANAGEMENT DECISIONS: Analysis/Oral Presentation Exercise
   Role: Manager
   Task: Make recommendations to senior management re. expansion of production
      capacity, financing, product mix
   Presentation: Written report & brief oral presentation—*videotaped*
   Skill Dimensions: Judgment, Problem analysis, Oral presentation, Written
      communication
   Time: 2 hours, 15 minutes

3. INTERACTION SIMULATION
   Role: Manager, Thrift Program Management section of a large bank
   Task: Business development and administration of thrift savings programs that
      corporations offer to employees as part of a benefits package
   Objective: Meet with employee whose performance has slumped recently and help
      him/her solve problems and improve performance
   Presentation: *Videotaped* interaction with trained role player
   Skill Dimensions: Control, Oral communication, Individual leadership
   Time: 1 hour

---

2. Objective Tests

Four objective tests were given. Each test contained one-third true-false and two-thirds multiple-choice questions taken from the test bank of *Management* (Aldag & Stearns, 1987). All eight sections received identical test questions, though varied in order. The first three tests were 50 questions selected by the two course instructors. The final exam consisted of 100 questions, randomly selected by one of the project directors from a set of 174 questions judged to be relevant to the actual course coverage by the course instructors.

Table 9.8
Learning Intervention: Time Allocation per Component

Component	Traditional		Experimental	
	Time	Method	Time	Method
Management Skill Development			1/3	Assessment Exercises
Content Knowledge Learning	2/3	Lecture-Text Quizzes	1/3	Team Learning Team Quizzes
Other: Pre- & post-assessments, tests, etc. Assessments	1/3	4 Content Exams & Assessments	1/3	4 Content Exams & Assessments

3. Student Course Evaluations

The Educational Testing Service's (ETS) Student Instructional Report (SIR) form was administered in accordance with the standard procedures to students in all eight sections. In addition to the comparing of results between the traditional and experimental sections, results from the experimental sections were also compared to ratings from the same instrument for the same two instructors teaching the same course using only the traditional method from the previous semester.

The Learning Interventions

The traditional treatment allocated two thirds of classroom time to content knowledge acquisition, using quizzes and a lecture-intensive method, whereas the experimental sections allocated only one third to content, using the team learning method with quizzes, and one third to development of basic management skills, using assessment-center-type learning exercises (Table 9.8). Both experimental and traditional sections provided students with identical review sheets prior to tests and used content knowledge quizzes.

Experimental

The experimental learning intervention (X1) was characterized by student participation in assessment exercises, use of team learning and content quizzes, and student/faculty discussion of content quizzes. Six learning/assessment exercises were used: value/goal setting, in-basket (complex), interaction, in-basket (writing), job selection interview, and small group decision making. The assessment-center-type exercises that were used involved students both in role play and in vicarious learning via assessment of teammates, using criteria specific assessment forms (Table 9.9). These were scheduled to approximately coincide with content knowledge coverage in the text. Thus, while traditional sections learned about a management principle or skill, the experimental sections learned both the principles and the applications.

Traditional

The traditional learning intervention (X2) covered the same textbook chapters and assignments and depended exclusively on the lecture-intensive method of teaching content knowledge. Both instructors were guided by how they had taught the course previously.

Methods of Analysis

To test hypotheses 1 (H1) and 2 (H2), a MANOVA analysis was performed on the pre- and posttreatment results ($2 \times 2 \times 14$ mixed design). The two between-subjects factors were Treatment (Experimental vs. Traditional) and Experience (Post- Only vs. Pre- and Post-). To test hypothesis 3 (H3), ANOVAs were used to compare the difference in means between the experimental groups (X1 and X2) and the traditional groups (X3 and X4) on student scores on the four content knowledge tests. ANOVA was also used to test hypothesis 4 (H4) to determine if any significant differences existed between experimental and traditional treatments on student course evaluations.

Results

Hypothesis 1 (H1) was supported. The MANOVA indicated a significant ($p < 0.001$) learning effect due to the experimental treatment (Table 9.10). This provided statistically significant evidence that the experimental treatment, as compared to the traditional treatment, was effective in increasing overall student performance on the target set of basic management skills as measured by the pretest-posttest difference on DDI's measures.

Hypothesis 2 (H2), which predicted that students taking the skills preassessment would score higher on the postassessment, was not supported. The MANOVA showed no significant difference ($p = 0.534$)

Table 9.9
Description of Skills Learning Exercises

1. Values/Goal Setting
   Role: Self in career context
   Task: Clarification of personal values and goal-setting re. abilities
   Skill Dimensions: Judgment, Problem analysis, Impact (motivation)
   Time: 3 class periods (50 min.) and 3 hours out of class

2. In-Basket Exercise
   Role: Manager, district government office
   Task: Evaluating and directing subordinates, project planning, etc.
   Skill Dimensions: Planning and organizing, Judgment, Problem analysis, Delegation,
      Control, Written communication
   Time: 3 class periods (50 min.) and 3 hours out of class

3. Interview and Analysis
   Role: HRD trainer, new employee, worker/mentor, or department
   Task: Interview and analyze new employee orientation program.
   Presentation: Written report of analysis and recommendations
   Skill Dimensions: Judgment, Analysis, Oral and Written communication
   Time: 3 class periods (50 min.) and 1 1/2 hours out of class

4. In-Basket Exercise
   Role: Middle-level manager, sales
   Task: Directing subordinates, dealing with customers and suppliers
   Presentation: Response in writing to the in-basket items
   Skill Dimensions: Judgment, Problem analysis, Written communication
   Time: 2 class periods (50 min.) and 1 hour out of class

5. Selection Interview
   Role: Personnel department, recruiter
   Task: Preparation and conduct of three selection interviews
   Skill Dimensions: Oral communication, analysis
   Time: 3 class periods (50 min.) and 1 1/2 hours out of class

6. Small Group Decision-Making
   Role: Sales manager (5 different roles, e.g., backgrounds)
   Task: Development of decision criteria and alternative solutions by group consensus
      (highly diverse member characteristics)
   Assessment: Day 1-Group role play, Day 2-Observe group, Day 3-Discuss Skill
   Dimensions: Oral communication, Analysis, Group leadership
   Time: 3 class periods (50 min.)

between the preassessment and postassessment sections and the postassessment-only sections (Table 9.9).

Table 9.10
Tests of Hypotheses H1 and H2: SSPSX MANOVA $2 \times 2 \times 14$ Mixed Design

Source of Variation	SS	DF	MS	F	Sig of F
Within cells	1909.42	3484	.55		
DIMENSIONS (14)	1690.83	13	130.06	237.32	.000
TRTMT BY DIM (H1)	28.61	13	2.20	4.02	.000
EXPER BY DIM (H2)	6.53	13	.50	.92	.534
TRTMT BY EXPER BY DIM	10.15	13	.78	1.42	.140
$N = 272$					

MANOVA 2×14
Treatment (Experimental vs. Traditional)
   with Dependent variables (14 Skill Dimensions)

	Canonical Cor.	*p*-value
Interaction:	.37	0.000
Treatment (2) with Skill Dimensions (14)		

Hypothesis 3 (H3) was supported. No significant differences were found between the traditional and experimental sections on the four content knowledge exams (Table 9.11).

Hypothesis 4 (H4) was likewise supported. No significant differences ($p = 0.30$) were found between the experimental and traditional sections on student course evaluations, measured by ETS's SIR (Table 9.12).

Discussion

Support of hypothesis 1 (H1) provides additional evidence that selected basic management skills can be learned in an academic setting and that the assessment center method is an effective pedagogy for undergraduate students. This finding confirms the results of the Phase I study.

The lack of support of hypothesis 2 (H2) suggests that, without timely and developmental feedback, learning effects of pretest assessment exercises will not be significant. Considering the extent of concern given to control of pretest effects (sequence effects and interaction of testing and treatment) in research design (Campbell & Stanley, 1963), it is surprising that this highly reactive seven-and-one-half hour pretest provided no statistically significant threat to internal validity. The results are, however, perfectly consistent with and explained by social learning theory

Table 9.11

Test of Differences on Content Knowledge Exams—H3

Design Test	Group	N =	Mean	F' =	p =
One	Experimental	141	83.5		
(100 pts.)	Traditional	132	85.5	1.07	0.71
Two	Experimental	141	82.2		
(100 pts.)	Traditional	132	83.2	1.27	0.16
Three	Experimental	140	80.7		
(100 pts.)	Traditional	131	82.3	1.21	0.28
Four – Final	Experimental	139	159.3		
(200 pts.)	Traditional	131	159.3	1.22	0.24
Combined	Experimental	141	402.8		
(500 pts.)	Traditional	132	408.5	1.00	0.996

Table 9.12

Tests of Differences in Student Course Evaluations

Hypothesis: H4
SAS ANOVA

Question: How would you rate the quality of instruction in this course?

Source	SS	DF	Mean S	F Value	Pr F	R-square
Model	0.49	1	0.494	1.08	0.30	0.005
Error	100.26	219	0.458			
Total	100.75	220				

Means: 1. Traditional ($n = 111$) 4.405
2. Experimental ($n = 110$) 4.50

Interpretation: No significant differences between experimental and traditional treatments on student instructional reports

(Bandura, 1977). Since no feedback of results from the pretest was given to students, any immediate learning effects were not reinforced and, thus, not retained.

Support of hypothesis 3 (H3) suggests that faculty concern regarding the deleterious effect that teaching basic management skills might have on content knowledge acquisition is unfounded. The results were consistent with the intuitive proposition that a synergy exists in student learning of content knowledge through applications that simultaneously develop relevant basic skills. Outcomes were also consistent with evidence from 20 years of experience with an ability-based learning program at Alverno College (Mentkowski & Doherty, 1984); namely, as students see the connection between content knowledge and "how they can use it out there" via skill applications, knowledge becomes more meaningful and important.

Support of hypothesis 4 (H4) suggests faculty concerns that students may react negatively to new methods, because they are different or because they place greater responsibility on the student for learning, are probably unwarranted.

Results of the current study clearly support the proposition that the assessment center method can be effective in teaching skill acquisition with no loss of content knowledge learning. However, the difference between experimental and traditional sections on posttest scores, while statistically significant, was of low magnitude (Canonical correlation = 0.37). Additionally, when differences were tested for the 16 individual skill dimensions, only 6 were statistically significant, the differences were minor, and the results were mixed. The experimental treatment thus was effective compared to the traditional treatment, but students developed in small increments and not consistently. Artificial and weak effects of experimental manipulation are common. In this case, student grades were dependent only on completing the postassessment exercise and not on the quality of their performance. This may partially explain the low magnitude of the experimental effects. Another explanation is that a single course can be expected to produce only minor gains in student skill development and then only for a limited number of management skills.

Examination of the normed data reveals that, although students compared favorably to the AACSB/DDI Skills Diagnostic Program's (SDP) norm group in Phase I of the study, when posttest scores from Phase II were compared to an external norm group of beginning and middle level managers, student skill levels were far below what employers may expect from graduates. These junior-level students may be expected to develop somewhat as they complete their program. However, since these skills are not addressed by business school programs, gains may be expected to be minimal. Obviously, if performance levels of our students are expected to measure up to those in the work force, more development is needed than can be expected in one course. The results, taken as a whole, thus strongly suggest the need for the adoption of a comprehensive abilities-based model for the entire business school curriculum.

Table 9.13
Assessment-as-Learning Model

Assumptions About Learning

Learning involves making an action out of knowledge—using knowledge to think, judge, decide, discover, interact, and create.

An educator's best means of judging how well a learner has developed expected abilities is to look at corresponding behavior—thinking behavior, writing behavior, inquiry behavior, appreciating behavior, for instance.

Learning increases developmentally, even in its serendipitous aspects, when learners have a sense of what they are setting out to learn, a statement of explicit standards they must meet, and a way of seeing what they have learned.

Essential Elements

   *Expected learning outcomes (including abilities)
   *Assessment as process involving multiple performances
   *Explicit criteria
   *Expert judgment
   *Productive feedback
   *Self-assessment

Principles of Assessment

 1. Assessment is an integral part of learning.
 2. Assessment must involve a sample of behavior.
 3. Assessment must involve a performance of an ability representing the expected learning outcomes of a course, a program, a department, and/or the institution.
 4. Assessment involves expert judgment based on explicit criteria.
 5. Assessment must incorporate structured feedback.
 6. Assessment must occur in multiple modes and contexts.
 7. Assessment must incorporate an external dimension.
 8. Assessment is cumulative.
 9. Assessment instruments must incorporate open-ended possibilities for demonstrating a given ability.
10. Self-assessment is an essential part of assessment as well as a goal of the process. It is an essential ability for the autonomous lifelong learner.

SOURCE: Alverno College (1986)

Development and evaluation of a new model for curricular and pedagogical reform is the goal of the future phases of this study. Such a model
will focus on the abilities-based general and program-specific student
outcomes. These outcomes will be the organizing principles for redesign

of courses and methods with extensive assessment of student performance, both within courses and comprehensive. The model's assumptions about learning are taken from Alverno College's assessment as learning model (Table 9.13).

The implications for future research include application of the model and method to the entire curriculum for a major, such as Management, and then generalizing the application to a variety of majors both within a college of business and in a variety of disciplines in other colleges of a comprehensive university. The final stage should be explicit definition of the entry-level criteria for abilities. These then can become the exit criteria for a university's general education program.

Conclusions

The study suggests that renewed progress in Competency-Based Management Education (CBME) may be achieved by business schools addressing the development of basic management skills systematically across the curriculum. This is a clear challenge made in *Perspectives on Education* (Accounting Education Change Commission, 1989). The required level of faculty and administrative planning, and matrix program coordination, is not evident in most business schools today. One logical response to this challenge is for groups like AACSB, the Academy of Management, the Organizational Behavior Teaching Conference and others to devote time at their conferences and meetings to focus on the combined issues of defining capabilities that can serve as curricular design objectives, systematic curricular reform, and new teaching and assessment methods.

10 Giving an Action Exam: An Evolving Art

John D. Bigelow

Many colleges of business are becoming increasingly interested in offering courses that accomplish not only cognitive learning goals, but also behavioral or skill goals. This interest has in large part been stimulated by the American Assembly of Collegiate Schools of Business (AACSB), which has identified a number of behavioral skills that a college of business might appropriately address (AACSB, 1984). However, one key problem in creating a skills-oriented course has been how to measure learning accomplishment. Traditional learning assessment methods, such as essay or multiple choice exams, written papers, and oral presentations, seem more adapted to measuring cognitive learning and provide little evidence about how well the learner can actually apply learning to behavior in live situations.

One response to the measurement problem is to create an "action" examination, which attempts to test how competently students can actually apply their learning in representative situations. This can be done by providing students with situations via videotape, written cases, or role plays, and asking them to apply course learning to respond competently. The instructor may then assess learning by scoring the actual behavior. During the past few years, a number of instructors have been experimenting with action exams in their courses (e.g., Damm, 1983; Day, Licata, & Stinson, 1987; DiStefano & Howell, 1987; Lee, Adler, Hartwick, & Waters, 1987-1988; McEvoy & Cragun, 1986; Waters, Adler, Poupart, & Hartwick, 1983).

I began giving action exams in my junior level Organizational Behavior course in the fall of 1982 and have been giving action exams since then. I have found that the giving of an action exam is not intrinsically a simple or routine process. Rather, I have found that while the basics are easy to learn, the exam interaction is often nonroutine and always rich with possibilities. One reason for this is that the student is moved from the traditional examination environment, which may be characterized as "placid" (Emery & Trist, 1965), to a "disturbed-reactive" environment, in which statements by the student—and examiner—affect the course of the examination dialogue. As I give exams I find I am extending myself more deeply into the examination dialogue and developing as an examiner. I find myself adding to my repertoire of responses, increasing my contact with individuals, and discovering new ways to extract benefit from the action exam process.

The purpose of this chapter is to share some of the learning I have accomplished in giving action exams to more than a thousand individuals, and thereby to provide interested instructors with a more detailed sense of what an action exam is and how it may impact on a course. First, I will describe how I currently give an action exam. Second, I will describe some of the rules of thumb I have developed in managing two aspects of the exam process: dysfunctional stress and student response tactics. Finally, I will discuss the impact of using an action exam on my courses and my role as an instructor.

Giving an Action Exam

There are two aspects to giving action exams in a course. The first involves preparation in the course prior to giving exams. The second involves the steps of actually giving the exam. Below, I describe each of these aspects in more detail.

Course Prework

Prior to the action exams, I do a number of things intended to orient people to the exam, what it is, and why it is important. In the course description handed out at the beginning of the semester, action exams are listed as occurring around weeks 8 and 9, and again during weeks 15 and 16 (exam week). In the course description action exams are described as follows:

Action Exams (2 exams × 3 situations × 15 points each). Each individual will take two action exams. The first will be over three chapters randomly selected from chapters 1-4. The second will be over three chapters randomly selected from chapters 5-8. Exams will be scheduled by sign-up.

Action exams are conducted in a 20-minute individual interview with the instructor. In the exam you are presented with a series of situations. In each you are asked to respond in a certain way, drawing on specific skills learned in the course (for a description of the focal skills to be tested, see goal statements in the "Managerial Skills" handout). For example, a situation may describe a friend coming to you with a problem, and you might be asked to role-play a supportive listening response. Following your response you may be asked to explain your response. The exam is computer-scored live by the instructor, based on criteria drawn from the chapters studied. Feedback about how you did and where you stand is given immediately following the exam.

I informally talk through the exam description in class and invite questions. I also offer the option of "testing out" of the creativity action exam. I state that if a person has done something creative that (a) is based largely on his/her own idea, (b) has some relation to business, and (c) the person has done something with it (not simply thought it up), that the person can write it up and submit it for consideration as an alternative to the creativity part of the action exam.

Another thing I do to prepare students for the action exams is to provide them with a fairly specific set of learning goals for the course. These are broken out by chapter, and focus on application of concepts in situations. For example, the learning goal for the communication chapter is: "In a given situation, to be able to select and orally deliver a listening response of a given type (i.e., evaluative, confrontational, diverting, reinterpretive, probing, pacifying, understanding/reflective) and to explain what that response is and why it is appropriate." In introducing each chapter during the semester I refer to the learning goal for the chapter and may remind students that it points to the essential skills that the action exam will test.

One other thing I do to prepare students for the action exam is to offer each group a "mock" or sample exam prior to the actual exam. In a mock exam I will ask for a volunteer from the group to take a sample exam question in the presence of the group. I stress that the mock exam does not count in any way and that it is likely that the person who takes the exam may not score highly, since he or she is not prepared. During the mock exam, I permit others in the group to coach the examinee. Following the exam, I encourage a short discussion and ask for questions. While not all groups will ask for a mock exam, this physical demonstration of exam dynamics seems more helpful than the written material in giving many students a sense of what the exam is.

The week before action exams I circulate a sign-up sheet in the classroom. This sheet lists my available time (with class time, office hours, scheduled meetings, and so forth blocked out), broken into 20-minute blocks, over the 2-week period during which the action exams will be given. I point out the sheet during class and encourage groups to sign up their members in single time blocks. This allows groups to learn from and support each other as group members take the exam. However, I do not require groups to sign up this way and permit individuals to sign up wherever they choose. I also encourage people to schedule at a time they can live with—I have noticed a tendency among some to schedule early and then shortly before the exam to reschedule for a later time.

I monitor the sign-up sheet and prevent large blocks of time from being contiguously scheduled by strategically X-ing out blocks. In general, I try to avoid giving more than four or five exams in a row without a break. This generally compensates for latecomers and slow exams—and occasionally provides me with a break.

Action Exam Steps

Action exams are given in my office. The materials I use are (a) a three-ring binder with a series of exam scenarios, (b) a computer with an exam administration program (I wrote this program and am willing to share it, but a checklist can be used instead), and (c) a chair for the student. When I first started giving action exams, I kept an audiotape of the exam in case a student challenged the exam. I found, however, that students never did challenge the exam and that I never used these tapes again; consequently, I quit making them. The exam itself moves predictably through a number of steps, described below:

Contact and Start-Up

When a student comes in, I greet him or her, invite him or her to be seated, and close the door. I then initiate some nonexam-related conversation. For example, I may comment about the weather, ask the person how the semester is going, or inquire about some aspect of his/her work. In essence, I try to establish personal contact with the person and get him or her warmed up. I may take from a few moments to a few minutes in this step, depending on the nervousness of the person and his/her willingness to converse.

Giving the Exam

I then open the exam book and point to a scenario. For example, in testing on the conflict chapter, the following scenario is one of a number that may be used:

> Your office neighbor talks very loudly on the phone. It is very hard for you not to be disturbed in your work. You have talked to him about it in the past, but it keeps going on. You are sitting in your office. It is happening once more, and you are quite irritated about it. You have decided to confront this person now.

I identify the chapter the scenario is intended to test, and ask the person to read the scenario out loud.[1] I do this to keep the person speaking, to reacquaint myself with the situation, and, in later scenarios, to allow time for scoring a previous response. When the person finishes reading, I will ask some question requiring application of course materials to either analyzing and/or taking action in the situation. In the event of a role play, I will play the part of the other. I will continue my end of the role play until either the person finishes or I feel I have enough information to assess the person's competence. I may then ask some questions about how the person's responses were based on what was learned in the course. For example, with the above scenario I will ask the person to choose an appropriate conflict resolution approach and then implement it, speaking to me as though I were the person he or she is in conflict with. Following the role play, I will ask the person what approach he or she chose and inquire as to why the person thought it was appropriate for the situation.

In the event of ambiguous or incomplete answers, I may ask one or more probing questions. When I feel I have enough information to score the question, I will move to the next scenario and repeat the process until all three scenarios have been completed.

Scoring

At the same time that I am giving the exam I am also assessing the extent to which the person is demonstrating competence, based on a set of criteria shown on the computer screen.[2] (If a computer is not available, these criteria could also be on a written checklist). I attempt to be unobtrusive when scoring, since the student may be trying to interpret my actions. I use a mouse to click score buttons on the computer screen (which the student cannot see). I try not to score actions during or immediately after their completion, so as to not tie my actions with the person's behavior. I may score during pauses in the dialogue or while the person is reading the next scenario. Often I will enter score "hypotheses"— guesses as to how the person will score—and modify them later if needed. My sense is that I am succeeding in being unobtrusive. For example, while I was feeding back scoring data from the computer screen at the end of one exam, the student looked in awe at the computer and asked, "Is that thing picking up my voice?"

Feedback

When the exam is completed, the computer shows on screen the scores the person earned during the exam and how the person is doing during the course. I recap both scores to the person and talk a little about how he or she might have scored higher. I make a point to be nonjudgmental and encouraging, even when the person has generated a lower score. When I began giving action exams, I initially felt a resistance to telling the person his/her scores face-to-face. I think I feared that the person would begin arguing for a higher score. In fact, this has happened only once in my experience. It seems that most people are simply concerned with hearing these results and are not in a frame of mind to debate them.

Coaching

In addition to simply feeding back to students about how they did on the exam, I find I am increasingly taking on a coaching role. I try to look at the whole person during the exam and note things he or she has done, even when they have no impact on the exam score. For example, some people have nervous habits, such as rocking backing and forth, rubbing finger and thumb together, twitching, playing with a pencil, or fidgeting with their eyebrows. Some people tend to look either at the table or over my head during role plays, or they may hide their eyes with their hair or the rims of their glasses. Some tend to talk at length and off the point. Some chew gum. I point out these behaviors and consider how they might affect the way others see them. Again, I am nonjudgmental and try to set a helpful tone. I might also comment on their level of skill development and where they might focus their developmental efforts. For example, I might see a particular person as needing to work on open listening, or responding effectively when criticized, or being more active in including me in the dialogue. I will point these out. If the person has done very well, I may state that he or she is in the top 10 or 5 or 1 of examinees to date and compliment the person on his/her performance.

Managing Exam Stress

Most students report experiencing stress, especially just prior to the exam. However, most students feel more stress than they show, and—again, for most—their stress quickly turns to energy during the exam. Some students do show dysfunctional effects of stress during the exam. For example, they may demonstrate difficulty in attending to the exam or understanding what is asked, inability to remember course materials, long pauses before responding (perhaps up to a few minutes), difficulty in mentally setting up a response prior to role playing, and or they may give verbal self-messages during the exam: "You didn't like that response," "I'm not doing well," "I'm not a creative person," and the like.

Often students experiencing dysfunctional levels of stress seem to be caught in a spiral: They are aware that their stress is impairing their ability to respond, and this intensifies their stress.

Of course, one can argue that these people are going to encounter many situations in their career that are similar to the action exam and they must learn to deal with their stress. Indeed, experiencing the effects of nervousness during the exam can be a valuable learning experience for students who have yet to encounter live interaction application of their learning. Nonetheless, stress can interfere with other competencies the person may have developed during the course and make it difficult to measure them. Consequently, I do what I can to reduce nervousness to a manageable level. As discussed earlier, I try to familiarize students as much as possible with the exam prior to their undergoing it. In addition, I try to relax them at the exam start with some preliminary light conversation and establish a nonjudgmental climate.

For most people, this is enough. However, perhaps 5% of examinees still show signs of dysfunctional stress. If so, I will provide the person some time and space to collect him or herself. I may comment that there is time to stop and think for a moment. If a person says that he or she cannot remember some course concepts, I will invite him or her to stop and think a minute or to describe the concept in nontechnical terms rather than try to remember an exact term. Sometimes this is enough to get the person working effectively—and sometimes not.

Managing Exam Response Tactics

Just as students develop methods for preparing for and getting through written exams, so do many develop methods for getting through an action exam. While some of these methods are also useful in managing realistic situations competently, some can be artificial, in that they can lead to increased ambiguity about the correlation between the person's behavior and my assessment of competence. The existence of student tactics in the exam points to the importance of the examiner's taking an active hand in managing the exam.

Fortunately, in contrast to a written exam, an action exam is *interactive*. This allows me to recognize the ambiguities that some tactics create and to continue the interaction to generate better data. The tactics I have seen students use fall into two broad categories: tactics for role playing and tactics for explaining what they did. Not surprisingly, students seem to have a broader repertoire of tactics for managing the conceptual parts of the exam than they do the interactional/role-play parts. Below, I list some tactics I have seen in each category and discuss what I have done in response.

Breaking Away From Role Plays

When asked to do a role play, some students will respond by starting a hypothetical discussion about what they would do in such a situation. Some students may start a role play but, before it is completed, break to a discussion of what they are trying to do. At such points I break in and prompt them to role-play, not just speak hypothetically.

Students may also try to compress the role play into fewer interactions by making several responses at once. For example, in a motivational interview, a person might ask several questions in succession before pausing for a response. If I see this happening, I have found it effective to respond to the first question and then ask what the second one was. This is a reasonable role play response, which stays in character and pushes the person to interact at a more realistic level.

Escaping Live Interaction in a Role Play

Some students pause for extended periods in the dialogue while they try to recall what they have learned and think of what they'll say next. Some will bring a blank sheet of paper and may jot down key diagrams or charts from the text during the role play. The effect of these tactics seems to be to move the exam away from "real time" interaction and more in the direction of a traditional exam, in which the student has time to think, reflect, and even write about what is asked. My guideline has been to accept any behavior that might be reasonably tolerated in a live business setting. This means that I do tolerate occasional pauses and some jottings but not consistently long pauses or extensive jotting. I have noticed that students who demonstrate high competence on the exam very often go through the exam quickly: They formulate their role plays quickly and go through them with few pauses, false starts, or long deliberations.

Rambling Until Stopped

Some students apparently work on the hypothesis that the more behaviors they show, the more likely it is that I will find something to score. This kind of response may have been learned first in the context of an essay exam. Thus, in the role play they speak broadly and at length. If I think I see this tactic used, I will interrupt the role play and ask the person to summarize or move directly to the point. I may also counsel the person to speak more to the point or to commit him or herself to one "best bet." If the person continues to use this tactic, I may count the person down on an "etiquette" criterion, tell the person we are running short on time, and/or counsel the person about overlong speaking after the exam's end.

Not Responding to the Question

Some students seem unskilled in managing a response. They may wind down a discussion around the question without tying back to it, or they may apparently implicitly decide that a different question is the real (or more answerable) question, and answer it instead. I think sometimes students will handle application questions using a rigorous approach and deny that any good application of materials can be made. Once I realize that a problem of this type is in the making, it is not difficult to respond to. I may validate the person's line of discussion by agreeing that it is pertinent, then prompt the person to respond to the question asked. Sometimes the person will need reminding of what that question is.

Explanations Based on Common Sense

When asked to explain his/her behavior in a role play, the person may provide an accounting that makes no reference to course learning, even if he or she was asked explicitly to develop a role play based on some course materials. I find this tendency to slide away from course materials into "common sense" as one of the most common dislocations in the exam process. My guess is that many people find it difficult to manage both conceptual application and live interaction together, and so simply do what they "normally" do. This kind of response creates problems when trying to assess course learning as opposed to the level of competence the person brings to the course. My response to this tendency has been to carefully prompt people beforehand to base their role plays on course materials and to ask for an explanation at the end. Behavior that cannot be accounted for using course materials is scored down, even if it is reasonable. My rationale is that the purpose of the course is to add to their repertoire of skills, not simply to validate what they always have done.

Retrospective Explanation

A tactic related to the above is to retrospectively "fit" behavior to some course concept. In some situations a person may conduct a role play based totally on common sense. When I ask how the person was applying course materials, he or she may appear nonplused for a moment, then reflect and find an interpretation of his/her behavior that is consistent in some ways with the materials. I have mixed feelings when students do this but will score it as though the behavior was designed from the start. At least it shows knowledge of the materials and quick thinking!

Minimal Responses

When asked to account for their behavior, some people provide minimal responses that hint at a useful answer but do not flesh it out. I think this tactic may be directed at eliciting from me a series of prompting questions, which can provide hints to the examinee as to which direction to take. I know this is occurring when I start feeling impatient and as though I have to drag things from the person. When I see this happening, I will simply reiterate my basic question and, when the person finishes speaking, ask if he or she has anything more to add. This puts the burden back on the person to decide on what needs to be done.

Enumerating Rather Than Choosing

Sometimes I ask a person to choose one most appropriate approach that he or she could have used in the role play. Sometimes a person will respond by enumerating all the possible approaches that the course materials list. I see this both as a carryover from the more tentative academic approach students may learn in some college courses, as well as an attempt to communicate to me that he or she knows the materials. When I see this happening, I will interrupt and ask the person to simply describe one other approach that he or she sees as most appropriate.

Explaining by Process of Elimination

Sometimes role behavior is based on a typology, for example, types of listening responses or conflict resolution approaches. When asked why they chose a particular approach, some people answer by arguing why all the other alternatives were not appropriate. This approach, possibly developed in the context of answering multiple-choice questions, may be an attempt to show me that they know the material. However, if I see this happening, I will interrupt the person, state that I do not regard an elimination of alternatives as an argument for taking a particular course, and prompt him or her to explain why the behavior was appropriate in itself, without reference to the alternatives.

Asking Questions

Some students will ask me questions in the process of formulating their responses. This is perhaps a carryover from the class situation where such questions are appropriate. The more obvious of these are easily caught; for example, in answer to, "What were the conflict resolution approaches?" I may simply smile and say, "That's for you to tell me." Other questions, however, may be somewhere in between questions about what they should have learned and questions about exam process. For example, a person might say, "I can apply Kolberg's model here—is that what you're looking for?" Or he or she might pause in a role play and ask, "Am I on the right track?" In these cases I have to pause and think if there is a legitimate ambiguity in the exam or whether the person's confusion stems from a poor grasp of the material. In the former example I will probably answer the question. In the latter example I will probably prompt the person to continue in the way he or she thinks best.

A more subtle way of asking questions is for a student to seek cues from me as to how he or she is doing. For example, a person may take a certain tack in a role play and then pause and look at me with a questioning look. It is important for me to not to succumb to this invitation and respond with an encouraging (or discouraging) look. What I tend to do is respond as though it were a part of the role play (e.g., "Is there something else you wanted from me, boss?").

Impact of Exam on Course and Instructor's Role

Instituting action exams has led to changes in how students see the course and how I spend my time. These in turn have led to a number of other changes, which have resulted in a new balance of how the various factors of the course go together. In particular, action exams have led to changes in student motivation, how I allocate my time, and the extent of my contact with individual students. Each of these changes is discussed below.

Student Motivation

An important change created by action exams has been in what students are energized to do. In many courses, a significant amount of student effort is driven by exams, which energize students to do things that they believe will result in satisfactory exam scores. The institution of action exams has led to a channeling of that energy toward activities that will help prepare for an action exam, as opposed to a written exam. Before I gave action exams, many students felt that experiential activities such as role plays or skill practice assignments were of low instrumental value, if not irrelevant. Now students are more highly motivated to carry these activities out, even though the activities may be unfamiliar and initially uncomfortable.

Allocation of My Time

Having an exam that I believe measures course learning well, I am less worried about class process and more able to allow students and student groups to take responsibility for learning activities. Although I continue to be central in many classes, I now allocate less time to direct class management and more to group work, where groups take control and are responsible for planning and motivating the behavior of their members. I see my role now as more (a) a learning manager, who delegates to groups some of the activities I used to carry out personally; (b) a coach, who helps people and groups to organize effectively; (c) an assessor, providing timely feedback to students about their learning progress; and (d) a symbolic manager, whose concerned presence provides a framework in which student groups can develop their autonomy. As a result of my assessor role, I am placing more emphasis on rapid feedback. As noted earlier, I provide feedback to students about how they did and where they are in the course immediately after each action exam. In addition, I work hard to provide detailed feedback to student groups about their papers within a few days of receiving them.

My Contact With Students

Action exams have resulted in a much closer contact between students and myself. Students know they will spend 40 minutes with me in individual interaction and therefore expect that our relationship will not be distant. Conversely, I find myself becoming increasingly student-oriented in my approach to teaching. I collect basic information about students' backgrounds and take photos of groups. I use this information to learn people's names and something about them. I find myself becoming increasingly developmental in my orientation. As discussed earlier, I do some coaching in the action exams. I see the exam as a competency assessment process that provides useful information to students, in addition to a grade. I am less evaluative of low performers. While I will not hesitate to give a low-performing person a low grade, I will accept that a person has made choices leading to low performance without judgment. Because I get to know students better than many instructors in other courses, I am increasingly asked to provide references. At semester's end, I invite students to visit me after graduation so that we can catch each other up. All of these dynamics work together to move the course toward a closer, person-oriented experience.

Conclusion

In this chapter I have described some ways in which I have evolved through the learning involved in seven years of giving action exams. By instituting action exams in my OB courses, I have effectively made a structural intervention, which in turn has led over time to systemic changes in the courses. These changes include movement toward a student-oriented teaching approach, a shift in teaching style toward learning manager, coach, and feedback provider, and increasing expertise in developing and managing action exams.

If I were to retrospectively create goals that my current course design fulfills, they would be to develop a skill-centered course in which (a) skill-learning outcomes are measured more directly; (b) the examination process is sustainable in a *normal university setting* with small- to medium-size classes; (c) learning measures are as valid as possible; and (d) the design and process of the course provide a positive modeling of the skills to be learned. I think the course design described in this chapter satisfies these objectives pretty well. However, there is some strain among these goals, particularly between (b) and (c). The reader may be able to think of a number of ways to improve on criterion (c); for example, through use of multiple raters (including other faculty or businesspeople), more exam situations, actors, multiple-skill action situations, videotaped review process, or external raters.

I think that incorporation of any of these ideas can improve the *validity* of the skill measurement process. However, they also reduce the *sustainability* of the process by increasing the amount of time, effort, and money required to carry it out. Consequently I have yet to see anyone carry out these ideas in a normal university setting for an extended period. Eventually, the innovator tires of the effort and goes back to more traditional examination procedures. For those interested in instituting a sustained action exam process, the implication is clear: Either obtain additional resources for the course or develop an action exam process that does not significantly add to the resources required of the course and the instructor. Certainly a sustainable action examination procedure will not be as valid as a procedure possible in a more time- and resource-intensive setting. Nonetheless, I believe that in a skills-centered course, a sustainable action exam procedure represents a dramatic advance over more traditional measurement methods.

Notes

1. Sometimes the preliminary conversation will unearth a situation relevant to an action exam question; for example, a recent encounter with a boss. I sometimes will use this reported situation in place of the written question.

2. I currently use HyperCard on the Macintosh as a means for keeping student data and giving action exams. Each student's record is kept on a separate "card" and is linked to the exam screens via on-screen buttons that can be clicked by the mouse. The program also can print out class scores in various formats and generate exam sheets. I am willing to share this program with others on a public domain basis. IBM users may be interested in looking into "Plus," a program for the IBM that reads Macintosh HyperCard files.

11 Examining the Exam: Ruminations on the Development of a Management Action-Skills Assessment Procedure

Glenn M. McEvoy

Higher education has come under increasingly intense scrutiny in the past decade as tight budgets have led legislators and concerned citizens to demand accountability from their educational institutions. Traditional *input* measures of educational excellence—such as student-teacher ratios, number of faculty with doctorates, SAT scores of incoming freshmen, number of volumes in the library, and breadth of the curriculum—have been questioned in terms of their evaluation usefulness. In their place, stakeholders in the educational process are demanding measures of *outcomes* or achievement (Grant et al., 1979).

Business and management education has not been exempt from either the criticisms directed toward higher education or the calls for increased accountability. In fact, the flagship degree of management education—the MBA—has been increasingly singled out as a possible *cause* of the lack of U.S. competitiveness in world markets (Peters & Waterman, 1982). Critics maintain that while American business education performs acceptably in building conceptual and analytical skills, it does poorly in preparing students for the interpersonal and behavioral components of a manager's job (Porter & McKibbin, 1988).

Competency Measurement and the Criterion Problem

In response to the calls for accountability, academic disciplines such as law and medicine have undertaken a competency-based approach to education, specifying what underlying traits, motives, self-images, and skills are required for successful performance outside the classroom, and then have attempted to develop those competencies in their students (Berk, 1986).

In the past 10 years, the American Assembly of Collegiate Schools of Business (AACSB) has spent more than a half million dollars investigating ways in which business schools can become more responsive and accountable to their stakeholders (Albanese, 1987). The first phase of this 3-phase project identified the learning outcomes desired of business school graduates by various constituents and categorized these into cognitive and noncognitive areas (AACSB, 1987).

At this point, the AACSB project ran head on into "the criterion problem." That is, once the desired outcomes were identified, the problem became one of determining how to measure those outcomes. Therefore, in Phase 2 and Phase 3, the AACSB (a) developed face-valid tests to measure management skills such as decision making, problem analysis, written and oral communication, leadership, self-objectivity, planning and organizing, and delegation; and (b) explored the reliability of, and administrator reactions to, the face-valid testing procedure. The testing procedure developed was a modification of the assessment center procedure used in industry and is presently available for purchase commercially from Development Dimensions International (AACSB, 1987).

Skills Measures for Individual Courses

The problem with the AACSB testing procedure is that it is time-consuming (1.5 days per student), expensive ($198 per student), and tests at the level of the entire curriculum (Dobbins, 1989). An individual instructor cannot afford to use an assessment center to measure skill learning in a single class. As a result, there has been some activity in the development of management action-skills testing procedures applicable to individual classes.

For example, Bigelow (1983), Lee, Adler, Hartwick, and Waters (1987-1988), and Waters, Adler, Hartwick, and Poupart (1983) have all developed and tested action-skill exams using primarily a role-play approach. Utah State University (USU) began a stream of research in 1986 designed to develop a behavioral testing technique and assess various ways of developing managerial action skills in business students. Procedurally, the USU skills test built on the approaches proposed by Bigelow (1983) and Waters et al. (1983).

Early psychometric results for the USU procedure were encouraging. The test was shown to be reliable, with interrater reliability coefficients ranging from 0.68 to 0.81 (McEvoy, 1988; McEvoy & Cragun, 1986, 1986-1987). Thus, one hurdle was overcome.

A second concern was with the nature of the construct of management action skills. The USU skills test procedure uses a checklist approach to measure the skills of communication, problem solving, delegation, conflict management, motivation, and performance feedback in role-play situations. Each checklist identifies and scores six behaviors that make up the overall skill, using a presence-absence approach as recommended by Cameron and Whetten (1983). (More details on this testing procedure are provided later in the chapter.) While some desirable behavior is the same across problem areas (e.g., active listening, joint problem solving), other types are different. Thus, to some degree, the USU scoring procedure assumes a "situationalist" perspective and uses a "focused ratings" approach where each skill area is broken into subparts that are rated separately. Regarding such a rating approach, Mead (1986) has noted that "although it is relatively easy to establish interrater reliability with these types of scales, there is a danger that the rating scales can be trivial and fail to represent the complexity of the . . . task" (p. 514).

Thus, the high interrater reliabilities achieved by the USU approach may be an artifact of the method used. An alternative measurement strategy would be more holistic, with a global or overall rating given in each skill area (Mead, 1986). McKnight (1988) has proposed such a "universalistic" approach to management action-skills assessment. He suggested that role plays in any management skill area could be scored, using a single universal scoring sheet that assessed 14 elements pertaining to the boss, the subordinate, and the process (e.g., Does the boss listen? Is the boss honest? Does the boss create a win/win situation? Is the subordinate motivated to improve?).

Because of this concern, the USU action-skills test was compared with a holistic rating approach, as suggested by McKnight (1988). The result, which is reported in detail in McEvoy and Cragun (1988), was a substantial and significant correlation ($r = 0.48$) between the two results. Thus, the results of the two approaches appear to converge even though they make different initial assumptions about the nature of managerial action skills. This provided an increased level of confidence in the focused ratings approach to the assessment of such skills.

Other Validity Concerns

The issue of validity is extremely complex. To be valid in our context the test procedure must be capable of assessing the criterion of "managerial performance." This criterion has been examined extensively over the past 50 years in industrial psychology and, it still remains illusive (Thornton & Byham, 1982). If we could measure all factors that contribute to managerial success and performance over time, we would be tapping the so-called "ultimate criterion." As this is impossible, researchers settle for approximations of this criterion. Specifically, the most common criterion involves the judgment of others recorded in the form of a rating.

In the case of students, a good approximation of the ultimate criterion would be performance ratings and record of accomplishment over an entire working career. Such a study would require about 40 years of longitudinal data—obviously a time frame too long to be practical.

Lee et al. (1987-1988) attempted to overcome this problem by having managers from local firms sit in on behavioral exams of their MBA students and provide an overall assessment of each student's interpersonal skills. They found acceptable correlations of $r = 0.56$ to 0.84 between managers' ratings and those provided by faculty using a detailed rating sheet, and labeled these correlations "validity coefficients." However, the correlation between similarly situated raters is generally considered evidence of reliability rather than validity (Bernardin & Beatty, 1984). Thus, additional evidence of validity is needed.

A short-term criterion that has potential in the case of students is a rating of on-the-job performance in the same areas assessed by the action-skills testing procedure. Validity of the competency test could thus be examined for students employed in management positions. Accordingly, the purpose of the next portion of this chapter is to present a preliminary empirical investigation into the validity of the USU management action-skills testing procedure using the criterion of on-the-job ratings.

Methodology: Action-Skills Test and the Criterion

This research examined the validity of the USU skills testing procedure by comparing test scores with the ratings provided by current supervisors, peers, and subordinates for students in management positions. Seventeen MBA students who were employed in management positions provided the sample for this preliminary investigation. They were recruited from a graduate class in human resource management that I taught in the summer of 1988.

These student-managers were tested in the following action skills using USU's current test procedure: interpersonal communication, performance feedback, delegation, conflict management, problem solving, and motivation.

The Action-Skills Test

The USU skills testing procedure requires about 20 minutes for each student. Three skill areas from the list above are chosen at random to be tested. When the student enters the testing room, he or she is presented with a stimulus scenario for the first skill area to be tested. A sample scenario in the area of problem solving might be:

> You are the manager of a prestigious ladies' clothing store. It is your responsibility, among many others, to schedule the work of all nine store employees. The owner of the store, John Fantasia, has a daughter named Joan. John hired his daughter to work in the store and has instructed you to let her have the hours she desires, which are weekdays until 5 p.m. Since the store is open evenings and weekends, and the number of employees is small, you have had to move several long-term employees to less desirable shifts to keep the store covered at all times it is open. These employees have not been happy about giving up their better time schedules to the boss's "spoiled punk-rock" daughter and have expressed their unhappiness to you in no uncertain terms. You feel certain that several of these valuable employees may quit if you don't do something about this problem. You decide to confront John Fantasia now.

The student is given 1 to 2 minutes to review the information in the scenario and prepare to play the role assigned. The instructor plays the other role. Generally, there is a trained graduate assistant in the room along with the instructor. As the role play develops, both instructor and graduate assistant score the student's performance, using a standardized checklist. Upon completion of the first role play, the procedure is repeated twice more with new scenarios in different skill areas. Student scores are the average of those assigned by the instructor and the assistant, and the total skills test score is the sum of an individual's scores on each of the three role plays. (All analyses in this chapter were performed with *total* action-skills test scores.)

Rating checklists have been developed for each skill area based on a review of the pertinent literature (see McEvoy & Cragun, 1986-1987, for a more thorough discussion of checklist development). Each checklist provides for scores from 0 to 10 on a single scale. A sample is provided in Table 11.1.

The course from which these student-managers were drawn was an off-campus course. For that reason, the usual USU skills testing procedure had to be modified slightly: A graduate assistant was not present at the time the test was taken. Rather, the test was tape-recorded, and the graduate assistant provided a skills rating after listening to the tape (versus making a "live" rating). Possibly because of this modification, the inter-rater reliability of the test scores was not as high as usual: $r = 0.64$.

The Criterion

A rating form containing each of the six performance dimensions (communication, performance feedback, delegation, conflict manage-ment, problem solving, and motivation) was developed. A sample is appended to this chapter. Terms used on the form were defined and behavioral examples provided. The form also asked for an assessment of overall management skills. All performance dimensions were assessed on 6-point scales (0 to 5).

These ratings forms were sent to each student-manager's immediate supervisor plus two peers and two subordinates in a good position to observe his or her performance. Ratings were returned directly to the researcher in a preaddressed envelope. In addition, student-managers provided a self-rating, using the same form.

Since two peers and two subordinates provided ratings for each stu-dent-manager, interrater reliabilities could be calculated for these two sources. Unfortunately, these reliability coefficients were disappointingly low. The highest was 0.35, and none achieved statistical significance. Thus, all subsequent interpretation of these ratings must be undertaken with extreme caution.

Results

Ratings from the two peers were averaged, as were the ratings from the two subordinates. These averaged ratings are referred to as the peer and subordinate ratings, respectively, in subsequent analyses.

Table 11.1

Sample Score Sheet for Assessing Behavioral Skills

Skill Area: Problem Solving

                                                                    Score

1. Establishes environment conducive to   ____   ____
    effective communication and explains   0   1
    the reason for the meeting.   0 = does not do or does inadequately
                                                    1 = does adequately

2. Asks other for his or her views on the   ____   ____   ____
    nature of the problem: 0   1   2
    a) Listens actively.   0 = does not do
                                                    1 = does
                                                    2 = does and demonstrates active
                                                          listening

3. States own views on the problem: ____   ____   ____
    a) Speaks assertively.   0   1   2
                                                    0 = does not do
                                                    1 = does
                                                    2 = does and demonstrates assertion
                                                          skills

4. Arrives at a mutually agreeable definition   ____   ____
    of the problem.   0   1
                                                    0 = does not do or does inadequately
                                                    1 = does adequately

5. Jointly resolves the problem using the   ____   ____   ____
    following steps: 0   1   2
    a. set/clarify goals and objectives;   0 = does not do
    b. generate alternatives;   1 = engages in some of these steps
    c. evaluate alternatives;   2 = engages in most of these steps
    d. select the best alternative and implement.

6. Sets a date and time for evaluation of the   ____   ____
    decision and follow-up.   0   1
                                                    0 = does not do or does inadequately
                                                    1 = does adequately

Overall assessment   ____   ____
                                                    0   1

                                                    Total Points _____

Table 11.2
Descriptive Statistics for Major Study Variables

Variable	Mean	SD
Supervisor rating (sum) (SUPERSUM)	24.5	6.8
Supervisor rating (overall) (SUPEROVL)	3.7	1.1
Peer rating (sum) (PEERSUM)	23.5	3.8
Peer rating (overall) (PEEROVL)	3.5	.5
Self rating (sum) (SELFSUM)	22.6	3.9
Self rating (overall) (SELFOVL)	3.3	.6
Subordinate rating (sum) (SUBORDSUM)	25.1	4.4
Subordinate rating (overall) (SUBORDOVL)	3.8	.7
Action-skills test score (ACTSKILL)	14.9	3.6

NOTE: $n = 17$

All analyses in this chapter were performed using both the sum of the dimension ratings and the overall management skills rating from each of the four sources (supervisor, peer, subordinate, self). Thus eight ratings, two from each source, were examined. Descriptive statistics for these eight ratings and the total skills test score are provided in Table 11.2. As can be seen, the amount of variance present in the peer, self, and subordinate ratings is relatively small.

Table 11.3 reports the intercorrelations of all study variables, including the action-skills test score. On the whole, correlations between the eight criteria variables were disappointingly low (see the first eight lines in

Table 11.3

Correlations of All Study Variables

	1	2	3	4	5	6	7	8
1. SUPERSUM								
2. SUPEROVL	.94							
3. PEERSUM	.34	.25						
4. PEEROVL	.26	.21	.90					
5. SELFSUM	.46	.55	.05	−.04				
6. SELFOVL	.74	.82	.13	.03	.79			
7. SUBORDSUM	.22	.30	.25	.06	.24	.16		
8. SUBORDOVL	.16	.25	.19	.07	.28	.17	.92	
9. ACTSKILL	.22	.38	.08	.12	.80	.61	−.07	.00

NOTES: See Table 11.2 for meanings of abbreviations.
$n = 17$
rs > .70, $p < .001$
rs between .55 and .70, $p < .01$
rs between .40 and .55, $p < .05$
rs between .31 and .40, $p < .10$
rs < .31, ns

Table 11.3). The two ratings provided by supervisors on the job (a sum and an overall skills rating) were correlated fairly highly with self-ratings (0.46 to 0.82) but only modestly with ratings by peers (0.21 to 0.34) and subordinates (0.16 to 0.30). Self, peer, and subordinate ratings were interrelated only slightly (rs ranged from -0.04 to 0.28, with a median r of 0.14). These modest intercorrelations prohibited the use of a composite single criterion against which to judge the validity of the skills test procedure.

The last line in Table 11.3 presents the data relevant to the question of the validity of the action-skills testing procedure. As can be seen, the test scores correlated highly with self-ratings (0.61 and 0.80), modestly with supervisor ratings (0.22 and 0.38), and hardly at all with peer and subordinate ratings (rs from -0.07 to 0.12).

Are the USU Skill Tests Valid?

Overall, this preliminary small sample investigation provided mixed evidence for the validity of the USU action-skills testing procedure. Correlations with skills test scores were impressive for self-ratings, respectable for supervisor ratings, and disappointing for peer and subordinate ratings. Of course, the peer and subordinate ratings used in this study did not demonstrate acceptable interrater reliabilities, nor was much variance present in the ratings, so the failure to find them related to the action-skills test may be attributable to psychometric problems with those measures. Clearly, more work is needed here.

Perhaps in future studies five or six peers and five or six subordinates should be involved in providing criterion ratings. This step should improve interrater reliabilities. Further work may also be needed on instructions to these raters, controls on which peers and subordinates provide the ratings, and the seriousness with which those chosen approach the rating task.

Also, a clear limitation of the present study is its small sample size ($n = 17$). A small number was adequate for a preliminary investigation of this type, but larger samples are needed in subsequent studies to avoid the problems of weak statistical power and capitalization on chance. The results obtained in the present study—both the finding of statistical significance for some correlations and the failure to find significance for other correlations—must be interpreted with utmost caution because of the small number of subjects involved.

Another explanation for the failure to find adequate and consistent correlations between the skills test and on-the-job performance ratings may be a weakness in the skills testing procedure itself. It is possible, for instance, that a 20-minute role play does not provide adequate time to accurately capture behavior that is reflected in on-the-job performance over an extended period of time. There has been speculation in the assessment center literature that some individuals may be able to "shine" over a 2-to-3-day period and still not make good managers. Of course, the generally well-proven predictive validity of assessment centers reduces the persuasiveness of this argument (Thornton & Byham, 1982), but if such a concern can be raised for a 2-to-3-day assessment center, then it clearly is a possibility for a 20-minute role play.

Perhaps future attempts at skill assessment need to take a broader course-long approach much like the traditional "class participation" grade, except based on demonstration of specific management action skills in class over the entire length of the course. In addition, future validation efforts need to adopt a longer time perspective. For instance, a useful approach may be to follow up 1 year after a student has graduated to see if there is any relationship between skills measured during college and skills demonstrated later on the job.

Of course, it is possible that only a modest correlation is to be expected between the skills test used in this situation and on-the-job performance ratings. The action-skills test is analogous in some ways to a "work sample" in personnel selection, where the stimuli and responses in the testing situation approximate those of the work environment (e.g., a typing test for typists). Bernardin and Beatty (1984) have pointed out that in such situations low correlations may be expected because of the different sources of variance present in the rating and work samples. Specifically, whereas performance on the job is a function of both ability and motivation, performance on the action-skills test may be primarily a function of ability because motivation levels are likely to be high and consistent across all participants in the test.

Perhaps this distinction between "will" and "skill" can be illustrated best by looking at the ratings of one particular student in the sample. This student performed very well on the action-skills test as a whole and on the dimension of delegation in particular. Yet, ratings from his subordinates were low. In explaining his low ratings, one subordinate wrote that this manager sometimes delegated work to others who were "incapable of integrating new ideas and techniques into problem solving." Other comments by this subordinate suggested that he viewed his manager as having the underlying skill needed to delegate effectively ("his analytical and problem-solving skills are excellent in most areas") but simply failed to use these skills in delegating.

The significant relationship between self-ratings and action-skills test scores may be an artifact of the methodology because students took the skills test score first and then rated their own job performance some time during the following week. Even though students did not receive feedback on how well they had done on the test, it is possible that their self-perceived performance in the skills test setting contaminated their own on-the-job ratings and led them to rate themselves more in line with performance in the work sample than they might have without that experience. Of course, other raters were not exposed to the action-skills test setting and hence may have been less familiar with what each of the performance dimensions meant operationally (even though these dimensions were defined in some detail on the rating form). Based on the low interrater reliabilities and low intercorrelations with other sources of performance data, it appears that peers and subordinates in particular may have been unclear as to the meanings of the performance dimensions.

Establishing the validity of any measurement is a complex and ongoing endeavor that involves more than a single step. Our concern at the outset is really one of construct validity: the degree to which inferences can be drawn about the underlying construct (managerial performance) from the results of the measurement process (action-skills test). Campbell (1976) suggested fully eight different ways in which construct validity could be assessed. One of these—correlational studies between variables theorized to measure the same thing—was the approach taken in this chapter. But clearly, there are many other avenues open to researchers in this area.

Conclusion

The ultimate objective for this stream of research is to help colleges of business become more responsive to their constituents. Many different approaches to the development of student managerial skills are possible: case study, lecture, discussion, experiential exercises, behavior modeling training, computer-assisted instruction, and so forth. However, before experimentation can begin with different educational methods, we must have a reliable and valid criterion against which to measure the relative success of these different approaches. Criterion development, a frequently overlooked step in educational improvement, was the focus of this research. Clearly, considerably more work remains to be done on this important topic.

Appendix: Sample Rating Form

Numerical ratings are to be assigned using a scale from 0 to 5 where:

0 = very poor performance compared to other peers
1 = below average performance compared to other peers
2 = average performance compared to other peers (STANDARD PERFOR-MANCE)
3 = above-average performance compared to other peers
4 = outstanding performance (better than 80% of peers)
5 = consistently superior performance (better than 95% of peers)

Note that the peer comparison group here is to be other managers with whom you are familiar.

**Numerical
Rating**

Skill Area 1: COMMUNICATION

Consider the extent to which she communicates a desire to listen, is empathic, uses an active listening approach when appropriate, owns her statements, shares feelings in a statement beginning with "I," uses neutral language to avoid defensive reactions, avoids dogmatic assertions, and is sensitive to the congruency of her nonverbal and verbal messages.   _____

Skill Area 2: PERFORMANCE FEEDBACK

Consider the extent to which he carefully observes performance-related behavior in others, provides negative performance information in a manner that does not cause defensiveness, uses descriptive—not evaluative—statements when conveying negative feedback that objectively describes what happened and the organizational consequences of the behavior, and uses problem-oriented (not people-oriented) statements.   _____

Skill Area 3: PROBLEM SOLVING/DECISION-MAKING

Consider the extent to which she asks others for their views on the nature of the problem, states her own views on the problem assertively but not aggressively, arrives at a mutually agreeable definition of the problem, resolves the problem through clarification of goals and objectives, generation and evaluation of alternatives, and follow-up with effective implementation of the decision. _____

Skill Area 4: DELEGATION

Consider the extent to which he selects appropriate subordinates to delegate to, clarifies desired outcomes, provides authority and resources to accomplish the task, assures the subordinate understands the assignment, informs all those affected of the delegation of duties, and provides appropriate follow-up. _____

Skill Area 5: CONFLICT RESOLUTION

Consider the extent to which she defuses potentially volatile situations, asks for others' perceptions of the problem and listens actively, states her own perception of the problem assertively, arrives at a mutually agreeable definition of the problem in terms of the underlying needs of both parties, and uses a confrontation approach to arrive at a satisfactory resolution to the conflict. _____

Skill Area 6: MOTIVATION

Consider the extent to which he assures that the problem is one of motivation (vs. communication, knowledge), determines the nature of any motivation problem, ascertains the motivational needs of other individuals, jointly sets performance goals, and finds ways to reinforce desirable behaviors in others through provision of valued outcomes contingent upon performance. _____

Skill Area 7: OVERALL MANAGEMENT SKILLS RATING

Considering all six dimensions above, how would you rate his or her overall management skills? _____

Why did you give this overall rating?

Part IV Insights Into Managerial Skills

There seems to be some convergence among studies about the important management skill areas, for example, communication, conflict management, influence,
and so on. Relatively little attention has been given, however, to the phenomenon
of skill. My impression is that we tend to implicitly rely on a "black box" view of
skills. In this view, primary attention is directed toward pedagogy and skill
measurement. What are skills? From a black box point of view, they are whatever
is taught and/or whatever increases between pretesting and posttesting. I worry
sometimes that skill areas such as communication, conflict management, power,
and the like become "garbage cans" into which instructors dump any materials
associated with the area. These materials, in turn, become the definition of the
skill. I'm also aware, from my own action exam experience, that an oral exam can
test retention of cognitive material, for example, understanding of a conflict model.
Thus it is possible to develop an "action" exam that reflects only the ability to use
one, possibly narrow, way of thinking about the skill.

Our image of skills may be overly influenced by corporate training, which
emphasizes "designed" skills, usually intended for well-defined job settings.
These tend to be procedural, convergent, unilateral, and short-term. Managerial
skills, on the other hand, are characteristically "natural" skills, which can be highly
contingent, varied in expresssion, interactive, and also long-term in their impact.

In sum, we are only beginning to learn about the nature of skills. What are we
learning? The five chapters of this section provide new insights into the nature of
managerial skills, and by extension, into the pedagogy of teaching managerial
skills.

In Chapter 12, David Coghlan and Nicholas Rashford suggest that skills are a
multilevel systems phenomenon. They propose that managerial skills can be
organized by four levels of organizational participation. They describe how this
model can be used in skill-training workshops and at the MBA level.

The next two chapters provide insight into both the skill learner and the kinds
of situations in which skills are practiced. In Chapter 13, Ray Rasmussen points
out that people enter skill-training courses with already developed practice theories, which may be dissonant with prospective learning. He describes active
listening practice theories that his students bring and how course materials may
not persuade these students to change their practice. In Chapter 14, Ken Keleman
and his colleagues propose that problem situations requiring managerial skills are
typically "messy" and usually require an interweaving application of several skills.
They describe an instructional approach that centers on holistic, ill-structured

situations. They discuss student response to this approach and provide an interactional appraisal form.

The final two chapters of the book provide the deepest challenges to the way we think about skills. In Chapter 15, Melvin McKnight asserts that skills are by their nature responsive and subconscious. He criticizes current skill-learning programs and describes a skills course that uses primarily coaching and practice to develop participants' skills. In Chapter 16, Robert Quinn and his colleagues refer to a number of other chapters in this book while developing the proposition that the current "transactional" approach to skills teaching must be complemented with a second-order, "transformational" approach. They describe not only the development and implementation of such a program at Ford but also its effects on managers.

12 Developing Key Intervention Skills on Four Organizational Levels

David Coghlan

Nicholas S. Rashford

Training and developing managers in skills that enable them to deal effectively with the multiple issues within an organization is a perennial task for OB teachers and trainers. In the systems approach, complex systems are divided into hierarchical levels of complexity (Miller, 1978). In organizations these levels are typically described as individual, group, intergroup, and organizational (Rousseau, 1985; Staw, 1984). Levels of organizational behavior are common in organizational behavior and organization development (OD) texts. In these texts they seem to be rather static notions, providing convenient headings under which particular elements of organizational behavior can be located. One approach, which we developed (Rashford & Coghlan, 1987), attempts to articulate and link together the different levels of behavior in organizations. It describes levels in a more dynamic framework of how people participate in organizations by defining them in terms of tasks and interventions and attempting to link them to provide a useful action-skills tool for managers. This framework is integrative in that it attempts to describe in a single paradigm the psychological processes of individual, group, and intergroup behavior with issues of technological and strategic management (Harrison, 1987; Ivancevich, Szilagyi, & Wallace, 1977; James & Jones, 1974). This chapter outlines that framework in terms of managerial action skills, and draws on experience in using it in management development workshops and an executive MBA program (Rashford & Coghlan 1988, 1989).

171

Four Levels of Organizational Behavior

The framework that we put forward (Rashford & Coghlan, 1987) describes four levels of participation in organizations (individual, face-to-face team, divisional/group, strategy/policy). These levels can be viewed as degrees or types of involvement, or as degrees of complexity, depending on whether one approaches the question from the point of the view of the individual moving toward the organization to participate or on the part of the organization viewing the commitment of individuals. From the point of view of the individual, the least complex approach is the relationship that the individual has with the organization. The more complex approach to participation exists in working out and solving the difficulties of a face-to-face working team. An even more complex involvement exists in terms of the group or divisional type of interface, where teams must work together to achieve complex tasks. Finally, the most complex, from the point of view of the individual, is the relationship of the total organization to its external environment in which other organizations are individual competitors, competing for scarce resources to produce similar products or services. On the part of the organization, the question is one of involvement. The most basic involvement is to get a person committed to the goals, values, and culture of the organization. The second level of involvement is to establish good, working face-to-face relationships in functional teams. The third level of involvement is the group or divisional level in which complex MIS and data systems must by used to extend the knowledge and coordinate the functions of complex working divisions or strategic business units. Finally, the most complex of all is the unified effort of all participants in an organization toward the end of making the organization profitable, growth oriented, and functional in its external environment. This set of complex behaviors, then, is separated into a cognitive map—a mental construct of different types of participation and involvement—by the use of the concept of levels of participation.

There are many interventions that could be utilized on each level to enable it to function effectively. The selection of a "key" intervention, as the one to best enable a particular level to achieve its task, emerges from the particular tasks and definition of each level. It is evident that the interventions are drawn particularly from the OD literature, whose theory and practice provide an action-research approach to facilitation change. It is essential for the contemporary manager to develop effective process skills (Schein, 1988). Our (1987) framework of organizational levels, constructed specifically around central process issues for the individual, the team, the group/division, and the strategy/policy levels, demonstrates how core skills must incorporate all four levels. Other frameworks that give particular attention to, for example, individual or team skills are not inconsistent with this framework. In this chapter, we offer our framework to further reflection and development of action-skills models.

Level 1 describes the Individual level. When it is in place and operating effectively, a person will allow the organization and its goals be a source of personal goal motivation. The individual will still retain his or her own individuality while "belonging" to the organization. The key intervention on this level is the career interview in which the dynamics of the life cycle, the work cycle, and the family cycle are located and place in juxtaposition so that the individual can locate his or her career in the context of his or her life.

Level 2 describes the Team level. When it is functioning effectively, there is an additional commitment to the organization to work together in a face-to-face team. The effective team acts as a unit working toward a common goal. Effectiveness in this concept means that a team is capable of finding and correcting its own dysfunctions. A successful team is only perceived as successful after it has successfully corrected its own dysfunction. The individual's task is to contribute to the team's functioning, while the team's task is to be a functioning unit. The organization's task is that the team be significant in its output. The key intervention on this Level 2 is that of team-building.

The Group or Divisional level is Level 3. This level is made up of several fact-to-face working teams that must function together to accomplish a divisional purpose, such as manufacturing, sales, or marketing, or it is a collection of individual work teams that provide a strategic business unit function for an organization. When the third level is in place, the group or division is capable of obtaining information and converting it into decision processes, enabling the implementation of complex programs or operations. The task of this level is to map the flow of information and partially completed work from one unit to another. The organization's task is to see that these units form an effective aggregate. The key intervention on this level is internal mapping, where dysfunctions in information or work flow are identified and corrected.

Level 4 is the Organizational Policy or Strategy level. It is the final fusion of these divisional groups together to form a working, whole organization. It must be capable of reflecting on its own strengths and weaknesses, as well as being engaged proactively in determining the opportunities and threats from the external environment. It matches these two in a selection process that determines programs, services, and products aimed at accomplishing the goals of the organization and servicing the external environment with its products and services. The key intervention is open systems planning, performed in terms of the organization's core mission, with its internal and external constituencies that make demands on the organization.

It is suggested that there is a close link between each level. For instance, an action taken on Level 4 can affect a team's functioning and lead to an individual's questioning his or her sense of belonging to the organization. So a triggering event on Level 4 must be dealt with on Levels 1 and 2. Effectiveness on Level 2 depends on Level 1 being in place, Level 3 depends on Levels 1 and 2, and Level 4 on all three. Our hypothesis is that such a delineation of levels in terms of definition, tasks, and key intervention provides a valuable diagnostic construct and repertoire of skills for the manager. The more static uses of the notion of levels does not attempt to build links between levels in this dynamic way.

Management Action Skills on Each Level

The framework helps unravel the complexity of the task of understanding how people function in organizations and provides a key to effective intervention on each level. This chapter focuses on the four key interventions—the career interview, team-building, internal mapping, and open systems planning—as core managerial skills needed to enable each level to function effectively. The learned ability to use these interventions appropriately and effectively constitutes a useful managerial skill. The conceptual background on which each intervention is based is provided.

Level 1 Skills: Individual

The individual adult's life cycle, work cycle, and family cycle provide the context of the individual's relationship with the organization and the issues of human resource management (Schein, 1978). The managers study the life-cycle concepts and make the transition to their own behavior as a laboratory for learning about the behavior of others. The first aspect of getting them involved is to have them reflect on their own life cycles and chart a history that traces their reactions to past behavior and feelings. They are invited to reflect on their own progress through the life, work, and family cycles in order to assess their own development and identify the key feelings associated with each stage in their experience. The critical insight comes with their basic assertion of the validity of the life-cycle information and difference in individual approaches to the stages. A second insight comes from seeing that an individual's experience is only one part of a bigger picture and so the need to understand others' experience to complete the picture.

The second focus is to apply the individual aspect of the adult life cycle to the workplace, using the concept of the career anchor, as described by Schein (1978, 1985a). After an explanation of career anchors, managers are introduced to the practice of the career interview. In the career interview the individual's history is explored through the narration of career and vocational choices juxtaposed with issues of personal values and the interaction of the life and family cycles (Schein, 1985a). The significant point of instruction in the career interview is allowing the interviewee ownership of his or her own career story as the interview attempts to be sensitive to the other's dreams and to draw a pattern from the interview (Schein, 1985b).

Learning is enhanced in two ways. First, the individual's self-reflection opens the door to bringing emotions and life issues into the world of work, and ties the effects of these issues back to job performance. The second point of learning is accomplished by the comparison of the individual's own career interviews with those of other participants. This provides the beginnings of a mosaic detailing the larger patterns of life cycles, anchors, career setbacks, dual careers, and other individual workplace issues. The proactive learning process comes from intervention in the growth and development of peers and subordinates.

Level 2 Skills: Team

There are three elements to this section. First, the key skill is to understand the significant difference between process and content in order to understand and experience team facilitation and repair. Inputs on group process and team-building are made in this context, using Schein (1988) and Beckhard (1972). Beckhard's team-building dynamics comprise four activities: setting goals and priorities, allocating work, examining the team process, and developing the interpersonal relationships. There are different perspectives on these activities—the leader's, the members', outcomes, and a third-party consultant's. Second, the face-to-face team skills a leader needs in the contemporary workplace are introduced. These skills include: self-insight, cross-cultural sensitivity, cultural/moral humility, proactive problem-solving orientation, personal flexibility, negotiation skills, interpersonal and cultural tact, repair strategies and skills, and patience (Schein, 1981). The final element focuses on the concept of process consultation (Schein, 1987). There are three parts to this element. First, the distinction between process and content is made. Second, the key elements of process are highlighted and examined. Third, the process of entering into a process-consulting relationship and intervening is explored. The process-consultation approach is much more than a technique of working with groups. It is a philosophy of working with human systems.

Particular skills sessions are devoted to cases and experiential processes to illustrate team dynamics and to strengthen the process-consultation skills of the managers. Structured experiences such as Tinkertoys™ or Construct O Straw can provide much of the Level 2 dynamics. The exercise is structured to provide the possibility for the experience of the development of teams and the observation of process. The processes are recorded on video. Debriefing focuses on both the team dynamics learnings and learnings on the consultation processes.

Level 3 Skills: Group/Divisional

The overall goal on this Level 3 is to understand and experience internal mapping processes (Beckhard, 1975). Descriptions of information systems, definitions of PERT, issues of work flow and the sharing of resources, systems fit and interteam power relations (Harrison, 1987) provide the conceptual framework on which Level 3 behavior is based. Level 3 intervention is, by its nature, a process that takes at least 1 or 2 years. It is fraught with complex mapping processes, dealing with the utilization of scarce resources, the tracking of complex engineering, and the design and application of product processes.

The key task in internal mapping is to plot the flow of operations and map the functions so as to develop a sense of where overlaps and dysfunctions occur. A second task is devoted to the practice of getting the larger picture from each map and setting goals for change processes and review. Individuals studied a case in which the engineering and design of prefabricated building projects provided examples for discussion. The work is best done in and between the actual work teams. One of the most successful interventions took place around the engineering group at AT&T Long Lines. The group mapped out the flow of work installing the new optic fiber transmission line step-by-step. The process extended over 2 years and had about 6,700 steps in seven stages. The mapping process pointed out how the process broke down between stages of the different engineering functions.

A second section is devoted to the topic of organizational learning (Argyris & Schon, 1978). Managers are introduced to the concepts of single- and double-loop learning, organizational double-loop learning, and intervention strategies. Case material is used in the application of these concepts. The focus here is to acquaint managers with the blocks to organizational learning that can be a feature of the Level 3 process.

Level 4 Skills: Strategy/Policy

The goal is to understand Level 4 by experiencing the organization's endeavor to exist and participate in a competitive environment. The first section is given to open-systems planning (Beckhard & Harris, 1977) and its application and the second to the definition and review of the concept of stakeholders (Freeman, 1984).

The 6 steps of open-systems planning are:

Step 1: Defining the organization's core mission
Step 2: Mapping the current demand system
Step 3: Mapping the current response system
Step 4: Projecting the future demand system
Step 5: Conceiving the desired future state
Step 6: Activity planning

The work is done in organizational or functional teams. Each step is gone through individually so that an overall picture of the organization in its present and future environment is painted. From this activity the notion of stakeholders is extrapolated. The team discusses the notion, clarifies the distinction between stakeholders and shareholders, and generates its list of stakeholders, evaluating which stakeholders are more significant than others. In one instance a top-level cabinet team mapped its stakeholder groups and gained considerable insight into a significant relationship with an outside body from which an important strategy was designed.

Conclusion

The aim of this chapter has been to share how organizational levels have been used in developing managerial skills, with a view to developing the understanding and further clarification of the framework itself and contributing to education, training, and development models. The pedagogy of an approach to management skills used in training and development programs and an executive MBA program (Rashford & Coghlan, 1988, 1989) has been described. The approach is built on a particular framework of organizational levels (Rashford & Coghlan, 1987). The framework attempts to link together how people participate in organizations and how there is a relationship between the individual's belonging, the team's functioning, the organization's functioning as an aggregate of interteam networks and how it relates and competes in an external environment. Each level focuses on a key actor—the individual, the face-to-face working team, the group-division, and the organization—and provides a framework for developing management skills. The framework focuses on the actual agendas of organizational life, the individual's struggle to fulfill life tasks, the team's effectiveness, the coordination of scarce resources, and the organization's survival.

We have found that participants in the workshops and classes have admitted to recognizing their own experience in the construct. The key intervention processes are an extension of the process-consultation approach, with its action-skills thrust toward diagnosis and intervention as simultaneous processes. As a framework it has proved to be a valuable and useful educational, training, and development model. The value of the training tool is in the application to actual management experiences in developing human resources as individuals and in teams, and in managing the complex interaction of an organization with its internal and external environment. The framework attempts to contribute to the development of an approach to management-skills development that integrates both process and content.

13 Issues in Communication Skills Training

R. V. Rasmussen

Over the past two decades, the need for managerial skill development in management training and business school education has been well documented (Scc AACSB, 1984; Albanese, 1987; Bigelow, 1983; Bradford, 1983a,1983b; Cameron & Whetten, 1983; Endicott, 1982; Golen et al., 1989; Hopelain, 1985; Katz, 1974; Knippen, 1988; Lee, Adler, Hartwick, & Waters, 1987-1988; Livingston, 1971; Mintzberg, 1975; Porter, 1983; Powers, 1983; Vance, 1986; Waters, Adler, Poupart, & Hartwick, 1983; Whetten & Cameron, 1983).

In particular, communication skills have been repeatedly emphasized as essential parts of management practice and skill-training programs (as examples, see Bennett & Olney, 1986; Bond, Hildebrandt, & Miller, 1984; Golen et al., 1989).

Perhaps prompted by this need, a variety of communication skill clusters have been developed that are based on organization research analyzing the skills managers use to conduct their work (e.g., Boyatzis, 1982; Flanders, 1981; Ghiselli, 1963; Livingston, 1971; Mintzberg, 1975).

Undoubtedly, further research and synthesis will unfold over the next decade, but at present there is sufficient consistency to lead Cameron and Whetten (1983) to present a list of skill characteristics that they feel represents "proven characteristics of high performing managers" and sufficiently summarizes the work of other researchers in the field.

Within this broad communication context, skills related to listening (e.g., active listening, paraphrasing) have been repeatedly identified as essential in their own right or as key components of broader skill clusters, such as interviewing, counseling, performance appraisal, and assertive-

179

ness (as examples, see Cameron & Whetten, 1983, p. 22; Golen et al., 1989, p. 51; Knippen, 1988, p. 40; Lee et al., 1987-1988, p. 13; Waters et al., 1983, p. 38).

This chapter is focused on examining training issues related to the particular skill of active listening. It was prompted by two concerns: first, by my observation of resistance exhibited by some learners to communication skills like active listening, and the consequences of that resistance on the learners' motivation to engage in skill-development exercises; and, second, by my observation of management training programs and training outlines presented in training and teaching journals, which allocate very little time to communications training, too little in my estimation for the problems of resistance to the surfaced and adequately dealt with.

The chapter is also prompted by concerns expressed by others who have also observed that difficulties are sometimes encountered in teaching a skill like active listening. For example, Hellriegel, Slocum, and Woodman state that "listening skills guidelines are much easier to understand than to develop and use in day-to-day interpersonal communication" (1983, p. 163); Knippen that "after spending years themselves doing something ineffectively it feels strange and uncomfortable to do it differently" (1988, p. 45); Axley that "incredulous questions . . . are often put to professors or consultants . . . who try to explain that words do not mean, people mean, and the companion notion that meanings are not transferred by communication" (1984, p. 432); and Katz that:

> Real skill in working with others must become a natural, continuous activity, since it involves sensitivity not only at times of decision making, but also in the day-to-day behavior of the individual. Human skills cannot be a "sometime thing." Techniques cannot be randomly applied, like an overcoat. Because everything which an executive says and does (or leaves unsaid or undone) has an effect on his associates, his true self will, in turn, show through. Thus, to be effective, the skill must be naturally developed, and unconsciously as well as consistently demonstrated in the individual's every action. It must become an integral part of his whole being. (1974, p. 33)

A major theme of this chapter is that successful skill development depends, importantly, on the learner's attitudes toward the skill. Although this is a common theme in the adult education literature (Wlodkowski, 1985), it has been given little attention in the communications training literature, which tends to be focused almost exclusively on learning activities (e.g., role play, simulation) and learning theories (e.g., Social Modeling Theory).

For purposes of narrowing the scope of the chapter, I elected to focus on the skill of active listening. While the focus is on a particular skill, it will be suggested that the concerns with active listening may well represent the kinds of attitudinal problems that might be encountered in teaching other communication skills. Thus, while narrow in focus, the chapter lends itself to speculations in the broader context.

Active Listening as Presented
in Text Materials and by Communications Researchers

Active listening is generally conceived of as a complex of verbal and nonverbal responses on the part of a listener that encourage an in-depth exploration of a speaker's thoughts and feelings. Verbal skills generally associated with active listening include paraphrasing, querying, passive listening, using door openers, acknowledging (both verbally and nonverbally), and using concentration techniques (Gordon, 1977, p. 78; Haney, 1986, p. 273). According to Rogers and Farson, an active listener "actively tries to grasp the facts and feelings in what he hears, and he tries, by his listening to help the speaker work out his own problems" (1955, p. 27). In short, active listening consists of a variety of associated skills designed to facilitate a nondirective problem-solving discussion.

Various rationales are provided to explain the importance of active listening. Perhaps the most common rationale is that it is useful in reducing miscommunication and misunderstanding. Communication and management texts virtually all share a communication process model indicating that sender and receiver choices with regard to encoding, channel selection, channel noise, and decoding combine to create the potential for message distortion. Redundancy and feedback measures (like active listening) increase the likelihood that the intended message is that which is received. This theme has been further extended by Axley (1984) and Haney (1986), among others, who state that miscommunication in organizations is pervasive and costly and that active listening is a preventative measure.

A second rationale provided to justify active listening is contained in the visions of the early and later human relations schools, which held (a) that employee counseling would provide emotional relief for workers, reducing obstacles to work performance; (b) that supervisors able to create "supportive relations" were more effective; (c) that "the ideal managerial climate is characterized by supportiveness, empathy, participation and trust" (Redding, 1972, p. 330). In short, active listening (along with other communication skills) enjoys a lengthy history of attention in the management literature.

A third rationale presents active listening as a quasi-coaching technique that facilitates problem exploration and problem solving on the part of a subordinate, work colleague, or important other and is used to implement a developmental-type appraisal interview (see Maier, 1976, for a full treatment of this topic, and Cederblom, 1982, for a review).

Section I: An Exploratory Study of Learners' Practice Theories

The investigation described below originated with my experience in teaching communication skills in 5 contexts: (a) private and public sector management-development workshops, (b) distance education for managers, (c) interpersonal communication labs, (d) MBA courses, and (e) undergraduate courses. The insights offered are based both on informal debriefing discussions with trainees in small groups and on unstructured interviews with six randomly selected learners from each of the five learning groups specified above.

The interviews ranged in duration from 17 to 85 minutes and were initiated with a nondirective question, asking interviewees to describe their personal reactions to the idea of active listening. Following the interviewees' self-initiated reports of issues related to active listening, a series of structured questions was employed to verify or disconfirm issues raised by other interviewees.

Among the biases held by the interviewer were that there would be a fair degree of resistance to the idea of active listening. While this expectation may have been transmitted to the interviewees creating an "experimenter demand" effect, the interviewer was also involved in teaching the skill of active listening and thus could as easily have been perceived as demanding favorable attitudes toward active listening. In short, it is impossible to estimate either the direction or the degree to which researcher expectancies affected the statements made by the interviewees.

Characteristics of Interviewees

The interviewees ranged in age from 19 to 54 (mean = 33.9) with four populations (managers in distance education, workshops, labs, and MBA students) being older (range 24 to 54, mean = 36.8) and undergraduate business students considerably younger (range 19 to 34, mean = 22.5). Omitting undergraduate students whose work experience was minimal, the mean number of years of work experience for the remaining groups was 6.4 years. Prior to conducting the interviews, the interviewer believed that younger, less experienced interviewees (e.g., undergraduates, managers with less experience) would feel more resistance to the idea and practice of active listening.

Random selection was done with a predetermined male/female ratio of 50/50 to ensure that gender differences, if they existed, would surface. Prior to the interview process, the interviewer believed that females would be more accepting of active listening than males.

All interviewees experienced essentially the identical approach to teaching communication skills in general and active listening in particular. The pedagogical approach has been described elsewhere (Rasmussen, 1984). Thus, all comments made by students may simply reflect the instructor, method, and materials used in the communications courses and not the concept of active listening. However, the courses were all rated very highly by learners. MBA students rated the course at 4.7 on a 5.0 scale, where faculty averages are in the 3.5 to 3.8 range. Managers in management development workshops rated the course at 4.5 on a 5-point scale, where 4 represented "very good," and 5 "one of my best management development courses ever." These consistently high ratings militate against, but do not preclude, the possibility that the instructor, method, and materials were the cause of the resistance.

The issues emerging from the interviews are presented in the spirit of Vaill's (1983) "practice theory," a concept similar to Argyris's "theory-in-use" (Argyris & Schon, 1974). According to Vaill, an actor's practice theory consists of "the models of situations and the relation to them which the actor develops in his mind. . . . [it is] literally, a personal theory guiding his practice, bearing some relation to public objective theories about organizational situations, but in no sense identical with them" (1983, p. 51).

While Argyris suggests that managers must be shown how ill-founded their subjective theories-in-use are, Vaill disagrees. He is convinced that "there is far more wisdom in practice theories than academic theory has yet begun to tap" (1983, p. 51).

Following Vaill's ideas, one goal of the present chapter was to identify "practice theories" underlying expressed resistance to the concept of active listening. This can lead to the development of the contingency theory of interpersonal skills to which both Bradford (1983b) and Vaill (1983) allude as lacking in current skill-development approaches. At the very least, it should lead to insights derived from trainee "wisdom" that can be used to anticipate training problems and develop training approaches to deal with those problems.

Themes Identified Through the Interviews

Most interviewees (86.7%) made comments that indicated that they had some level of concern about the idea and practice of active listening. While more strong resistance was expressed by younger, less experienced interviewees (as expected), there were no apparent differences between male and female interviewees (contrary to expectation). Overt manifestations of resistance either observed in courses or described by interviewees include joking about the skill, incorporating satirical paraphrases into their conversations (e.g., "Do you mean to say that what you really meant was . . ."), avoiding using active listening in daily conversations, and ridiculing fellow learners who are attempting to use active listening in conversations. As one interviewee put it, "I'm so nervous about being caught [paraphrasing] . . . I can't concentrate . . . when I'm out with [other students in the MBA class]. . . . I keep a low profile so that they won't give me the gears."

Through the interviews, the author has identified several themes underlying the interviewees' stated resistance to using active listening in their day-to-day conversations. The order of presentation of the themes is not meant to reflect on their relative importance. The percentages stated in the thematic reports below correspond to whether the interviewee spontaneously mentioned the issue without having been prompted or whether the interviewee agreed with the issue after having been prompted by the interviewer.

Theme 1: Good communications involves "give and take."

Most interviewees either spontaneously stated (53.3%) or agreed when asked (33.3%) that effective communication requires "give and take" and that a person initiating a discussion of a problem is implicitly demanding advice. Someone who is listening actively is not doing his or her share. Merely reflecting, rephrasing, and summarizing another person's feelings and thoughts does not suffice. Giving involves giving ideas, suggesting solutions, asking the question that causes a light to go on. As one person put it, "I feel that I have to tell my friends what I think. Why else are they raising the issue in the first place if not to get my ideas?"

Gordon's (1977) book contains some support for this theme. Although he does not systematically explore sources of resistance to active listening, he does present a list of questions asked by learners that stem from what he believes are common misunderstandings about the skill. For example, the question "Can't I ever use roadblocks" (1977, p. 69) could be reasonably interpreted as an indication that learners often want to respond by giving advice or by making responses other than active listening.

Theme 2: Communications "techniques" are manipulative.

Most interviewees stated (36.7%) or agreed (41.7%) that active listening lacks spontaneity and/or is manipulative. Interviewees focus both on a sense of fraudulence and a sense of conscious, strategic responding. Consistent with this, some interviewees (8.3%, 36.7%) view active listening as a mechanism for leading people to say what one wants them to say.

In contrast, most interviewees (21.6%, 66.7%) felt that responses that are recognized to be problematic by communications experts and by the interviewees themselves (e.g., moralizing, sarcasm, blaming, advice) are spontaneous and natural and, while undesirable, are a cut above being manipulative. In short, the interviewees' practice theory suggests that spontaneity is as or more important than communication modality.

Theme 3: Listening is passive and a sign of weakness.

Many interviewees (23.3%, 48.3%) felt that active listening represents a passive, nurturing stance. More females (31.7%, 56.7%) than males (15%, 40%) expressed this position. Some female interviewees stated that they have consciously distanced themselves from nurturing roles—or at least from entering additional situations in which they are expected to take a nurturing stance. Speaking to this point, one female interviewee said, "I have a difficult enough time holding my own. If I don't go nose-to-nose with those guys [other managers in her organization], they'll walk all over me." In short, their practice theory suggests that it is more important to be seen as assertive than as a good listener. While communications experts would probably take exception to the assumption that assertiveness and listening are mutually exclusive, the fact that it is part of the interviewees' practice theories is instructive.

Related to this, needing someone to help clarify a problem is seen by some (5%, 26.3%) as a sign of weakness or inadequacy. They felt that problems ought not be shared. This suggests that interviewees have not bought into what Eisenberg and Witten have called "the ideology of openness" (1987, p. 418).

Theme 4: Paraphrasing is parroting and a waste of time.

To many interviewees (53.7%, 15%), active listening in the simple form of paraphrasing seems overly repetitive and a waste of time. The listener is seen as merely repeating (with minor variations) what the speaker just said, and the speaker then merely repeats him or herself. On an emotional level, this perception of listening as circling around an issue is experienced as irritating and frustrating. As one person put it, "I get impatient and think, 'What are we waiting for? Let's get on with it.' " Interviewees also reported (36.7%; 45%) that there would not be sufficient time in the workday to extend conversations with extensive paraphrasing.

In part, the interviewees may be reflecting a practice theory that problem solving should be straightforward, that people ought to be able to say what is on their minds and move to a solution in a fairly linear, rational fashion.

Fitting with this theme, Gordon reports that learners ask whether they "need to feedback every message" (1977, p. 69).

Theme 5: Active listening is unnecessary because miscommunication is infrequent.

This theme relates to the communication process models that are contained in the communications chapter of virtually every management text. In general, the models indicate that a message recipient may not receive the meaning intended by a message sender because of difficulties in the encoding, transmission, and decoding processes. Most texts go on to state that work relationships and organizational effectiveness may be affected adversely unless message redundancy measures are taken. One such measure is active listening.

Many interviewees (11.7%, 73.3%) felt that the communication process model is interesting and probably useful. However, very few agreed (11.7%) that they often experience difficulties arising from misunderstanding. This stance is consistent with Axley's (1984) belief that the conduit metaphor of communication is pervasive, which is a simplistic belief that meaning is easy to transmit from person which is anchored in four (incorrect) assumptions: (a) that language transfers thoughts and feelings from person to person, (b) that speakers and writers insert thoughts and feelings into words, (c) that words contain the thoughts and feelings, and (d) that listeners and readers extract the thoughts and feelings from the words.

Theme 6: Second-party facilitation is not desirable.

While willing to admit that they are caught up in personal dilemmas that are sometimes difficult to resolve, few interviewees (only 11.7% when asked) believed that such dilemmas are commonplace. Related to this, few interviewees (8.3%, 23.3%) accept the social value of joined problem exploration in the style suggested by active listening. Most (26.7%, 61.7%) felt that the best way to help a close friend is by showing sympathy, not through a nondirective listening approach. Many (13.3%, 35%) believe that it is inappropriate, or even dangerous, to get involved too deeply with the work or social problems of anyone except one's close friends. When asked, few (5%) believed that the simple act of active listening on the part of a relatively unskilled peer could be very helpful in resolving those problems.

Putting the Themes in the Perspective of Management Training

The themes identified above are subject to several limitations. First, a qualitative approach to understanding the issues related to active listening doesn't provide a measure of the extent of the problem. Second, because the learners interviewed were participants in the interviewer's courses, they may well not generalize to learners in other courses. Related to this, the learners may have been responding to the interviewer's expectations, or the interviewer may have mapped the information generated during the interviews to fit his preconceived ideas.

Despite these limitations, the findings contribute to an understanding of the attitudinal underpinnings and sources of resistance to learning the skill of active listening and are of sufficient interest to warrant discussion in the literature and further systematic investigation.

The interviewees revealed that they have resistance to the concept of active listening and the reasons given are interesting and varied. Were such attitudes found to be pervasive, one could postulate on the part of learners an unwillingness to spend the time necessary to master a skill like active listening or a learning stance of "going through the motions" if forced into a nonvoluntary skill-building practice session. While each theme may display a lack of understanding of the concept or an ill-conceived practice theory, the themes may also reflect a wisdom that goes beyond the academic theory.

Section II: Implications for Training Design

The ideas offered in this section are based on the assumption that there may be a good deal of resistance to the concept of active listening and, thus, that it is worthwhile to explore issues in workshop design that affect that resistance.

As a means of exploring workshop design issues, Vaill's (1983) practice theory is used as a key element of a process-oriented training model (Table 13.1). Trainees arrive at the training sessions with practice theories that may or may not be consistent with the communication theory to be employed in the workshop. The first step in training (beyond needs analysis) often is cognitive in nature, consisting of an exposure to materials explaining and demonstrating the concept of active listening. These would include communication models, persuasive arguments made in text and by the trainers, text and media examples of the concepts in practice (e.g., transcripts), modeling by the trainer, and empirical evidence. As a consequence of exposure to the concept, the learners' practice theories can be expected to surface. Learners will experience dissonance to the extent that the materials fit with their practice theories.

Different practice theory themes might be expected to be in the foreground for different learners. For example, in light of the evidence offered above, a female might relate to materials in terms of interpersonal issues like strength/weakness. The consistency of the materials with the learner's practice theory, and the degree to which the materials deal with surfaced inconsistencies, will determine the learner's attitude about the concept and motivation to engage in skill practice sessions on a committed level.

The training model is useful as a guide for systematically examining practice theory and attitudinal issues-related training design. In the sections below, the adequacy of each element is examined. The examination is meant to be exploratory, not exhaustive.

Cognitive Materials: Are the Models Adequate?

Cognitive materials available in texts and on various forms of media (videotape, audiotape, film) may not be adequate to convince learners that active listening is important or that it would accomplish the outcomes predicted by the experts. The most pervasive model found in management texts is the communication process model. It implies that misunderstanding is pervasive and costly.

Table 13.1
A Training Process Model

---

1. Trainees arrive with practice theories at subconscious level

2. Concepts are presented
   — text and models
   — modeling by trainer
   — empirical evidence

3. Trainees surface practice theories
   consistent → engage in skill practice exercises
   inconsistent → resistance to skill practice

4. Special activities to deal with resistance are introduced

There are several problems with the process model as a justification for active listening. First, active listening is but one of many measures that could be used to prevent miscommunication. Second, the model fails to indicate the degree to which (lack of) active listening plays a role in miscommunication. Third, the model fails to provide different, convincing contexts in which active listening might be employed to solve miscommunication problems. Fourth, there are no contingencies. For example, in a conflict situation, it is difficult to conceive that active listening alone could help in preventing miscommunication or in finding a solution. In such a situation, the way one presents his or her version of the issue may be as or more important than active listening.

Cognitive Materials: Is the Evidence Compelling?

When arguing for the need of measures like active listening, communications materials often cite examples of problems that have stemmed from poor listening. Axley (1984), for example, states that "miscommunication is the normal state of affairs in human communication" (p. 432). He also states that miscommunication is dangerous "particularly in settings such as organizations in which great numbers of lives and material resources can be affected" (p. 434). Using specific anecdotes, Haney (1986) quotes a top business executive who suggested that "billions of dollars are lost in waste and duplication clearly induced by miscommunication" (p. 6) and cites estimates by managers that miscommunication consumes from "25 to 40 percent of their budgets" (p. 6). Finally, he uses examples both horrific (e.g., two pilots bailing out of their two planes at the command by the wing leader, "Bail out, your plane is on fire") and inconsequential (e.g., a sign reading "Eat here and get gas") as evidence that miscommunication is costly. However, neither author offers other than anecdotal evidence.

A nonexhaustive and nonrandom selection of 70 management texts found on my bookshelves revealed that most (90%) have communication chapters and most (92%) of these chapters contain a version of the process model of communication, but that no evidence (except anecdotal) is provided in any of the chapters. As a consequence, readers (and trainers) are left with the types of anecdotal evidence mentioned above. Furthermore, a survey of the literature failed to find a single study in which the questions of pervasiveness and cost of miscommunication were addressed.

Cognitive Materials: Are the Examples Convincing?

Management and communication texts contain a variety of examples, including transcripts demonstrating active listening. These may not be adequate to convince learners that active listening is a practical skill. For example, 50% of the interviewees in the present study were shown a transcript contained in a leadership text by Gordon (1977, p. 69) and asked for their reactions. The transcript begins with a subordinate presenting a problem. The supervisor's responses consist entirely of paraphrasing. Nearly all interviewees (91.6%) stated that they didn't believe that the transcript was realistic, that the supervisor's responses were genuine, or that the outcome would have been so positive. The lack of "give" on the part of the supervisor and the smoothness of the discussion bothered many of them. Interestingly, Gordon goes on to give answers to questions typically framed by trainees in response to reading such transcripts (e.g., "Do I need to feedback every message . . . ?"; "Can't I ever use roadblocks . . . ?"; and "Can I trust that others can always solve their problem . . . ?"). These questions and Gordon's attention to answering them indicate that trainees may indeed respond negatively to such transcripts.

To further investigate the impact of text materials, the other 50% of the interviewees were shown the Gordon transcript and a transcript taken from Maier's (1976) text on the performance appraisal process. Unlike the Gordon transcript, the Maier transcript consists of a mixture of active listening and directed probes. All interviewees expressed a preference for the Maier transcript, stating that it was more realistic and that the outcomes were more feasible.

In sum, transcript examples may interact with trainee practice theories in ways that shape trainee attitudes toward the concepts being demonstrated. Thus, it might pay to create or select transcripts that demonstrate different issues. For example, one that shows assertiveness coupled with active listening might serve to convince females that active listening does not necessarily connote weakness. At the very least, research is necessary to determine how trainees react to transcripts used in training sessions. Transcripts might also be constructed and tested for trainee reaction.

Modeling: Some Considerations

Modeling may have a high payoff in terms of demonstrating the efficacy of certain communication styles like active listening and in promoting social learning. In fact, interviewees (18.3%, 70%) reported that they thought the instructor's style was very effective, especially with respect to active listening. However, the interviewees also reported (8.3%, 46.7%) that they thought the workshop or course context was very different from the organizational context, implying that the same skills may not work in the organizational setting.

Other problems with modeling were demonstrated through a series of modeling experiments I conducted. Three styles of interviewing (active listening, probing, and advising) were employed with three volunteers who presented real back-home problems. The other workshop participants acted as observers and were asked to both report their reactions in terms of preference and explain their reactions. I did not reveal which of the three styles was preferred, and I attempted to model probing and advising styles in positive ways. In almost every case, the volunteer presenters in the active listening mode reported more satisfaction and more progress with the session than did presenters in the probing and advising modes. However, the observers preferred the probing mode and rated the active listening and advising modes equally. Their explanations followed to some extent the themes presented above.

One conclusion that can be tentatively drawn from these two sets of experiences is that modeling as a mechanism for shaping positive attitudes toward active listening may be confounded by role, context, and stage of development. For example, it may be that learners will not understand the potential power of active listening unless an expert models it directly with them (learning role). Simplistic modeling in role plays and as trainer-leader may not suffice to convince learners that the skill will transfer to the workplace (context). Modeling may work only in the stage of a

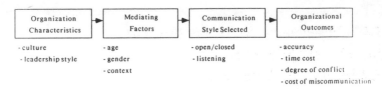

Figure 13.1. A Contingency Model of Communication

workshop when the trainees have bought into the skill and are focused on learning how to do it (stage of development). Prior to that time, they may be so focused on reacting in terms of their practice theories that the intended social learning process is negated.

Conclusion: Toward a Contingency Model of Communication

Vaill (1983) has stated that practice theories can be used to develop a contingency theory of interpersonal skills. While I consider the practice theories surfaced through this study to be exploratory, and not exhaustive or complete, the findings contribute to the development of a contingency model of communication (Figure 13.1).

Organizational characteristics such as culture and leadership style would influence organization members' choices with respect to communication style. Mediating variables such as gender, age, and the communication context (e.g., a conflict situation versus a conversation between colleagues) would account for variations in styles.

Individual styles collectively would influence the efficiency of communication (accuracy, cost in terms of time spent communicating, degree of conflict, cost of miscommunication). Individual styles would also determine, in part, the degree to which the member feels respected or powerful.

Following Vaill's ideas, the wisdom contained in learners' surfaced practice theories can lend to the development of a contingency model. The present study indicates that such an idea is sound and that further systematic research is warranted.

14 Experiences With Interaction Skills Development: A Situational Approach

Ken S. Keleman

Kathi J. Lovelace

Joseph E. Garcia

Schools of Business are being encouraged to shift their educational focus, adding skill application as a complement to the more traditional cognitive or analytical instruction (e.g., Porter & McKibbin, 1988). In responding to this need for change, attempts to improve instruction in managerial competencies have generally pursued a skill-competency approach. Whetten and Cameron (1984), for example, proceeded by (a) identifying relevant competencies or skills, then (b) designing an instructional package to teach these specific skills.

We have worked with such skill-focused materials for several years in our courses and have been impressed with the learning gains our undergraduate students displayed, as compared with our more traditional Organizational Behavior instruction. Still, we were left with uneasy feelings when we watched seemingly skilled students act ineptly in new interaction situations where we felt they should display mastery. Students who had previously done suitable analysis and displayed appropriate skills often appeared to flounder when they faced similar but unpracticed situations.

In an attempt to reduce this apparent generalization or transfer problem, we have changed our instructional focus to a situational approach as contrasted to a skill-component approach. A brief description of our experience follows, including our basic reasoning, instructional methods, and some general observations.

The Nature of Managerial Problems

Our first question was to ask why students had problems transferring skill learning across interaction situations. When we reflected upon this, it became apparent to us that problems do not come to managers in neat packages with labels such as "this is a delegation problem," but are, by contrast, "messy." For example a situation may be a complex interweaving of time-management, stress-management, and conflict-management issues that are unique to the specific situation. Because of this complexity, the interpersonal interaction problems managers face are perhaps best technically labeled as "ill-structured" problems. Ill-structured problems are defined as those problems in which the problem solver contributes to the definition and resolution of the problem, using information generated from initial unsuccessful attempts at a solution (Simon & Hayes, 1976).

Ungson, Braunstein, and Hall (1981) suggest that effectively solving ill-structured problems is the management metaproblem. Clearly, interpersonal problems constitute a large portion of this problem solving. Consequently, the choices between a skill-based, as compared with a situationally based, orientation for teaching interpersonal competence might be reinterpreted as a "part versus whole" learning issue. As Wexley and Latham (1981) note, whether a "part" or "whole" teaching/learning strategy is superior depends upon (a) task complexity (difficulty), and (b) task organization (the degree of interrelationships among subsets of the task). These same authors also note that for highly organized tasks, the "whole" method seems to be more efficient.

Instructional Considerations

It was with such thoughts that we decided to focus on "whole" situations, to increase the variety of situations, and to restrict the focus to interpersonal interactions. Concurrently, we shifted emphasis to a basic "systems" problem-solving model (see, e.g., Church, Smith, & Schell, 1988-1989) within the behavior modeling/action learning approach we used for teaching skills.

Interaction Skills Focus

We have been emphasizing the interpersonal interaction skills of management students for the past 3 years in our undergraduate course development. Fundamentally, two guideposts led us in this direction: (a) the substantial amount of interpersonal interactions required in managerial jobs, which may entail 50% to 80% of a manager's time (Luthans, Hodgetts, & Rosenkrantz, 1988; Mintzberg, 1973), and (b) the important adverse consequences of ineffective interactions, documented at the extreme by derailed executives (McCall & Lombardo, 1983). This is not to suggest that other skill domains (e.g., self-knowledge, personal stress management) are not important. We simply felt that with limited instructional time we could have more leverage or address more variance in managerial performance by focusing on interpersonal interactions.

Assessment Procedures

As we were committed to a behavior modeling/action learning approach, an initial problem was to develop an appropriate assessment system. As Bigelow (1988) points out, the assessment procedures appropriate to traditional instruction (e.g., papers, essays, multiple-choice exams) provide little information as regards the interaction skills of a student. A number of instructors who teach skill-based courses attempt to create more appropriate assessment procedures in the form of "action exams" (e.g., Bigelow, 1988; Damm, 1983; DiStefano & Howell, 1987; Lee, Adler, Hartwick, & Waters, 1987-1988). Generically, this measurement approach requires that a student display appropriate skills and behavior given a stimulus set such as a role play or case. The instructor or other assessors observe and evaluate the behavior on one or more dimensions appropriate to the interaction. We adopted this action exam strategy since it seemed to fit with our interaction focus.

In our case, the development of a workable assessment form has been a continual concern. Our forms have varied from overly simplistic to overly complex. The form we are currently using is depicted in Table 14.1. It addresses three major interaction attributes. The "Interaction Flow" section draws attention to a systematic interaction process in terms of the content and direction of the interaction. This is based on a systems model of problem solving. The "Interaction Outcomes" section addresses the viability of interaction outcomes. This was based on Fisher and Ury's (1981) work with the Harvard Negotiation Project. The "Communication" section contains a description of the communication underpinnings. These reflect the utilization of requisite communication skills necessary for interpersonal interactions. They are consistent with skills suggested in skill-component approaches to effective communication (e.g., Whetten & Cameron, 1984).

Accompanying the development of an assessment procedure was the concurrent issue of creating appropriate role-play stimuli. In our case, we had been using a number of short cases that had required students to analyze situations using specific Organizational Behavior models or frameworks. It was fairly easy to rewrite these into a role-play format that provided a purpose for interaction around important managerial issues. These role-play scenarios represent a wide variety of organizational settings and problems, for example, manufacturing and service firms in the private sector as well as public and not-for-profit firms. The scenarios usually have a central issue, for example, stress management, but require multiple skills for successful execution as an interaction role play. A sample scenario is presented in the Appendix.

Instructional Procedure

We are currently using the following 5-phase procedure in our skills course:

Phase 1: Preliminary Comments

To prepared the students for the role-play interaction process, we encourage the students to have "fun" with the role plays. We point out that *play* is an integral part of the term *role plays* and indicate that students can practice behavior in this nonthreatening environment without serious consequences.

Additionally, we discuss the causes and effects of goal-path multiplicity in interpersonal problem solving. We note the different assumptions the role players make as well as situationally induced differences. Students are reminded that it is common for actors to attribute success and, in particular, failure to the environment while observers tend to attribute success and failure to personal characteristics of the actor. We use this actor-observer difference (Jones & Nisbett, 1972) to highlight the impor- tance of effective feedback and to point out that a person's performance in a role play and his or her value as a person are distinct. In sum, Phase 1 serves to frame students' expectations about the role-play problem-solving process.

Phase 2: Establish Discriminations

This step helps students to understand the appraisal form in Table 14.1. We discuss each of the elements on the form to develop a common understanding of the terms and behavioral processes. Students are told this form will be used to appraise role-play interactions in the course. To supplement descriptions, we use videotapes (made of other students) to display interactions. We carefully conduct stop action "walk throughs," showing how the observation form can be coded and providing the rationale for each assessment. We pick examples with widely varied styles to start with so that the students may build observation and discrimination skills. In sum, Phase 2 provides students with observation, discrimination, and labeling skills.

Phase 3: Practice

The next step is to allow the students to practice various role plays. We do this by having them perform role plays in class, either in small groups or on videotape. We then ask the actors and observers to evaluate the interactions for themselves, using the observation form. This exercise provides students with the opportunity to practice different approaches and get quick feedback. Again, we point out that there can be a number of successful approaches to problem-solving interactions and that the key is to choose an effective approach that takes into account individual preference as well as situational differences.

Phase 4: Students as Actors

After practicing in class, we have each student complete a videotaped role play. The student is assigned a role play and may execute it with any partner that he/she desires. To ensure attention to relevant conceptual material, the student is asked to complete a "plan" prior to taping his or her role play. In this plan the student (a) describes the role-play situation, (b) points out the major issues, (c) specifies what outcomes are expected from the interaction, and (d) summarizes the anticipated flow of the interaction. Before the plan is complete, students are encouraged to try out their role play and adjust the plan where needed.

Table 14.1
Observation and Appraisal Form for Use in Class and by Instructors and
Others as Evaluators

Observation and Appraisal Form

Role Play title _____ Date _____

Name _____ Section _____

Please watch the interaction then record your observations and comments on this form.
Your observations will be used for discussion. Please make your rating by marking the
"o" which best corresponds to your judgment. Omit non applicable items.

Interaction Flow: Complete and effective →
                          Somewhat apparent and effective →
                       Absent or ineffective →

	Absent or ineffective	Somewhat apparent and effective		Complete and effective
1. Opening, rapport	o	o	o	o	o
2. Meeting framing	o	o	o	o	o
3. Legitimate needs of Role 1 discussed	o	o	o	o	o
4. Legitimate needs of Role 2 discussed	o	o	o	o	o
5. Solutions mutually developed	o	o	o	o	o
6. Specific behavior and system changes	o	o	o	o	o
7. Closing summary, restatement	o	o	o	o	o

Comments:

Interaction Outcomes   Complete and effective →
                          Somewhat apparent and effective →
                       Absent or ineffective →

	Absent or ineffective	Somewhat apparent and effective		Complete and effective
8. Serves interests of both parties	o	o	o	o	o
9. Takes "community" interests into account	o	o	o	o	o
10. Is durable, lasting will be carried out	o	o	o	o	o
11. Is tied to objective criteria	o	o	o	o	o
12. Maintains or improves the relationship	o	o	o	o	o

Comments:

Communication:

Complete and effective →
Somewhat apparent and effective →
Absent or ineffective →

	Absent or ineffective	Somewhat apparent and effective		Complete and effective

13. Nonverbal behavior	o	o	o	o	o
14. Congruence	o	o	o	o	o
15. Descriptive communication	o	o	o	o	o
16. Positive regard	o	o	o	o	o
17. Problem focused	o	o	o	o	o
18. Praise appropriately	o	o	o	o	o
19. Establish ownership	o	o	o	o	o
20. Balances participation	o	o	o	o	o
21. Active listening	o	o	o	o	o
22. Keeps on task	o	o	o	o	o
23. Style flexibility	o	o	o	o	o
24. Appropriate intimacy	o	o	o	o	o
25. Maintains composure	o	o	o	o	o

SOURCE: Keleman, K. S., Garcia, J. E., & Lovelace, K. J. (1990). *Management Incidents*. Dubuque, IA: Kendall/Hunt. Reproduced with permission.

For this first videotaped assignment, we assign a small percentage of course points but select a random subset of the cuts to review and discuss in class. This social consequence provides more than sufficient motivation to encourage quality work by most students.

Phase 5: Second Iteration

Later in the term, when students have had a number of opportunities to practice, they are assigned a second role play to plan, practice, and videotape. This second taping is graded for a large percentage of course points. We evaluate each tape separately, using the observation form in Table 14.1. A copy of the form completed by the instructor serves as the student's feedback on the assignment.

Beyond this 5-phase procedure, we find that students become interested in receiving additional personal feedback. As a whole, the activity serves as an opening for students to explore and improve their own interpersonal styles in a variety of situations.

Some Observations

To date we have not systematically collected data that would speak to the relative effectiveness of this instructional approach. We have, however, made a number of informal observations.

First, regarding overall effectiveness, we regularly teach the undergraduate managerial skills course. We have noted a marked improvement, even within one quarter, in the ability of students to size up a new situation and interact effectively. We also teach subsequent senior-level elective courses with strong interaction components. We have the impression that students who have been through the redesigned junior-level skills course are more willing to initiate a problem-solving interaction. These students also conduct themselves more effectively in interactions than did students 4 years ago, when we were teaching more traditional Organizational Behavior courses. In addition, student comments have been quite positive, as have casual comments from other instructors.

As Bigelow (personal communication, 1989) points out, when confronted with new situations, students tend to rely on their lay theories. This tendency has been evidenced in class discussions, and it has prompted a shift in our classroom teaching strategy. Discussions of role plays in class have become situation focused, with Organizational Behavior theories and models as the complement rather than the drivers. Even though the common thread across situations is the systematic problem-solving orientation, we find plenty of opportunity to discuss content and skill-specific issues.

As with any course, students are initially concerned about grading, as were we. Currently, we use a form similar to that shown in Table 14.1, and our grading is basically normative. However, having graded hundreds of hours of videotape to date, we feel we have a reasonably good idea of what to expect on an absolute level. When we develop a new scenario, we co-review tapes to establish common anchors for grading and feedback purposes. Discussions of student videotapes in class provide a good opportunity to review behavioral data and communicate expectations to students. Such discussions appear to lead to a number of "ah ha!" experiences, and we find that students accept our evaluations quite well.

Student stress can be a problem initially in the videotaping. Students who have not previously been videotaped may appear nervous and distracted during the first taping. To minimize the student stress, we allocate only a few points for the first videotaping and encourage systematic preplanning and practice with their role-play partner before taping. We anticipate that this reduces stress, as compared with "live" action exams, but on occasion, the trade-off is in terms of the "freshness" of the interaction.

A major problem we have encountered to date is a problem particular to any action exams. Action exams, in any form, take a considerable amount of time to grade. We have yet to discover the kinds of economies of scale that multiple-choice questions provide for content centered courses. On the positive side, however, when we have watched two to four tapes of a student throughout the course of a quarter, we feel that we really know our students.

An additional problem we have occasionally encountered involves situations where a student may competently deal with a role-play situation and yet not fulfill a number of the evaluation criteria depicted in Table 14.1. In fact, certain situations prohibit receiving high grades on all categories (e.g., having to notify an employee that he or she is being laid off makes it difficult to display behavior that would score high on item 8, "Serves the interest of both parties"). As a result, we have resorted to reconciling our evaluation within the context of the situation. By this we mean that a rating of complete and effective for a particular dimension will be rated more or less rigorously, depending on the nature of the role-play situation assigned to the student. This practice makes it important for us to co-review scenarios as a form of validity checking. Our future plans include inviting managers from firms who hire our graduates to participate with us in calibrating our evaluations.

Conclusion

In sum, the shift to situation-based skill development represents a major progression in our instruction. Given our feedback from students to date, we are confident that the change has been worth the investment. Perhaps as important, as instructors we have learned a considerable amount about effective and ineffective interactions through this approach to managerial skills development.

Appendix: Sample Role Play Scenario

Skyjack Airlines

Background

Both persons work for a Skyjack Airlines, a major air carrier which has developed a reputation for poor service due to overbookings, mechanical failures and late arrivals. Role 1 is Skyjack's gate clerk supervisor at a large midwestern "hub" airport and is responsible for 10 gates. As supervisor, Role 1 is responsible for the safe, orderly and effective passenger boarding and deplaning by gate clerk personnel. The gate clerks, one of whom is Role 2, work directly with the public and handle the details of boarding, assigning seating, announcing pertinent information to passengers, and so forth.

Role 1: Gate Clerk Supervisor

As gate clerk supervisor, one of your missions is to improve the public's perception of your airline. This has become even more important in recent months. There have been several near miss accidents in the industry, including one highly publicized case involving your company. Airline fliers have become increasingly more demanding while at the same time, you are trying to help your gate clerks be effective "ambassadors" for Skyjack.

Yesterday you had occasion to observe an incident at Gate 17 where the flight to New Orleans (Flight #987) was delayed for three hours due to mechanical difficulties. The ground repair crew was carefully replacing a malfunctioning altimeter, a very important task.

In the terminal, the passengers, many of whom had made connections from other cities, became restless and concerned with the status of their plans. The gate clerk, Role 2, followed standard procedures, informing the waiting passengers of the delay. Unfortunately, the repair crew underestimated the complexity of the repair and the expected departure time was postponed several times. After waiting for two hours, several passengers asked to be told the cause of the delay. The clerk phoned the repair crew and then relayed over the public address system that, ". . . the plane was broke and the mechanics had to call out for parts, and as soon as they got it back together they would be ready for boarding and take-off."

SOURCE: K. S. Keleman, J. E. Garcia, & K. J. Lovelace (1990). *Management Incidents*. Dubuque, IA: Kendall/Hunt. Reproduced with permission.

This announcement caused an uproar. Several passengers made loud comments about broken airplanes, and a number asked the gate clerk to check to see if they could switch bookings to a flight on another carrier to New Orleans.

Having witnessed some of the uproar, you feel compelled to meet with this gate clerk to have a talk about yesterday's incident.

Role 2: Gate 17 Gate Clerk

Your job is to effectively manage the flow of passengers on and off airplanes at your gate. In addition you spend considerable time answering all sorts of questions about flight schedules, ticket information and various facilities in the airport. Lately things have been quite busy. Just yesterday, for example, there was a big problem with Flight 987 to New Orleans. The plane was delayed for three hours. As a result, the waiting area was filled with tired, hungry, and disenchanted fliers. Many had come from other parts of the country and were already anxious to continue their travel.

During the delay, you received a series of inaccurate estimates from the repair crew about when the plane would be ready. It seemed like every fifteen minutes or so they would call and revise their estimates to a later time. Eventually, some passengers wanted to know what was going on so you called the repair crew. They told you they had decided to replace the altitude meter or something. Not knowing what one of these gizmos does, you announced to the waiting passengers that something was broken, had to be replaced, and the part was on its way. That seemed to upset quite a few people. You anticipated that this would happen anyway since they had been waiting over two hours.

Your boss, who saw part of the uproar, asked you to come meet with her/him to talk over yesterday's situation.

15 Management Skill Development: What It Is. What It Is Not.

Melvin R. McKnight

This chapter is written in response to the announcement at the 1989 OBTC Conference that OBTS is embarking on a project to develop a model program for teaching management action skills. I am very much in favor of such a program; however, I am also much concerned. I see a great lack of conceptual clarity in the literature as to what such skills are and how they are developed. In my view, most of what has been labeled as skill development is only marginally related to what skill development actually is and requires. I would include the most popular texts, which tout skill development as part of their title, in this marginal category. Just recently, I received a book in the mail about supervisory skill development. Since I have been teaching such a course for the past 4 years and am always on the lookout for new material, I was delighted to receive the book and eagerly began reviewing it. Much to my dismay, I failed to find more than a few exercises in the entire book that actually had anything to do with developing supervisory skills. I am afraid that unless we get some clarity around this issue before beginning the OBTS project, it too will wind up being misguided. I am hopeful that this chapter will begin to bring such clarity.

What Skill Development Is

Two things characterize skill knowledge and distinguish it from conceptual knowledge. First, it is responsive in nature. Second, it is a product of the human subconscious. Most of the confusion in the literature has resulted from the failure to recognize these two characteristics.

Perhaps the best analysis of the nature of skill knowledge is found in Michael Polanyi's little book, *The Tacit Dimension* (1966). Polanyi refers to the fact that the human mind has a wonderful ability to create programs that automate behavior. He uses the ability to drive a car as an example. If we are driving down the road at 70 miles per hour and a truck suddenly pulls out in front of us, we do not stop to analyze the situation and decide on a course of action. Rather, we *respond* out of our tacit knowledge of how to drive—*without any forethought at all*. If our tacit knowledge is adequate and the situation permits, we miss the truck. If not, and we survive, we have an opportunity to continue our acquisition of the skill of driving.

This type of knowledge is also what the behaviorists, such as B.F. Skinner (1974), refer to as *conditioning*. It is the subconscious knowledge of an appropriate response to a given stimulus, and it is evoked automatically by the stimulus without the intervention of conscious mind. We are all very highly programmed beings in this regard; we have such programs for walking, eating, talking, and many other routines of our daily lives, and we could not function without them.

The point is that "people skills"—the ability to be influential with people—have this same structure. For example, if I am working as a production superintendent and a very upset shop foreman confronts me and starts yelling, I do not remember which leadership style is appropriate in a situation like this and try to use it. If I even try to do it that way I will quite properly be dismissed as a phony. Rather I respond, out of my tacit knowledge of how to be a leader/manager, *without any conscious forethought at all*, just as I do when I am driving and a truck pulls out in front of me. And what I do will work, or not, depending on my degree of skill at the time—the quality of the behavioral programs I have developed for dealing with such a situation. Management skills are *responsive*. The biggest confusion in the literature concerning them comes from a failure to recognize this fact.

Second, skill knowledge is a property of the subconscious part of the human mind, rather than being, in any sense, conceptual. It takes the form of *awareness* and can be acquired only from experience, not from conceptual learning. A skill-development course therefore has to be a course in awareness.

We can understand what this means by again referring to Polanyi (1966). He notes that tacit knowing has a structure that always consists of two terms. We attend from something to something. The something we attend *from* Polanyi calls the "proximal" term. The something we attend *to* he calls the "distal" term. For example, we attend from the particulars constituting the act of driving (manipulating the gas pedal, gearshift, steering wheel, and so on) to the comprehensive act of driving. The key characteristic of tacit knowing is that the proximal term (which we attend from) is always subconscious. Polanyi says, "We know the first term only by relying on our awareness of it for attending to the second." For example, when we get into our car and put our key in the ignition, we do not think, "Now I must turn the starter, now I must depress the clutch, now I must step on the gas, and so forth." Rather, we hook into our driving program, and it takes over. We do all those things without being focally aware of doing them—we are aware of them only in terms of the comprehensive act of driving itself. In fact, our conscious mind is often occupied elsewhere—talking to a companion, thinking about something, and so on. Because of this, Polanyi says we have a knowledge that we cannot tell. Another example he uses is recognizing a face. We can all do it, but we cannot even begin to say how we do it. Certainly when we meet someone for the first time, we do not try to memorize the shape of the nose and mouth, the distance between the eyes, and other features so we can recognize the person again. Rather we recognize them in terms of the comprehensive entity that these particulars jointly constitute—we attend from these particulars (the proximal term) to the face itself (the distal term). It is precisely because we cannot specify the knowledge that is in the subconscious that the police have turned to "face kits" and artists to aid victims or witnesses of a crime in developing likenesses of suspects.

This is also the reason why people who are skillful at something are unable to say, conceptually, what they do; for example, it explains why we have found that skillful leaders are unable to tell us what leadership skill consists of.

Polanyi further says that it is in terms of *meaning* that things enter into their appearance. He offers the example of using a tool: "We are attending to the meaning of its impact on our hand in terms of its effect on the things to which we are applying it." Again, the point is that human skills have this same structure. When my upset shop foreman confronts me, I am attending *from* my subconscious programming concerning how to be influential with people (particularly upset people) to this particular situation. It is only in terms of the *meaning* of my acts that I am aware of them—in terms of their impact on the other who is confronting me. As I try something and it is *meaningful* for me, that is, it is effective, I become programmed to utilize that sort of act again. As I try something that is not effective, that behavior begins to be "extinguished" (in behaviorist terms). Over time, this process results in the acquisition of increasingly more effective behavioral programs, which result in higher levels of skill. The essential thing to realize, however, is that it is learning that is taking place entirely in the subconscious.

Finally, Polanyi notes that one can acquire a skill by a process he calls "in-dwelling." By carefully watching a skillful instructor and attempting to emulate what he or she does, a student is "in-dwelling" in the skill the instructor is exhibiting. This can result in at least a partial direct transfer of the subconscious programming the instructor is using to the student.

What Skill Development Is Not

Against this background, we can begin to see what is misguided in much of the skill-development literature. In the interest of time, I am going to limit this analysis to one text: *Developing Management Skills*, by Whetten and Cameron (1984). I have selected it not only because it is one of the more popular skill-development texts available, but also because I believe it to be the best. Nevertheless, relative to an understanding of the nature of skill knowledge as outlined above, it is quite off the mark. The major problem is the confusion of subconscious awareness with conceptual knowledge.

Whetten and Cameron use a modification of the behavior modeling approach to training. About this model they say:

> The learning model used most widely for skill training in industry usually consists of four steps: first, the presentation of principles (sometimes called behavioral guidelines or key actions steps) based on data collected from successful practicing managers or derived from general theories of human behavior; second, demonstration of the principles to participants by the instructor, a videotaped incident, or written scripts; third, opportunities to practice the principles in role plays or exercises; and fourth, feedback on personal performance received from the instructor, experts, or peers. (page 3)

They then make three modifications to this basic model: (a) they emphasize conceptual learning, (b) they have added a preassessment activity at the beginning of each chapter, and (c) they have added an application activity at the end of each chapter. About the first of these they say:

First, we have emphasized conceptual learning, since it is important to understand the whys behind the hows. This enhances one's ability to adapt to changing circumstances and also prepares one for a vital function of management—teaching those skills to others. (page 3)

They implement this by having a section in each chapter of their book called "Skill Learning," in which they present theories and research findings from the social and management sciences. My point is: That is not what skill learning is! And because of that, it is not true that it will "enhance one's ability to adapt to changing circumstances."

To clarify this point, consider the Whetten and Cameron approach to learning the skill of "Improving Employee Performance Through Motivation" (chap. 6). Under the motivation subheading of the "Skill Learning" part of the chapter, they say:

The real challenge of managers is to design incentive systems that encourage high performance and also engender high employee morale.

To accomplish this objective, managers should use two general approaches to employee motivation. First, they should examine the overall system of rewards in their organization from their subordinates' point of view to ascertain its potential for motivation. This is best done using diagnostic questions derived from expectancy theory. . . .

The second approach focuses on shaping employee behaviors so they are consistent with the expectations of management. It is referred to as operant conditioning or reinforcement theory. (p. 310)

Skill learning is then presented as in-depth discussions of these two motivational approaches, including an 8-point plan for shaping behavior using behavior modification. Following this, the "Skill Analysis" section provides two cases to be analyzed, using expectancy theory and operant conditioning, and the "Skill Practice" section uses a case as an opportunity to practice using behavior modification for the analysis of, and development of a plan to change, behavior using the 8-point process. Now, I have no objection to such an educational exercise, because I believe it does have value. But we need to recognize that the skill it teaches is *only* that of applying these particular theories to diagnose situations and develop plans for remedying them; only if we are willing to assume that motivational skill is entirely conceptual and consists of nothing *but* this ability can we say that we are actually teaching motivational skills.

Again, my point is that *this assumption reflects a fundamental misunderstanding of what skill learning is.* I have found in my work that there is indeed a motivational skill—the ability to relate to employees in a way that inspires them to want to do their best—and I have even found "operant conditioning" from behaviorism to be one of the best theoretical systems for helping me to understand it. However, motivational skill is far more organic than the form of behaviorism used by Whetten and Cameron would permit. One must realize that *everything* is a stimulus—physical gestures, facial expressions, smiles, vocal inflections, and so forth. To apply operant conditioning to this skill in a conceptual fashion, one would have to have a reinforcement schedule that included and permitted control over all of these very subtle, and for the most part subconscious and therefore involuntary, phenomena. It is precisely because such control is impossible that we need to recognize the type of skill learning Polanyi describes; only a skill-development approach that can include these very important subconscious phenomena can offer a path for truly becoming skillful. Indeed, if there really were no more to motivational skill than the ability to apply expectancy theory and operant conditioning (in the form of reinforcement schedules), how could we possibly account for the thousands of supervisors in industry who are, in fact, skillful at motivating their people, yet who have never heard of either theory?

In using their model, Whetten and Cameron also confuse skill development with what I would call "pre-skill training." As noted earlier, a key feature of skill knowledge is that even people who are skillful cannot tell you conceptually what they do. It is therefore not possible to come up with a set of "action steps" for any skill. The part of the learning process to which Whetten and Cameron's first step (presentation of principles) applies is actually therefore pre-skill training, which establishes the foundation for skill learning but is not skill learning itself. For example, we can describe to a student the actions that one must perform to drive a car, and this knowledge is obviously necessary as a foundation for the skill of driving. But we would hardly say that anyone who can perform these elementary acts is a skillful driver; no matter the level of conceptual understanding, *every* new driver of a vehicle employing a clutch experiences jerky starts at first. Only practice and the programming of the subconscious that results from experience will bring the skill.

Finally, Whetten and Cameron fail to recognize that the learning loop involved in skill development is a very tight one—it consists of many iterations, each of which may be only seconds in duration. Thus, to structure a text such that each chapter consists of one iteration of the loop—with a section dedicated to each phase of the learning process (presentation of principles, demonstration, practice, and feedback)—is again to seriously misunderstand the nature of the skill-learning process. This criticism also applies to most of the experiential learning movement in Organizational Behavior. The most widely used learning model in that literature has been some form of that presented by Kolb, Rubin, and McIntyre (1971), in which learning occurs in a continuous process of concrete experiences, reflective observation, abstract conceptualization, and active experimentation. This is, in fact, accurate as a model of the process of experiential learning by which skills are acquired *if it is properly understood*—as a process in which each iteration lasts only a short time and learning comes about as a result of much repetition. But to structure a text so that exercises consist of one iteration (usually conceptually focused) is again to seriously misunderstand the nature of true skill learning.

The error of assuming that skill knowledge is conscious and conceptual, rather than being subconscious and responsive, can be understood more clearly by considering what happens if we apply the traditional approach that Whetten and Cameron embrace to the task of learning the skill of skiing. To do so we would first need to acquire the knowledge we will teach. We would do so by sending a scientist operating within the passive, observational model of the traditional sciences to the ski slope. The scientist would need to find a good slope and very carefully, and very accurately, observe everything the skiers do as they come down the slope until he or she had sufficient observations for his or her statistics to be valid (this would require about 400+ observations). The scientist would then write a book about how to ski that sets forth, faithfully and well, everything he or she has observed. This would be a very interesting book, would it not—a book about how to ski written by a spectator.

Now we, as college professors, have students who are nonskiers who wish to learn to ski. We require that they buy that book, study it diligently, and then take an exam over its contents. If they get a 100% score, we congratulate them and send them forth as skiers. But are they now skilled skiers? In fact, have they actually learned anything at all about how to ski? Of course they have not! Our teaching was nothing but an illusion. The matter is hardly a trivial one—this is exactly how we traditionally attempt to teach the skills of motivation and leadership.

Our skiing example demonstrates several things. First, it shows clearly why we do, in fact, need to be actually teaching skills in our OB courses.

We need to recognize what is a skill and teach it as such, not confuse skill knowledge with conceptual knowledge and create the illusion of education when, in fact, none has taken place. Second, this example shows clearly that our traditional approach embraces two basic fallacies. The first is that observational knowledge is sufficient to the task of learning a skill. The second is that memorizing something, even a book written by a professional skier, will in itself be enough to result in acquiring a skill. Both are untrue.

Observational knowledge is not incorrect. It is right as an accurate observation of (for example) what it looks like to watch someone ski. However, it is the wrong knowledge. The knowledge of what either skiing or leadership looks like is not at all the knowledge of how to do it. That knowledge is what Polanyi says it is—*the subconscious awareness of the meaning of one's acts on one's environment.* It is the "operant conditioning" of the behaviorists. And it can be learned only from experience—by experimenting with one's behavior in situations like those for which one is developing the skill—and learning subconsciously the meaning of one's acts until those acts become skillful. This is not at all to say that observational knowledge, and particularly the knowledge given by an expert, cannot be helpful. Indeed, it can be very useful within the proper context, that is, if one is practicing skiing at the same point in time that one is reading about skiing. But it cannot be a substitute for true skill learning.

Implications for a Skill-Development Program

Polanyi's understanding of the skill-development process offers a new perspective on the "managers are born and not made" controversy, for it suggests that management skills certainly can be acquired, not by memorizing a book, but over time as a natural outcome of the experiential learning process. After all, we have all learned to drive, to walk, to talk, to eat, to ski, to play tennis, and to acquire many other such skills, and it has not taken us terribly long to do so. It also makes it clear how the mind can empower us to handle a very great deal of diversity in our day-to-day lives and, in so doing, exposes what is perhaps the greatest shortcoming in the cognitive approach. It is simply not possible to memorize enough theories to know how to consciously deal with every situation that might possibly arise. We would go crazy even trying. Rather, one acquires skill by using the conscious mind in a very different way—to learn from experiences in the world in order to generate effective conditioned response mechanisms.

This makes it very clear that skill learning absolutely must be student-centered and experientially oriented. There is a role for cognition here, but it must be in service to experience, not the other way around, as is often done in so-called "experiential learning exercises," where an experience is rigged to teach the meaning of a theory (as in the Whetten and Cameron motivation exercises described earlier). Rather, one experiments with behavior, becomes aware of the meaning of one's behavior, and then uses cognition to develop hypotheses about how one might change it to be more effective. For example, after a fall while making a turn, a skier might decide more weight should be put on the downhill ski next time. Similarly, one might decide to try to be more patient with an employee following an encounter that did not work out as one had hoped. These are indeed hypotheses, but they are experiential—they refer to the possible outcomes of one's acts. When we interject a traditional conceptual theory into this process (as Whetten and Cameron do repeatedly), we run the risk that the theory will make the students forget their experiential referent, particularly if we test them on the content of the theory. In other words, a traditional, "external" theory might be useful if it helps the student develop a better behavioral hypothesis to try for the next iteration in the learning process; but if it becomes *a substitute for that process*, as it is virtually set up to be in the Whetten and Cameron book, the result is certain to be confusion and a short-circuiting of skill learning.

Because of this, I think the only model really appropriate for skill teaching is that of coach. A coach watches closely while a student practices a skill. The coach interrupts the performance when he or she sees a lesson to be taught, then helps the student become aware of the meaning of the actions the student has just performed in the context of their effectiveness in achieving a desired result, and the student tries again. As the process is repeated, the performance gradually becomes more skillful. The coach might also demonstrate how to do the performance skillfully, so the student can learn by "in-dwelling" in his performance (as noted above).

As this process takes place, there is also a growing awareness on the part of the student of the implications (meanings) of various behaviors he or she might engage in when confronted with a particular situation. Thus, a higher sort of learning takes place also—one that results in the student's behavioral programs increasingly becoming conscious and therefore choiceful. This phenomena was pointed out to me in a recent letter from John Bigelow (1990) in which he describes it as follows:

In my own work on skills, I think it is true that much of skill competence involves the acquisition of skill programs such as you describe. I see this as a necessary step in a person developing complex behavior systems which can be executed in real time. However, I would also include a higher level of skill competence in which these programs are selected and arrayed in an unfolding interaction. For example, in a listening situation a person may need to choose between reflecting back what a person says or providing some helpful advice or information. I would suggest that here the person is working on a more conscious and less programmed level. If we observe such a person, we may observe hesitation, eye shifts, etc., indicative of cognition as the person makes a conscious, perhaps difficult, decision.

I have observed exactly the same phenomena in my work, and my students have even talked about that choice process. While the process clearly does involve cognition, it does not appear to involve the sort of analysis that we normally think of when we use that term. Rather, it is an almost instantaneous (and I think intuitive) weighing of a situation, selection of a particular behavioral program, and then surrender to that program. The awareness that makes this possible seems to be a natural outgrowth of the skill-development process.

Finally, there is also such a thing as conceptual skill in a more traditional sense (and it is this that the Whetten and Cameron book is actually teaching). Conceptual skill determines what one can do with the conceptual knowledge one possesses. For example, a student could possess a quite complete knowledge of accounting yet lack the skill necessary to utilize that knowledge to design an effective accounting system. In many management activities, conceptual skill is parallel to the responsive type of skill Polanyi describes. For example, a leadership performance often involves both the conceptual skill of articulating a sense of direction or vision, and the responsive skill of communicating it such a way that others are committed to it and motivated to give it their best.

However, even conceptual abilities, in themselves, consist of both knowledge and skill components. As Polanyi suggests, when we begin to learn a subject such as accounting (this is my example—he again uses learning to drive a car), the knowledge of accounting is initially external to us—we attend *to* it. At some point, however, a transformation takes place such that we begin to attend *from* that knowledge to the design, for example, of an accounting system. It is at this point that skill learning becomes possible, and for this reason it is also at this point that knowledge begins to be *empowerment*, that is, that management education is truly effective. My work in using the model of skill development outlined in this chapter suggests that in teaching conceptual skills, this transformation *must be required* or it does not take place; that is, students must be required to use what they learn to attend to external problems. When only objective tests are used in a course, knowledge is tested just *before* this critical transformation takes place, and unless some other assignment requires the transformation, the skill necessary to do anything with the knowledge is never acquired. The virtue of the case method is that it does develop this skill component of managerial knowledge.

The "Being Dimension"

There is one other major issue that is critically important to a successful skill-development program. This concerns the psychological context in which skill development takes place. There is a second type of knowledge in the human subconscious—a yet deeper knowledge that determines one's state of being at any given point of time. I call it "being knowledge" after Abraham Maslow (1963), who first identified it (at least implicitly), and also to make it clear that it truly is a form of knowledge. One's state of being is therefore changeable over time (if one understands the programming process and recognizes that the task is one of reprogramming the mind).

This dimension is critically important because management is a holistic phenomenon—one manages as a whole person. We always communicate what we are and where we are in very subtle, often nonverbal ways, and there is no possible way to avoid doing so. This aspect of a manager's behavior creates the climate, and thus forms the context, through which he or she must utilize skill and perform the more cognitive parts of the job. Further, one's state of being affects behavior on a subconscious level where it is not consciously controlled by the manager. I usually introduce the notion of this type of knowledge by asking if anyone has ever worked for a boss with an ego problem, an insecure boss, or a boss who was always in a negative place. Then we discuss what these bosses do—that is how does a boss with an ego problem, or an insecure boss, or a negative boss, manage subordinates, and what happens to the work climate and quality of work as a result. The discussion always makes it very clear that such bosses are destructive for subordinates, for the quality of working life, for the quality and often quantity of work performed, and ultimately for themselves.

This dimension also interacts with skill; such managers are destructive precisely to the extent that they are skillful at dealing with people. The more skillful they are, the more destructive they are. The danger is therefore that a skill-development program that does not explicitly include education on the "being" dimension may actually wind up being destructive.

At first glance, the "being" dimension might seem difficult to teach, but actually it is not. Whereas skill knowledge corresponds to the "operant conditioning" of the behaviorists, being knowledge corresponds to "classical conditioning." The difference is that operant conditioning is the subconscious knowledge of the *reaction* of our human environment to our acts, whereas classical conditioning is the subconscious knowledge of the *universal* environmental contingencies that confront all managers. Thus, being knowledge is a knowledge of universal *values* rather than of universal facts; it is an awareness of the true value of things for effectiveness as a leader/manager and is universal in the sense that every leader/manager faces these same contingencies. For example, an ego problem is destructive for managerial effectiveness for all leader/managers in the same way (because it operates on consciousness to make one try to manage employees for the sake of one's ego rather than for group objectives). The awareness that an ego problem is destructive is an example of being knowledge.

This type of knowledge is concerned with the implications of the various values one might embrace, and one teaches it simply by making students aware of these implications or contingencies. For example, a student who is made aware of the destructive potential of an ego problem is much less likely to develop one in the course of his or her career than one who does not have that awareness. It is beyond the scope of this chapter to do more than provide this brief outline of the nature of a course aimed at teaching this type of knowledge; however, such a course is no more than a transformation of a traditional OB course (with a great increase in the relevancy of the course to the students). I have been teaching OB this way since 1978 and have demonstrated through empirical research that the course is effective in helping students become more psychologically healthy (McKnight, 1979).

Experiences With Our Skill-Development Program at NAU

We are now in our fifth year at Northern Arizona University with a skill program organized according to the understanding of skill development outlined in this chapter. I will briefly outline how that program is set up and then close by summarizing some lessons I have learned thus far from this attempt and, in general, from my work in trying to understand the human subconscious.

Our program is constructed on the coaching model and consists of a sequence of three courses, the first two of which are required for all management majors. The first course is a traditional OB course. When I teach this it is the "being foundation" course, although not all of the professors teaching the course teach it in this way. The second course is titled "Line Management" and is the basic management skills course. It is a course in leading/managing people effectively for organizational objectives. The third course is titled "Senior Practicum in Management," its prerequisite is completion of the other two courses. Students in this class meet with student teams in the other classes and serve in the role of coaches. The program is set up this way primarily because of a constraint that it require no more resources than the more traditional program it replaced. It was also very clear to us that we could not hope to be effective with it unless we could get more individual attention to the students than one instructor for each 40 students. The obvious solution was to train students as coaches. In our design there is one coach for each team of six to eight students.

All of the instructors teaching the skills course meet with the student coaches once a week and essentially do with them what the coaches will be doing with their student teams later in the week. For the most part this involves modified role plays, where the modification is that no one is ever allowed to play any role other than himself or herself in the situation with which he or she is working. The reason for this is that learning skill knowledge on the subconscious programming level can take place only when one is doing one's best to handle a given situation, as oneself, and learning from the experience.

Coaches and student teams are given the challenge of developing their team members so that they become the most skillful team in the class. Twice each semester, teams meet in "skill meets" to determine which teams have been most successful. These are modified role plays carried out before the entire class and evaluated for skill by peers, coaches, and instructors.

Conclusion

In closing, let me summarize what I have learned from my work with skill development:

1. The understanding of the skill-development process outlined in this chapter is clearly valid. A skill program organized according to it is clearly effective at increasing the interpersonal skills of students as leaders and managers. In fact, I have found that skills are a great deal more teachable than I believed before we started the program; I have watched a number of students become far more skillful in one semester than I would have thought possible.

2. The key to making it work is coaching. This is still the weakest link in our program; however, things are continuing to improve over time. There is a long-term learning phenomenon in a program like this—the better a class of coaches is, the better the students they are teaching will be when they become coaches. Ideally, I think one would interface undergraduate and MBA programs (or Ph.D. and MBA programs) such that the coaches were drawn from the higher program. Unfortunately, we do not have a large enough graduate program at NAU to be able to do this.

3. The keys to making coaching work well are selection and training. Not every student should be a coach; it requires a certain degree of self-development to be effective at it. I therefore think there should be some control over the selection of coaches if possible. In any case, the training function needs to be developed to whatever extent resources permit. The better the coaches are, the better the program will be. I do think that one coach for each six to eight students is an effective ratio.

4. Skill development requires practice on the part of the students. It only happens when one engages in acts that have the structure of tacit knowing described by Polanyi, that is, one must attend from his or her knowledge to a problem or situation for skill development to take place. Because this is the key moment in skill learning, a skill-development course must be structured so that each student has an opportunity for adequate "air time."

5. The role of the instructor in such a class is also that of a coach. This involves demonstrations of effective ways to handle situations, fishbowl role plays in which the instructor takes various roles—subordinate, supervisor, and the like—and plays the role so as to teach. For example, I sometimes deliberately make mistakes so students can see what happens when I do. When playing the role of subordinate, I usually take advantage of any mistakes the students make and exaggerate the consequences so they can clearly see what can happen.

6. There is always a transferable component in skill development. For example, one can learn thinking skills in accounting and later transfer much of that ability to another field. Similarly, one can learn conflict-resolution skills, and they will empower one to be more effective at delegating, communicating, and so on. In fact, teaching skill development tends to obscure our traditional subject-matter divisions. The skill of motivation, for example, is operative in every supervisory act—delegation, discipline, communication, and so on—and so is the skill of leadership.

7. Although I have not had the opportunity to do so, I think there would be a significant advantage in combining the teaching of the being and skill dimensions in a single course. Instead of the two separate courses I now have, I would like to experiment with a basic and advanced course, each of which combines the two dimensions. I think there would be a synergistic effect that would make the courses more powerful.

8. While one cannot say conceptually what is in the subconscious, it does appear to be possible to access at least some of this information through projective techniques. This is particularly true for the being knowledge component of subconscious knowledge. For example, I have found that people can say what effective leadership is (and universally so—everyone gives similar answers) if projective questions are used. I think one of the most exciting frontiers in this work is the development of better projective techniques for accessing subconscious information. I have hopes that eventually we can use such techniques to obtain accurate assessments of skill knowledge.

9. Skill development together with development on the being dimension becomes what I call "personal power"—the power of an individual to be effective in influencing his or her environment. That, ultimately, is the deciding difference between highly successful people and the "also-rans." Our work suggests that personal power can be acquired quite rapidly if one understands the process involved and engages in it consciously.

16 Education and Empowerment: A Transformational Model of Managerial Skills Development

Robert E. Quinn

Neil B. Sendelbach

Gretchen M. Spreitzer

> If, as I suggest, most of these [managerial development] programs are good, why do I not become the supermanager of my aspirations? At various times I've learned how to approach my job as a total business system, how to quantify and measure everything, how to plan strategically, how to manage change, how to manage my time, how to get results by motivating others, and umpteen other proven approaches to successful management. . . . All this leaves me confused as hell. My management instincts have been watered down. I've now been conditioned to stop in the middle of some management activity and try to remember which techniques might apply. The different management techniques seem to meld into an anti-synergistic mixture, in which the sum is less than the totality of the parts.
>
> —Michael Brown, as quoted in Sandelands (1990)

Managerial development appears to be in a quandary. A key assumption across many of the chapters in this volume is that traditional cognitive approaches to managerial development are insufficient and that managerial skills development has much to offer. This line of reasoning is not new. Boyatzis (Chapter 7) suggests that this movement away from

AUTHORS' NOTE: We would like to thank Kim Cameron, Michael Thompson, and Ernie Savoie for invaluable comments on earlier drafts. The views expressed in this chapter do not necessarily fully represent the views of the Ford Motor Company.

219

traditional cognitive approaches took root in the early 1960s under the label *affective learning* and has reborn now as competency-based learning.

Contemplating 30 years of effort, we might assume that much has been accomplished. This assumption, however, may be overly optimistic (Bigelow, 1990). Whetten, Windes, May, and Bookstaver (Chapter 2), for example, review the past 10 years of literature on skills development with some disappointment. They suggest that many see the teaching of managerial skills as a very limited cult movement. The majority of faculty members are ignorant of the content and suspicious of the methods in skills courses. These courses have difficulty spreading to a wider base, they argue, because of course size assumptions, differences in teaching methods, student discomfort, political implications in business schools, the lack of widespread familiarity and demand on the part of business, and the infrastructure of the greater educational world. In short, teaching skills violates the core assumptions of traditional management education at nearly every level and hence has made little progress as a widespread innovation. It is seen as unproven and too radical.

To this discouraging situation McKnight (Chapter 15) brings the argument that current assumptions about skills education are, however, not radical enough. Building on Polanyi (1966), he claims that skills knowledge is both responsive and subconscious. He suggests that individuals have metaprograms that direct behavior. In responding to an interpersonal situation, a metaprogram is evoked and an individual responds somewhat spontaneously. Over time these metaprograms develop and change. Using the Whetten and Cameron (1984) skills text, *Developing Management Skills*, as a point of criticism, he argues that the use of cognitive information in the skill-development process is of very limited use.

On one hand, McKnight fails to understand the mission of Whetten and Cameron and all other authors of skills texts. Precisely for the reasons specified by Whetten et al. (Chapter 2), skills texts must be structured to at least be comprehensible to the "opposition." Publishers are well aware of potential markets and are simply not going to produce a book so radical that it will be rejected outright. The Whetten and Cameron book has done more to advance the cause of skills education than any other volume. Many authors of skills texts understand McKnight's message. They, however, believe that they must make some compromises in order to be heard.

On the other hand, McKnight provides some very important insights into the nature of skills development. Skills learning should be student-centered and experiential. The educator's role is not professor, but coach.

The student experiments with a behavior, becomes aware of its meaning, and uses cognition to develop hypotheses about how to behave more effectively. Each experiment slightly alters or reinforces the metaprogram. Theory is useful only if it assists in generating more and better alternatives for the next trial. Skill learning is possible, and knowledge becomes the source of empowerment.

In essence, what McKnight is advocating in his discussion of metaprograms is deep change, or what is sometimes called second-order or paradigm change (Bartunek & Moch, 1987; Levy, 1985). A central assumption in such arguments is that metaprograms both serve and bind us. While they help us to know and understand some things, they blind us to others. Over time our maps of reality become increasingly less accurate and our strategies increasingly less effective if they do not change as reality itself changes. When individuals are supported in the difficult task of reassessing reality, and thus altering their metaprogram or paradigm, they become more aligned with reality, more self-empowered, and more effective. One reason for this increased effectiveness is that they are not only able to develop new skills but they are also better able to utilize the skills they already have. What McKnight is advocating, then, is a different, more transformational approach to skills building.

Two Models of Skills Development

For the past 30 years a cognitive, competency-based model for managerial skills development has dominated the field. We label this traditional approach first-order, transactional skills development. The objective of this first-order model is to develop specific skills through traditional teaching methods. The goal of this type of skills development is to nurture and maintain existing paradigms and the status quo. This model assumes a stable, certain, and somewhat predictable environment. This type of skill training is the focus of many of the chapters in this volume and has traditionally been the focus of the few skills courses in business schools.

In the past few years, many have come to view the transactional, first-order model of skills training as limited. In this chapter we introduce a second model of skills training and development, which is complementary to and builds on the first model. While this second model recognizes the need for traditional skill development, it focuses on transformational, second-order skill development (Levy, 1985). The objective of this transformational model is to stimulate individual paradigm changes and to empower individuals to take charge of themselves in the organization and initiate change (Jantsch, 1980; Sheldon, 1980). In contrast to the first model, an assumption of this model is that the environment is ambiguous and uncertain; therefore, skills must be dynamic and transformational for individuals to effectively adapt to a changing environment.

The outcome of this second model of skills development is empowerment. By empowerment we mean managers who take risks, who initiate action, who make changes, and who have a personal vision for themselves within their organization. Empowerment is a radical departure from more traditional approaches because it challenges many of the assumptions inherent in managerial development within business schools.

Empowerment: Exploring an Analogue

To more fully understand both second-order, transformational change in university life and the barriers inherent in this type of change, we turn to an analogue. The analogue is corporate America. We focus first on the generally accepted assumptions of management education in corporate America by examining that which is most false. We then turn to a radical management development program to find new insights about change. Here we begin with some basic assumptions.

Assumption 1: Facing unprecedented levels of change and continuous demands for increased organizational responsiveness, American corporations are widely concerned with developing the skills of middle managers.

Though some organizations are taking this task to heart, many have not. In many companies middle managers are to American corporations as students are to American universities—disempowered and ignored. During the past 10 years the ranks of middle management have been decimated due to downsizing efforts (Cameron, Freeman, & Mishra, 1990; "Caught," 1988). While their resources have dwindled, individuals are now doing the work previously assigned to two or three people. Although there are some noticeable exceptions, most companies tend to take for granted their middle managers. Relatively few organizations have introduced development programs to help their middle managers respond to new situations and make deep changes. As a result, middle managers tend to be burned out and unresponsive.

Assumption 2: Given the pressures for increased organizational responsiveness and the questionable state of middle managers, most executives are anxious to institute programs and teach middle managers to be transformational, or at least innovative, leaders.

Innovation and transformation entail high levels of risk. Many executives have no previous experience, nor incentive, for change; rather, most have been socialized in the assumptions of preserving equilibrium. Like the average management professor, they are tied to tradition. Interestingly, here the tradition is skills, though primarily first-order, transactional skills. However, the notion of a course that would bring the fundamental, developmental changes suggested by McKnight (Chapter 15) is first, difficult to comprehend and second, difficult to sell. Hence skills, only in the most traditional sense, are what is taught.

Assumption 3: Middle managers, anxious to grow and develop, are desirous of skills training.

To a great extent this assumption also tends to be false. In many organizations, middle managers are frustrated. Organizations tend, first and foremost, to disempower people. Providing new skills to a disempowered manager simply increases frustration. The greatest dissatisfaction is that the middle manager is not allowed to use the skills already possessed. Like the typical business student, the middle manager has to learn to "play the game." Just as the typical student is accused of "not wanting to learn," so the middle manager is accused of "not wanting to lead." Nothing, however, could be further from the truth. Both want to learn, grow, and have impact. Both, however, have learned that their respective systems tend to constrain such efforts, and consequently their metaprograms reflect the environments they encounter.

Assumption 4: If the above problems could be resolved, skills training would result in more effective organizations.

Here again, the answer seems to be disappointing. Just as most management professors do not teach self-discovery, interpersonal relationships, and leadership (see Boyatzis, Chapter 7), most corporate training efforts deal with these topics only superficially. Transformational topics tend to be taught in safe, transactional ways. Just as most leadership researchers are not transformational people, most corporate educators fail to be visionaries capable of helping participants discover their way into new metaprograms or paradigms. Even when they are capable and dedicated to the implementation of second-order, transformational-skills development, chances are they will not be permitted to do so unless sanctioned by key organizational leaders who commit the company to these efforts. Skills programs thus tend to provide more highly skilled transactional managers, better able to preserve the status quo, and thus more likely to exacerbate the original organizational problem.

A New Approach

The above picture of management development is not promising. But the situation is far from hopeless or irresolvable. Empowerment and deep change in the underlying philosophy of management development can be cultivated when a more transformational, second-order model is integrated with more traditional models (Conger, 1989; Conger & Kanungo, 1988). This very process is underway at the Ford Motor Company. A radical approach to middle management development has been designed, developed, and implemented. Instead of focusing on maintaining equilibrium, this program promotes change and new direction. It stimulates the capacity for transformational behavior. In the spirit of continuing the corporate analogue described above, in this next section, we will describe this more transformational, second-order approach to management development at Ford.

Historical Background

One of the most dramatic business turnarounds of the 1980s occurred at the Ford Motor Company. One key factor in the turnaround was Ford's investment in its people, its human capital. In the early 1980s, a major program called "Participative Management and Employee Involvement" was instituted to increase participation across all levels of the organization, from the assembly line worker to the line supervisor to top management. By 1987 Ford Motor Company had extended its transformational efforts and had successfully implemented a development program for the top 2,000 executives in the company. This program was established as part of the overall transformation process evolving at Ford as a result of the crisis the company had experienced in the early 1980s. This effort provided a forum for executive dialogue and reinforcement for the strategic direction the company was charting.

Although this effort was successful, it was viewed by top executives as inadequate. The question was asked: "What are we doing to prepare the next generation of leaders?" Failing to satisfactorily answer this question, the company recognized the need for a developmental program for its middle managers. This provided the basis for the design, development, and implementation of the Leadership Education and Development (LEAD) program.

From the beginning the LEAD program was different. It continued to build on the company's other transformational efforts but also extended its horizons. It continued to break the mold of traditional management development programs. Instead of following the traditional, internal "staff" route of program development by the Employee Relations Staff group in the Employee Development Office, individuals from the staff initiated and coordinated the involvement of a cross-company effort. A steering committee made up of executives from different operating units was constructed to investigate whether some corporate-wide development program would be necessary for the next tier of management. From focus group interviews with potential targeted participants, the steering committee found overwhelming support for a managerial development program targeted at the company's middle management. The focus groups indicated that the middle managers as a whole felt neglected and uncertain of their role in the overall transformation of the company.

With this support, the steering committee then turned its attention to the content and process of the program. The committee decided that a program integrating aspects of both the top management strategically oriented program and the supervisory skills-oriented program was necessary. The emerging need from the interviews and the contemporary literature was for training in leadership, empowerment, and managing and creating change. The committee reviewed several leadership/management programs available commercially and decided that a Ford-specific program would be more appropriate. The committee established basic criteria for the program. These criteria include: (a) the program should provide integration with other company efforts; (b) it should reinforce the Ford Mission, Values and Guiding Principles; (c) it should be targeted for participation by all middle management; (d) it should be application-oriented; and (e) it should provide a cross-functional and international perspective.

Program Design and Development

Given these criteria and the focus on leadership, empowerment, and change, the committee initiated an international search for appropriate theories and models. Through this review, the Competing Values Framework (CVF) (Quinn, 1988) was seen to provide the most insight and utility. Many of the problems articulated by the middle managers had a paradoxical nature. "I need help to become more creative and innovative, but I also need to stick to schedules and maintain structure in my department." "I need to nurture and develop my subordinates but must also focus on enhancing the bottom line." When viewed in the perspective of the CVF, these seeming contradictions became reframed as understandable and manageable.

At this time, the faculty at the University of Michigan were invited to become involved in the program. This collaboration required the design participants themselves to be transformational and become empowered. The implicit question was how intensive would the collaboration be? Would the university faculty take ownership of the project with Ford providing support and resources? Would Ford maintain ownership but elicit theoretical contributions from the faculty? Or would it be a more true collaboration with both sides sharing ownership through the design, development, and implementation of the program? Each option provided specific benefits. The first two options were basically traditional approaches requiring little risk. The third, true collaboration, represented a radical approach for both institutions.

Both Ford and the University of Michigan had successfully developed education and training programs in the past, using the two more traditional approaches. Moreover, both institutions questioned whether they in fact could collaborate. Nevertheless, both were curious about the potential benefits of collaboration: (a) greater capability to utilize expertise of individuals from both institutions, (b) improved integration between the "academic" theoretical perspective and the "real world" issues and applications, (c) a potentially greater impact on the participants than could be achieved by either organization "going it alone," and (d) the opportunity to build a bridge between the two institutions by reframing their differences as strengths. But collaboration also entailed risk. Collaboration would require two very strong and independent institutions to work together, to create an environment where both were dependent on the other. By definition, the purpose and goals of both institutions were different. Further, neither group had a commitment from its respective organization for what could be a 3- to 5-year commitment of resources and personnel.

The spirit of the program won them over. The decision to proceed in the design and development of the program collaboratively can be seen as a transformational action by both the Ford steering committee and the faculty from the university. The decision empowered the individuals involved; the risks were clear and the benefits potentially significant. There was the opportunity to create a new process that could model an ongoing, value-adding relationship between business and industry and the academic community. Yet if the resulting design were not approved, the developers would have expended much time, energy, resources, and personal commitment for a "failed effort" or one that might be just traditional.

To start the process, several design meetings were conducted with a host of participants from both institutions. First, the basic parameters and processes of the program needed reexamination in view of the collaboration. After examining various needs and options, including extensive discussions with managers at all levels, the group concluded the necessary skills were not the traditional, basic behavioral skills, but rather the more transformational, second-order skills.

In keeping with the above discussion of typical assumptions, this decision was radical and important. What was recognized here was that traditional skill training was an equilibrium-preserving activity, and what was needed was not more *information* but more *transformation* (De Bono, 1971). Conveying the right "form" to passive middle managers by training-experts was the tradition. Recognizing that middle managers are really the experts and that only they can determine the right "form" for any given situation calls for an approach that entails creativity, empowerment, and risk on the part of designers, participants, and the company (Kanter, 1982; Nonaka, 1988).

The design group also decided that while the program was to focus on the issue of leadership, the leadership focus needed to have a context—a context in the company's strategic issues (Davis, 1982). Ford was striving to align the whole of the organization around several key issues, and these became the context for the program. Learning, thinking, and managerial-leadership are the content for the program, while key strategic issues of customer focus, quality, and continuous improvement are the context.

Throughout the program, the participants are provided general concepts and principles, which they are then required to translate into the company context. Two different group configurations are used: (a) groups that are

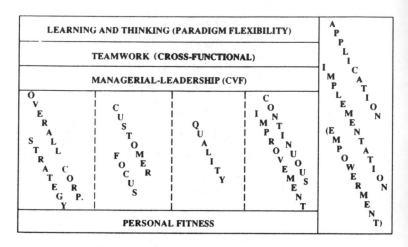

Figure 16.1. Content of the LEAD Program Core Session

mixed cross-functionally, and (b) groups that are functionally similar. The cross-functional group configuration provides a broader overall company system perspective, while the functionally similar configuration provides a deeper understanding of specific issues and challenges.

The focus on application and implementation of the program's concepts and principles supports another innovation. To reinforce the emphasis on application, the program was designed in stages. The basic content and context were established in the first stage, the core session. During the core session the participants are encouraged to reflect on how the content and context apply to their specific job responsibilities. Figure 16.1 represents the basic design themes for the core session of the program. At the end of the core session, each participant is asked to record insights and learnings and develop action plans for application. The core session is followed by the interim period, a 6- to 8-month period when the participants return to their normal job responsibilities. After 6 to 8 months, the participants are reconvened for a follow-up session.

The follow-up session extends the content and context from the core session. The new focus at the follow-up is the specific experiences of the participants during the interim period. Figure 16.2 illustrates the foci of the follow-up session. While the themes are the same, the purpose is now to analyze the experience, assess current conditions, and determine required next steps. This program is the first at Ford to incorporate a

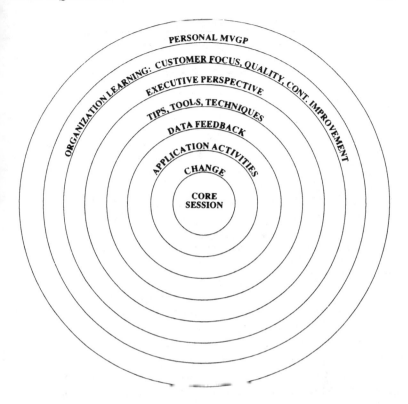

Figure 16.2. Follow-Up Session Themes

structured follow-up process. In terms of changing metaprograms and empowering middle managers, this part of the design is crucial. It is during the 6-month period that participants are able to test their new mind-sets by attempting to take new initiatives. During the follow-up they are able to present and compare their failures and successes.

Another aspect of collaboration by the design and development team was the issue of program delivery. As with the design and development, several options were available: Ford presenters, university faculty presenters, or a collaboration between Ford and university presenters. Once again, the collaboration option was selected. Each day of the session involves two program faculty presenters—one from the university and one from Ford. The faculty member frames the content and provides a theoretical background; the Ford executive provides context to the issue and discusses current company initiatives. This dual presenter process provides both the rationale and logic as well as the credibility of the message.

Equally important was the need to design the program so that not only did it have meaning for Ford middle managers from many countries but also that some sessions could be delivered in overseas locations, yet with an international mix of participants.

Program Processes

Process is the key to the transformational approach of the program. A transactional approach would be one defining the situation for the participants and prescribing an action/skill approach. The LEAD program process allows the participants to determine both the nature of their specific situation and the type of action they believe they can and should initiate. The process of allowing the participants to choose the type and degree of action is critical to the empowerment process.

Here again we see a divergence from normal approaches. Here the assumption is that the participants know more and know better than the organization. This ability to determine their own applications in their own job setting is critical to the empowerment process.

While the design and development of the program had many unique features, the product processes reflect interesting aspects that have contributed to the program's success. First, the program is providing overall organization alignment on key strategic issues. This is difficult with a company as large as Ford and with such strong functional ties. The objective is to provide a broad perspective and then to allow the individual participants to determine for themselves applications specific to their area of responsibility.

In many ways the participants are as diverse as those attending public education. They come from all functions (manufacturing, engineering, finance, general council, supply and distribution, sales, and so on), all nationalities (American, Canadian, European, South American, Asian), and from various staff levels of responsibility (from individual contributors managing major programs, to managers of major operations with responsibility for many people). This wide diversity requires program processes that allow for individual participant interpretation of program content.

The Impact of the Program on Middle Management

We have discussed the impact of the program on those involved in the design and delivery of the program. But what impact has the program had on its participants? How are they different as a result of their participation? Has the program achieved what it intended (i.e., empowerment)?

When the middle managers first come to the LEAD program, many describe their role in the organization as highly constrained. To a great extent, they see their job as simply "following the rules" and "seeing that the status quo and the system are maintained." These managers, much like business students in the classroom, learn to play by the rules and focus on fulfilling what is expected of them. The managers articulate their struggle with barriers that inhibit them from being responsive middle managers. From a series of interviews, surveys, and factor analyses, the five types of barriers emerge: (a) a lack of strategic vision in their unit; (b) the inevitability of organizational conflict and consequentially low commitment, trust, and teamwork; (c) the bureaucratic culture; (d) personal time constraints; and (e) the disempowerment of their co-workers. These barriers are common in most large organizations. The result of these barriers is middle managers who tend to feel disempowered and virtually ignored in the organization. Taking a traditional skills approach to people who feel so disempowered would only increase their sense of disempowerment. Clearly, the traditional cycle must be broken.

At this point, the managers participate in the core session of the LEAD program and then return to their jobs with action plans for the interim period. Few changes in the individuals' work units accompany the LEAD program. Nevertheless, when the middle managers return for the follow-up session of the LEAD program, there is substantially less focus on how organizational and individual barriers inhibit their effectiveness. Instead, the middle managers share examples of strategies they developed to help them overcome those barriers, strategies they developed to facilitate their own and others' empowerment.

From interview data, surveys, and factor analyses, four types of strategies emerge. First, they describe strategies for personal attitude changes as a means for reframing their environments. For example, one manager described a strategy whereby he made a conscious effort to reframe threatening situations as potential opportunities. He focused on remaining optimistic in spite of seemingly insurmountable barriers. Second, they articulate strategies for challenging organizational mind-sets by bringing up new ideas and questioning consensus. One manager described how she became a devil's advocate, continuously challenging her work group to question the way that things were done in their unit. Third, they reveal strategies for building trust and commitment among their co-workers. Many managers discussed the importance of breaking down "chimneys," or cross-functional barriers. Fourth, they share strategies for taking initiatives and trying new things, many times bypassing the traditional, hierarchical approval process. Overall, they perceive their role expectations to be expanded and enriched with less focus on traditional, transactional skills and more focus on transformational skills.

What stimulates the middle managers to change? What happens in the LEAD program to energize the managers in such a positive way? In this chapter, we argue that these middle managers have become empowered. The dual process of both overall alignment and individual application has resulted in significant empowerment of the participants to determine an application based on their own judgment. The participants feel empowered as they are able to choose the initiative, based on improved perception of company direction, and have a broader understanding of the overall systemic impact. A process of managerial empowerment is described below.

The Process of Empowerment

The primary objective of the LEAD program is to stimulate paradigm changes in the middle managers about their role in the organization. This objective is the first step in the empowerment process. The program serves as a stimulus for the managers to think deeply about how they can refocus their perceptions of themselves and their work role. As one manager described it, "The program forced me to reevaluate my core values, goals, and methods of operating as a means for reinforcing them and/or changing them. I made a conscious effort to become aware of my paradigms and then expanded my own and others' mind-sets toward change." Another manager described a co-worker who had been through the LEAD program as "born again, having a complete attitude change. Where he previously fought any mention of change, [this manager] immediately began preaching the virtues of having a mind-set favorable to initiating change." This first stage of the empowerment process involves an in-depth personal evaluation and cognitive reframing, which allow the middle managers to see themselves and their environment through different lenses (Bartunek

& Moch, 1987). This deep change may be thought of as a second-order personal transformation, a change in the individual's metaprogram

As a result of this self-transformation, the individuals perceive themselves and the organization in a new light. This fresh interpretation is then accompanied by new approaches to old problems (Bartunek, Gordon, & Weathersby, 1983). In this stage of the empowerment process, the middle managers initiate new patterns of action. They experiment with out-of-the-box thinking and behavior. They take risks, try unorthodox methods, and are more creative and innovative. In this stage old habits tend to be broken, and many times action is taken without going through traditional channels. There is greater trust in oneself and reliance on intuition and "pure guts" (Manz, 1986).

One manager said "I felt like I could try new things without going through the bureaucratic approval process. I didn't feel like I had to monitor every detail. I could trust my own intuition and believe that I was doing the right thing." In this stage of empowerment, the managers often have dramatic stories to tell about their new patterns of action. For example, a loan-approval process in Ford's credit company, which took 2 days for completion before a manager attended the LEAD program, was revised by the manager so that it took only 8 hours. Shortly thereafter, the manager further modified the approval process so that it now takes only 4 hours. In most cases, these new patterns of action are second-order or revolutionary changes instead of the more typical first-order, incremental changes the managers had previously felt compelled to initiate.

In most cases, these new patterns of action are reinforced by the managers' superiors, and the process of empowerment continues. However, in other cases, the managers' new patterns of action are not supported or nurtured by their superiors for a variety of reasons. As a result, these managers become disenchanted with their new paradigms and regress to their previous behaviors.

In cases where the new patterns of action are reinforced, the managers reflect on and learn from their new experiences. Where the new pattern of action was successful, the manager draws on that success for future action. In cases where the new pattern of action was not successful, the manager learns from his or her mistakes and grows and develops. In this stage of the empowerment process, individuals recognize the importance of a continuous learning mind-set and the need to remain flexible and adaptable in order to be responsive to a changing and ambiguous environment. One manager said, "I learned how to nurture ambiguity and complexity in order to deal with the constantly changing environment."

Another manager described a changed perspective on making mistakes, "I realize that it is okay to make mistakes, and when I make mistakes I try to think about how I can learn from them." In this stage of empowerment, cognitions become increasingly complex, which allows for greater learning and growth (Bartunek et al., 1983).

In the process of empowerment, managers become more self-confident and energized. One manager said, "I feel excited and invigorated about my role in the organization. My co-workers say that they noticed a difference in me. They say I am more self-confident and relaxed, that I have a special glow." The managers feel highly integrated with and committed to the organization.

What is more, this energy is transmitted to those around the empowered manager. The managers describe how they nurture and coach others to become empowered. "I empower others, helping them grow, develop, learn, and make decisions, giving them ownership of activities and wide areas of responsibility." These empowered managers report more communication with their colleagues, more social support, and more good citizenship behavior. In this way, the process of empowerment is synergistic. It draws individuals together to higher levels of effort. As transformational leaders transform their associates, empowered individuals empower their associates. In this way, empowered individuals band together to become an empowered work group.

As empowered individuals interact with one another, they develop new perspectives and have new experiences. For example, the managers describe how they share success stories and help one another diagnose situations to develop appropriate strategies. In addition, they build networks to expand their power base in the organization. These new perspectives and experiences then stimulate the managers to once more redefine their self and role, and the process of empowerment begins again.

Consequently, the process of empowerment is regenerative and deviation-amplifying (Weick, 1979). It is dynamic and cyclical. It is transformational at multiple levels. It begins by transforming individuals' sense of self, stimulates them to try new behaviors, helps them develop a continuous learning mind-set, and increases their self-confidence. This empowered individual, then, works to draw others into the process of empowerment so that they too become empowered. The result is an empowered work force, which contributes to a more responsive and effective organization. This process of empowerment is illustrated in Figure 16.3.

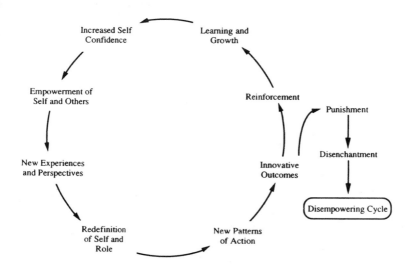

Figure 16.3. Cycle of Empowerment

It is important to note, however, that not all participants are positively affected by the program. A small number are disenchanted and cynical about the program from its beginning. Others feel stimulated to become empowered, but then return to their work group and receive no support or reinforcement for their newly learned paradigm. As a result, these individuals become disenchanted and regress to past behavior. As one disillusioned middle manager indicated, "This entire program is a fraud. The program is nothing like it is portrayed to be. No one here wants middle managers to be leaders." However, these individuals represent only a small minority of program participants, substantially less than 5%.

Conclusion: Implications for Training and Development

At the beginning of this chapter, we outlined two different models or approaches to skills development. The first model reflects traditional approaches to skills development. It is transactional and develops primarily first-order, transactional skills. The second model is complementary to and builds on the first. It focuses on transformational, second-order skills development. The LEAD program is highly consistent with this second, more transformational model. The program's objective, like the objective of this second model, is to stimulate individual paradigm changes and to empower individuals to take charge of themselves and initiate change, deep change. Like the transformational model of skills development, the LEAD program helps managers learn how to manage ambiguity and uncertainty. Rather than prescribing action, the program encourages the managers to assess a given situation and to think for themselves, to take risks, and to try new behaviors (Baird & Thomas, 1985).

Though designed to develop middle managers in a large corporation, the LEAD program is a useful analogue for managerial skills training in the business school classroom. It provides clues on how the second, more transformational model of skills development can be integrated into the curriculum of business schools. Moreover, the LEAD program and this second model of skills development are both found to be highly consistent with the four assumptions outlined at the beginning of the chapter.

In response to Assumption 1, which asserts that American corporations are concerned with the development of managerial skills, this transformational model of skill training requires a high degree of commitment to the manager. It is student-centered and experiential. The educator's role is not teacher, but coach. This model provides overall organizational alignment and stimulates students to become empowered and to experience deep personal change. Its goal is to re-energize or unfreeze managers as they face unprecedented levels of change and continuous demands for increased responsiveness.

In response to Assumption 2, which asserts that executives are anxious to institute programs and teach managers to be transformational and innovative leaders, this model of skill training is transformational by design. Its primary objective is to induce managers to reflect deeply about their self-paradigms and to transform those paradigms if deemed necessary. The goal is to simultaneously develop transformational leaders and transactional managers. Here the focus is not on following the existing rules and maintaining the status quo. Instead, individuals are encouraged to be cognitively complex and to question the way things are done in the organization (Quinn, 1988, p. 10). Evidence of individual transformation resulting from this second model of skill training is provided above in the assessment of the impact of the LEAD program.

In response to Assumption 3, which suggests that managers are anxious to grow and develop and are desirous of skill training, the second model of skill training is very much individually oriented. It allows individuals to integrate their personal values and needs. It is introspective and allows individuals to draw on and expand on their individual core competencies while also developing new competencies (Prahalad & Hamel, 1990). Instead of requiring conformity to a given managerial paradigm, it allows individuals to develop and nurture different paradigms.

Finally, in response to Assumption 4, which asserts that skills training results in more effective organizations, this transformation model prepares managers to be responsive to the changing and uncertain environment. By expanding managerial role expectations to be both anticipatory and reactive, visionary and reinforcing, strategic and executionary, and participatory and directing, managers will be able to contribute to greater organizational responsiveness and thus organizational effectiveness. Beyond the need for "hard" management skills, this second model also emphasizes the need for self-discovery, interpersonal relationships, and transformational leadership. These more "soft" skills are viewed by many to be critical to individual and organizational effectiveness given greater environmental instability and change (Nonaka & Johansson, 1985). We do not, however, advocate the abandonment of traditional skills training. Instead, we suggest that traditional, transactional training must be supplemented with the complementary focus of the second, more transformational, model.

Unfortunately, this transformational model of skills training and development is not easily implemented. There are no recipes for successful implementation and little precedent to follow. In fact, this model violates many of the core assumptions of traditional management education at nearly every level. It is radical, requiring risk on the part of both the receiver and the sender, the student and the teacher. It requires experimentation and trial-and-error processes. Moreover, it requires trust and openness to new ideas.

The LEAD program reviewed here is delivered in the organizational context of one organization: the Ford Motor Company. Intriguing challenges for researchers, educators, and other organizations include whether variations of this model can be fashioned to have similar impacts when delivered to young "premanagers" in a business school setting, or in a setting of managers from many different organizations assembled in an executive development program.

Our experience indicates that it would be highly desirable to extend, with appropriate reshaping, the Ford learnings to other settings. The benefits are impressive and long range. This transformational, second-order model of skills training, we believe, is the key to developing managers who will be able to manage in the 1990s and beyond. Managers trained in transformational skills will have the cognitive complexity necessary to effectively manage ambiguity and uncertainty in their working environment and in their jobs. This transformational model will help managers become aware of not only the costs and benefits of managerial paradigms but also the importance of paradigm change in order to respond to changing circumstances. In addition, this model of skills training will help managers become self-initiators, change-makers, and risk-takers— all essential self-empowering skills. The end product is a more productive work force and effective organization.

Afterword

John D. Bigelow

What is the current status of the "skills movement"? What have we learned since 1983? I see three major conclusions that can be culled from the chapters of this book:

Conclusion 1:
The "skills movement" is alive and active.

In 1983, the long-term viability of university-based skills programs was still very much in question. Since then a number of developments suggest that skill-based programs will not only persist but also increase in the longer term. First, skill-based programs are enduring. This book describes a number of skills programs that have been installed and are in operation. Some, such as the Urbana-Champaign program, have persisted for nearly a decade. An additional example not mentioned in this book is the University of Pittsburgh skills program (Damm, 1983), which has been active for more than 8 years.

Second, resources for skill teaching are increasing. Whereas in 1983 the only textbook was the new Whetten and Cameron book (1983), there are now at least three additional texts and skill resources (Keleman, Garcia, & Lovelace, 1990; Lewis, Garcia & Jobs, 1990; Quinn, Faerman, Thompson, McGrath, 1990; Robbins, 1988)—and others are in process. Apparently, book publishers see a market in this area.

Third, skills programs are receiving support. The AACSB continues its support for dealing with skills as a part of college learning. They have pioneered a skill-testing procedure and have sponsored the recent Porter and McKibbin report (1988), which reaffirms the need for skills. In 1989, the eight largest public accounting firms committed to $4 million over 5 years to stimulate relevant curricula, including communication and interpersonal skills. The Organizational Behavior Teaching Society has established a committee that aims to establish some model skill-development programs.

These developments suggest that skills courses will both continue and increase in number in the foreseeable future.

Conclusion 2:
Our repertoire of skill pedagogies is increasing.

In 1983, little was known about how to teach action skills. The Whetten text made the 5-step training-based model of preassessment, learning, analysis, practice, and application available to instructors (see Chapter 2). This model has been implemented in the classroom through use of self-appraisal instruments, conceptual materials, analysis of written/video cases, role plays, and practice in life settings.

Several chapters of this book suggest that there exist alternative approaches to teaching action skills. Some of the key approaches described in this book are listed in Table A.1.

While all these approaches are reported to enhance skills, it is clear that they accomplish a variety of skill-learning objectives. For example, the humanistic and IPCC approaches emphasize the thinking-through, goal-setting, and action-planning aspects of skillfulness. The outdoor challenge, actor-enhanced role plays, and situational practice approaches emphasize the real time "acting in a situation" aspect of skillfulness. The transformational approach addresses higher order thinking that may inhibit the exercise of skills.

Conclusion 3:
There is more to skillfulness
than we previously thought.

In 1983 managerial skills appeared to be a collection of relatively straightforward behavioral procedures, which could be applied to a wide variety of situations. We are finding, however, that skills are not as easy to recognize as might have been expected. In Chapter 11 we saw that skill examinations, supervisor ratings, peer ratings, and subordinate ratings all may lead to differing assessments of a person's managerial skills. In the

Table A.1
Alternative Skill Learning Approaches

Approach	Description of Skill-Learning Process	Chapter
Skill-specific	skills are learned singly through case analysis, role-play practice, and practice assignments	2
Outdoor challenge	group activities in which wilderness challenges are collectively dealt with	3
Humanistic	use of literature and current events in conjunction with learning logs to consider how to deal with managerial situations	4
Actor-enhanced role plays	interactional practice with trained actors	5
Interactive Personal Computer Cases (IPCC)	a computerized case unfolds through a series of decisions, with feedback following each decision	6
Situation-specific	holistic situations are dealt with, requiring application of a variety of skills in concert	14
Situational practice	subconscious skills are developed and refined through repeated situational practice	15
Transformational	in addition to skill learning, an emphasis is given to empowerment	16

previous section we saw skill pedagogies accomplishing a variety of learning objectives, some of which are not customarily associated with skills.

In fact, many of the chapters of this book suggest that we revise some of our assumptions about what is required to act skillfully. These are some of the revisions that I see.

1. *Skillfulness means situational effectiveness.* A common assumption in skill courses has been that skillfulness means skill mastery. We are finding, however, that there is a long leap between skill mastery and the ability to use skills in a realistic situation. In Chapters 4, 6, and 14, we see a shift from a focus on skill mastery to a focus on handling situations. To use a carpentry analogy, this would be equivalent to a shift from mastering a hammer to more emphasis on projects in which a hammer may be required. While the idea of focusing on the situation is not new (e.g.,

Mockler, 1971), we are seeing more interest in the kinds of situations in which managers must act skillfully (e.g., Chapter 12).

2. *Skillfulness is based on effective practice theories.* In most university courses students begin without any knowledge of what is to be learned. This is not true in skills courses. Chapter 13 reported that people develop their own practice theories, which inform their behavior and which may compete with course learning. Consequently, it is important for skill courses to make students aware of their current practice theories, encourage critical examination of their current practice theories, and provide course learning as enhancements of current theories—not simply alternatives to them. If this is not done, course learning will not "take": Students will learn what they must, then go out and do what they've always done.

3. *Skillfulness often requires thinking on one's feet.* We have tended to think of managerial skills as the relatively straightforward application of established procedures. Chapters 5 and 6 portray skill situations as a series of interactions in an unfolding situation. During interaction a person may obtain new information requiring a reevaluation of the situation, may find that the approach he or she is using is not yielding the desired results, or may find that he or she has no ready-made solution to the emerging situation. In such instances the person needs to reevaluate his or her goals and approach and possibly even invent a new approach. Skillfulness, then, does not simply mean refined application of skill procedures. It also means being aware of the situation, being flexible, and possibly being creative during the course of interaction.

4. *Skillfulness is improved by practice.* A widely accepted tenet of skill training is that we learn from experience. Chapter 15 provides some insight into this learning process by pointing out that much of skillfulness lies in one's ability to readily implement skill "programs." Such programs are often complex in formulation, requiring, for example, an integration of verbalization, intonation, timing, and nonverbal cues. Because of their complexity, skill programs cannot be rationally "figured out"—they must be learned by repeated execution. Thus, while a skills course should include time to work at the practice theory level, it also needs a component where skills are refined through practice.

5. *Skillfulness may be inhibited by higher level dynamics.* We have been slow in acknowledging that there are psychological barriers that may inhibit skill learning and application. In Chapter 16 we see that a person may learn skill approaches but not use them. In revision 2 above, it was suggested that a person may not use a skill because it conflicts with his or her practice theory. There are other reasons why a person may not apply

what he or she knows. First, the person may be fearful, for example, of looking incompetent, eliciting strong feelings, losing control, or revealing his or herself. Another possible skill inhibitor is a low sense of self-efficacy and correspondingly low expectations that any effort will be successful. Fears and low expectations, then, can act as barriers to taking skillful actions, even when a person believes that a particular action is appropriate. Because skillfulness requires practice, these barriers create a vicious cycle, which must be overcome for a skills course to be effective.

The overcoming of inhibitors may be an essential ingredient of the wilderness experience approach described in Chapter 3. In a study of how executives develop on the job, McCall, Lombardo, and Morrison (1988) comment, "Learning was something these managers did because they had little choice but to take action—stab at problems even if they weren't sure what they were doing, because doing nothing was surely unacceptable" (p. 63). Outdoor challenge seems to be one way to stimulate learning, by making inaction unacceptable.

Agenda: Making Skills Courses More Effective

What are the next steps for the managerial skills movement? There are a number of things that skill teachers might do to become better organized as a group; these might include, for example, obtaining an "interest group" status at the Academy of Management or elsewhere, organizing a conference on skills, assembling a skills advisory board, developing some standards around skill teaching or testing, and maintaining a roster of skill-teaching activities (David Whetten has done some work on the latter). All these activities presume that skills teachers have some common goals and that the expected payoff of organizing is worth the effort.

I think the one activity that would provide the most payoff for skill teachers would be to take what we are learning about skills and skill teaching and use this knowledge to make our skill courses more effective. Below, I outline what a "second generation" skills course would look like.

1. Goals. The goals of the course are twofold: first, for participants to understand what it means to be skillful in managerial situations and, second, to surface, assess, and develop participants' key management-relevant practice theories.

2. Course activities. The course begins by considering the kinds of situations with which managers must deal and the consequences of being skillful or

not. Participants then investigate their own practice theories and assess their adequacy in these situations. They then target key practice theories for development, diagnose barriers to becoming more skillful, and establish a program of study and practice to enhance their skillfulness in these areas. Support groups are formed on the basis of these individual programs. These groups can expect to videotape, debrief, and share their practice sessions with the class.

3. Conceptual materials. A series of readings are available as resource materials. These readings include a taxonomy of management situations, practical discussions of how to be skillful in managerial situations, skill pedagogies, treatises on inhibitors to skill learning and what may be done about them, and a bibliography of further reading. Class participants commit themselves to studying particular readings insofar as they fit with their particular program.

4. Assessment. This is done through (a) submission of a portfolio of accomplishments and (b) through an action exam designed to test the participant's effectiveness in target situations. The action exam does not look for any particular procedure; rather, it seeks to determine whether the participant has established appropriate goals in the situation and reasonably accomplished them. The exam may also test the participant's ability to respond skillfully to novel events that may be reasonably expected to occur. More conventional testing procedures may be used to test for conceptual understanding.

The elements of this course are drawn from practices described in this book. This design differs from customary course practices in four ways. First, it requires participants to establish their own learning activities on the basis of investigation into their own practice theory. This is necessary if the course is to impact on participants' actual practice theories. This approach assumes that participants can obtain enough insight into their own practices so that they can recognize their strengths and weaknesses. Further, it assumes that they can and will develop a program that will positively impact on their skillfulness. One can think of ways in which this process can go wrong, for example, a student who develops a program on the basis of minimizing discomfort, a shallow sense of self, or grades maximization. Some coaching may be needed.

Second, the course deviates in that it values evidence of increased skillfulness over evidence of content mastery as the basic indication of course learning. Instructors who are accustomed to content-oriented courses may feel uncomfortable with this.

Third, the course deviates in that learning assessment is largely through an action examination process, rather than through more traditional examination procedures. Moreover the action exam differs from the currently used process-oriented action exams in that it requires that participants set appropriate goals and make reasonable progress in accomplishing them—even if events take unexpected turns.

Finally, the course deviates in that the role of the instructor is different from that of an instructor in a more academic course. The instructor will spend much less time in managing actual learning activities. On the other hand, he or she will spend much more time monitoring processes, providing guidance, and engaging in action examination procedures. In many respects the changes in the instructor's role parallel contemporary changes in managers' roles.

A course of this description has some key potential advantages over current skill courses. It focuses on holistic managerial situations in which a number of skills may be brought to bear. It increases the likelihood that participants' actual practice theories are developed and that skill learning will continue to be used after the course ends. Scarce class time is focused on highest-priority skill areas. Skills are assessed in terms of effectiveness, which is probably a better indication of skillfulness than testing for application of skill procedures.

Can such a course be implemented viably in a university setting? Can we find instructors who can teach this course? Are instructor activities within reasonable bounds of effort and varied enough to allow sustained involvement, year after year? Will university systems support a course that deviates from the norm in these ways? Similar questions were raised with "first generation" skills courses in 1983. In my opinion, finding the answers to questions such as these is one of the highest-priority issues confronting the action-skills movement today.

Conclusion

This book began with the premise that universities have emphasized theoretical knowledge to the exclusion of other types of knowledge. The chapters of this book have explored different facets associated with the teaching of practical knowledge. During the past decade the skills movement has established a foothold, and we are in the process of making significant improvements in our ability to enhance peoples' skillfulness.

What new issues are we likely to encounter in the next decade? First, the question of ethics in skill use is likely to become more significant, particularly when we get into issues of persuasion, influence, and the possibility of "manipulation." Perhaps this one point where Habermas's

(1968) "emancipatory" knowledge becomes pertinent. Second, we are likely to become more concerned with skills as a theme cutting across disciplines, for example, skillfulness in management of accounting processes or in cross-cultural situations. Third, we're likely to see opportunities to link up with outcomes programs. Would it be desirable for skills courses to provide evidence for university level outcomes programs? Certainly this would require more attention to interrater reliability among action-skill testers. Finally, we're likely to begin finding that managerial skills are very much intertwined with other, longer term management-development processes, such as development of a more holistic perspective and displacement of caring from self to firm.

In sum, it has been a very good decade for the skills movement. Hopefully, in 1999 we will be able to point to an equivalent amount of progress.

References

AACSB (American Assembly of Collegiate Schools of Business). (1984). *Outcome measurement project of the Accreditation Research Committee (Phase II: An interim report)*. St. Louis, MO: Author.

AACSB. (American Assembly of Collegiate Schools of Business). (1987, May). *Outcome measurement project. Phase III report*. St. Louis, MO: Author.

Accounting Education Change Commission. (1989). *Perspectives on education: Capabilities for success in the accounting profession*.

Albanese, R. (1987). Outcome measurement and management education. *Academy of Management Newsletter, 17*(2), 12-15.

Albanese, R. (1989). Competency-based management education: Three operative and normative issues. *The Organizational Behavior Teaching Review, XIV*(1), 16-27.

Albanese, R., Schoenfeldt, L. F., Serey, T. T., & Whetten, D. A. (1987). *Education for management competencies: Approaches, new developments, and issues*. Symposium presented at the Academy of Management Meeting.

Aldag, R., & Stearns, T. M. (1987). *Management*. Cincinnati, OH: Southwestern.

Alverno College Faculty. (1985). *Assessment at Alverno College*. Milwaukee, WI: Alverno College.

Andrews, J. D., & Sigband, N. B. (1984). How effectively does the new accountant communicate? Perceptions by practitioners and academics. *Journal of Business Communication, 21*, 15-24.

Argyris, C. (1982). *Reasoning, learning, and action*. San Francisco: Jossey-Bass.

Argyris, C. (1985). *Strategy, change and defensive routines*. Boston: Pitman.

Argyris, C., & Schon, D. (1974). *Theory in practice*. San Francisco: Jossey-Bass.

Argyris, C., & Schon, D. (1978). *Organizational learning: A theory of action perspective*. Reading, MA: Addison-Wesley.

Axley, S. R. (1984). Managerial and organizational communication in terms of the conduit metaphor. *Academy of Management Review, 9*(3), 428-437.

Baird, I. S., & Thomas, H. (1985). Toward a contingency model of strategic risk taking. *Academy of Management Review, 10*, 230-243.

Bandura, A. (1977). *Social learning theory*. Englewood Cliffs, NJ: Prentice-Hall.

Bartunek, J. M., Gordon, J. R., & Weathersby, R. P. (1983). Developing "complicated" understanding in administrators. *Academy of Management Review, 8*, 273-284.

Bartunek, J. M., & Moch, M. K. (1987). First-order, second-order, and third-order change and organizational development interventions: A cognitive approach. *The Journal of Applied Behavioral Science, 23*, 483-500.

Bates, B. (1987). *The way of the actor*. Boston: Shambhala.

Beckhard, R. (1972). Optimizing team-building efforts. *Journal of Contemporary Business, 1*(3), 23-32.

Beckhard, R. (1975). Strategies for large systems change. *Sloan Management Review, 16*(2), 43-55.

Beckhard, R., & Harris, R. (1977). *Organizational transition: Managing complex change.* Reading, MA: Addison-Wesley.

Bennett, J. C., & Olney, R. J. (1986). The communication needs of business executives. *Journal of Business Communication, 8*(3), 5-11.

Bennis, W., & Nanus, B. (1985). *Leaders: The strategies for taking charge.* New York: Harper & Row.

Benson, G. L. (1983). On the campus: How well does business prepare graduates for the business world? *Personnel, 60,* 61-65.

Bentson, C., & Kaman, V. S. (1989). *Acting in and acting out at an assessment center: The design and implementation of role play simulations.* Presentation at the 17th International Congress on the Assessment Center Method, Pittsburgh, PA.

Berk, R. A. (Ed.). (1986). *Performance assessment.* Baltimore, MD: The Johns Hopkins University Press.

Bernardin, H. J., & Beatty, R. W. (1984). *Performance appraisal: Assessing human behavior at work.* Boston: Kent.

Bhogal, M. (1988). Out of the office and into the world. *Accountancy, 102*(1140), 110-111.

Bigelow, J. (1983). Teaching action skills: A report from the classroom. *Exchange: The Organizational Behavior Teaching Journal, 8*(2), 28-34.

Bigelow, J. (1986). Using microcomputers in teaching OB. *Organizational Behavior Teaching Review,* 71-88.

Bigelow, J. (1988). *Giving an action exam: An evolving art.* Paper presented at the 15th Annual Meeting of the Organizational Behavior Teaching Society, Los Angeles, CA.

Bigelow, J. (1990). *Managerial skills: Not what we think they are.* Paper presented at the Organizational Behavior Teaching Conference, Richmond, VA.

Bloom, B. S. (1956). *Taxonomy education objectives: Handbook I, cognitive domain.* New York: David McKay.

Bond, F. A., Hildebrandt, H. W., & Miller, E. L. (1984). *The newly promoted executive: A study in corporate leadership.* Ann Arbor: The University of Michigan Graduate School.

Boyatzis, R. E. (1982). *The competent manager.* New York: John Wiley.

Boyatzis, R. E., & Kolb, D. A. (in press). From learning styles to learning skills: The executive skills profile. *Journal of Managerial Psychology.*

Boyatzis, R. E., & Renio, A. (1989). The impact of an MBA program on managerial abilities. *Journal Of Management Development, 8*(5), 66-77.

Boyatzis, R. E., Renio, A., & Thompson, L. (1991). *Developing abilities in an MBA program.* Unpublished paper, Weatherhead School of Management, Case Western Reserve University, Cleveland, OH.

Boyatzis, R. E., & Sokol, M. (1982). *A pilot project to assess the feasibility of assessing skills and personal characteristics of students in collegiate business programs.* Report to the AACSB. St. Louis, MO: AACSB.

Bradford, D. L. (1983a). Introduction to this special issue on teaching managerial competencies. *Organization Behavior Teaching Review, 8*(2), 7.

Bradford, D. L. (1983b). Some potential problems with the teaching of managerial competencies. *Organization Behavior Teaching Review, 8*(2), 45-49.

Bradford, D. L., & Cohen, A. R. (1984). *Managing for excellence.* New York: John Wiley.

Bray, D. W., & Grant, D. L. (1966). The assessment center in the measurement of potential for business management. *Psychological Monographs, 80* (Whole No. 625).

Burke, M. J., & Day, R. R. (1986). A cumulative study of the effectiveness of management training. *Journal of Applied Psychology, 71*, 232-245.

Byham, W. C. (1982). How assessment centers are used to evaluate training's effectiveness. *Training, 19*, 32-35.

Byrne, J. A., Norman, J. R., & Miles, G. L. (1988, November 28). Where the schools aren't doing their homework. *Business Week*, pp. 84-86.

Caie, B. (1987). Learning in style—Reflections of an action learning MBA programme. *Journal of Management Development, 6*(2), 19-29.

Cameron, K. S., Freeman, S., & Mishra, A. K. (1990). University of Michigan School of Business working paper.

Cameron, K. S., & Whetten, D. A. (1983). A model for teaching management skills. *Exchange: The Organizational Behavior Teaching Journal, VIII*(2), 21-27.

Campbell, D. T., & Stanley, J. C. (1963). Experimental and quasi-experimental designs for research. In N. L. Gaga (Ed.), *Handbook of research on teaching* New York: Rand McNally.

Campbell, J. P. (1976). Psychometric theory. In M. D. Dunnette (Ed.), *Handbook of industrial and organizational psychology* (pp. 185-222). Chicago: Rand McNally.

Campbell, J. P., Dunnette, M. D., Lawler, E. E., III, & Weick, K. E., Jr. (1970). *Managerial behavior, performance, and effectiveness*. New York: McGraw-Hill.

Carnovsky, M., & Sander, P. (1984). *The actor's eye*. New York: Performing Arts Journal Publications.

Caught in the middle: Six managers speak out on corporate life. (1988, September 12). *Business Week*.

Cederblom, D. (1982). The performance appraisal interview: A review, implications, and suggestions. *Academy of Management Review, 219-227*.

Church, H. J., Smith, V. M., & Schell, B. H. (1988-1989). Managerial problem solving: A review of the literature in terms of model comprehensiveness. *Organizational Behavior Teaching Review, 12*, 90-106.

Cohen, S. L. (1980). The bottom line on assessment center technology. *Personnel Administrator, 25*, 50-56.

Conger, J. A. (1989). Leadership: The art of empowering others. *Academy of Management Executive, 3*, 17-24.

Conger, J. A., & Kanungo, R. N. (1987). Towards a behavioral theory of charismatic leadership in organizational settings. *Academy of Management Review, 12*(4), 637-647.

Conger, J. A., & Kanungo, R. N. (1988a). *Charismatic leadership*. San Francisco: Jossey-Bass.

Conger, J. A., & Kanungo, R. N. (1988b). The empowerment process: Integrating theory and practice. *Academy of Management Review, 13*, 471-482.

Cresswick, C., & Williams, R. (1979). *Using the outdoors for management development and team building*. U.K.: Food, Drink and Tobacco Industry Training Board.

Crooks, L. A., Campbell, J. T., & Rock, D. A. (1979). *Predicting career progress of graduate students in management*. Princeton, NJ: Educational Testing Service.

Curtis, D. B., Winsor, J. L., & Stephens, R. D. (1989). National preferences in business and communication education. *Communication Education, 38*, 6-14.

Daft, R. L. (1978). A dual-core model of organizational innovation. *Academy of Management Journal, 21,* 193-210.

Damm, R. C. (1983). Measuring skills: The University of Pittsburgh experience. *Exchange: The Organizational Behavior Teaching Journal, 8*(2), 35-36.

Davis, S. (1982, Winter). Transforming organizations: The key to strategy is context. *Organizational Dynamics,* 64-86.

Day, W. A., Licata, B. J., & Stinson, J. E. (1987, May 26-29). *Developing management skills using competency-based management education: Student reactions and concerns.* A session presented at the Organizational Behavior Teaching Conference, Bentley, MA.

De Bono, E. (1971). *Lateral thinking for management.* New York: American Management Association.

Development Dimensions International (DDI). (1985). Final report: Phase III, report to the AACSB. St. Louis, MO: AACSB.

DiStefano, J., & Howell, J. (1987). *Multiple methods for evaluating management skill development.* Paper presented at 14th Annual Meeting of the Organizational Behavior Teaching Society, Waltham, MA.

Dobbins, G. H. (1989). An examination of outcome measurements in higher education. *The Academy of Management News, 19*(4), 12-13.

Duncan, W. J. (1983). Planning and evaluating management education and development: Why so little attention to such basic concerns? *Journal of Management Development, 2*(4), 57-68.

Dunnette, M. C. (1971). Multiple assessment procedures in identifying and developing managerial talent. In P. McReynolds (Ed.), *Advances in psychological assessment* (Vol. II). Palo Alto, CA: Science & Behavior Books.

Eisenberg, E. M., & Witten, M. G. (1987). Reconsidering openness in organizational communication. *Academy of Management Review, 12*(3), 418-426.

Emery, F. E., & Trist, E. L. (1965). The causal texture of organizational environments. *Human Relations, 18,* 21-32.

Filley, A. C., Foster, L. W., & Herbert, T. T. (1979). Teaching organizational behavior: Current patterns and implications. *Exchange: The Organizational Behavior Teaching Journal, 4*(2), 13-18.

Finkle, R. B. (1976). Managerial assessment centers. In M. Dunnette (Ed.), *Handbook of industrial and organizational psychology* (pp. 861-888). Chicago: Rand McNally.

Fisher, R., & Ury, W. (1981). *Getting to yes: Negotiating agreement without giving in.* Boston: Houghton Mifflin.

Flanders, L. R. (1981). *Report 1 from the Federal Manager's Job and Role Survey: Analysis of responses by SES and mid-management levels executive and management development division.* Washington, DC: U.S. Office of Personnel Management.

Freeman, R. E. (1984). *Strategic management: A stakeholder approach.* Marshfield, MA: Pitman.

Friedman, G. (1989). *Women in management: Competence and career development.* Unpublished doctoral dissertation, Case Western Reserve University, Cleveland, OH.

Gahin, F. S. (1988). Executives contemplate the call of the wild. *Risk Management, 35*(7), 41-51.

Ghiselli, E. E. (1963). Managerial talent. *American Psychologist, 18,* 631-642.

Goldstein, A. P., & Sorcher, M. (1974). *Changing supervisor behavior.* New York: Pergamon.

Golen, S., Lynch, D., Smeltzer, L., Lord, W. J., Penrose, J. M., & Waltman, J. (1989). An empirically tested communication skills core module for MBA interviewees, with implications for AACSB. *Organization Behavior Teaching Review, 13*(3), 45-58.

Gordon, R. A., & Howell, J. E. (1959). *Higher education for business.* New York: Garland.

Gordon, T. (1977). *Leader effectiveness training.* New York: Bantam.

Grant, D. L., Katkovsky, W., & Bray, D. W. (1967). Contributions of projective techniques to assessment of management potential. *Journal of Applied Psychology, 51,* 226-232.

Grant, G., Elbow, P., Ewens, T., Gamson, Z., Kohli, W., Neumann, W., Olesen, V., & Riesman, D. (1979). *On competence: A critical analysis of competence-based reforms in higher education.* San Francisco: Jossey-Bass.

Haney, W. V. (1986). *Communication and interpersonal relations* (5th ed.). Homewood IL: Irwin.

Harrison, M. (1987). *Diagnosing organizations.* Beverly Hills, CA: Sage.

Hart, G. L., & Thompson, P. H. (1979). Assessment centers: For selection or development? *Organizational Dynamics, 7,* 63-77.

Hellriegel, D., Slocum, J. W., & Woodman, R. W. (1983). *Organizational Behavior* (3rd ed). New York: West.

Henderson, D. W. (1981). Learning public management skills through an assessment system. *Innovations in Teaching Public Affairs and Administration.* Provo, UT: Brigham Young University.

Hinrichs, J. R. (1969). Comparisons of "real life" assessments of management potential with situational exercises, paper-and-pencil ability tests, and personality inventories. *Journal of Applied Psychology, 53,* 425-433.

Hopelain, D. G. (1985). Teaching organization behaving. *Organization Behavior Teaching Review, 10*(3), 63-76.

Howard, A. (1974). An assessment of assessment centers. *Academy of Management Journal, 17,* 115-134.

Howard, A., & Bray, D. W. (1988). *Managerial lives in transition: Advancing age and changing times.* New York: Guilford.

Ivanevich, J., Szilagyi, A., & Wallace, M. (1977). *Organizational behavior and performance.* Santa Monica, CA: Goodyear.

Jacobs, R. L., & Baum, M. (1987). Simulation and games in training and development: Status and concerns about their use. *Simulation and Games, 18,* 385-394.

Jaffee, C., & Frank, F. (1978). Assessment centers: Premises, practicalities and projections for the future. *Management International Review, 18,* 43-53.

James, L. R., & Jones, A. P. (1974). *Organizational structure: A review of structural dimensions and their conceptual relationships with individual attitudes and behavior.* Fort Worth: Institute of Behavioral Research, Texas Christian University (Technical Report 74-19).

Jantsch, E. (1980). *The self-organizing universe: Scientific and human implications of the emerging paradigm of evolution.* New York: Pergamon.

Jones, E. E., & Nisbett, R. E. (1972). The actor and the observer: Divergent perceptions of the causes of behavior. In E. E. Jones, D. E. Knaouse, H. H. Kelley, R. E. Nisbett, S. Valins, & B. Weiner (Eds.), *Attribution: Perceiving the causes of behavior.* Morristown, NJ: General Learning Press.

Kaman, V. S., & Bentson, C. (1988). Roleplay simulations for employee selection: Design and implementation. *Public Personnel Management, 17,* 1-8.

Kanter, R. M. (1982, July-August). The middle manager as innovator. *Harvard Business Review,* 95-105.

Katz, R. L. (1974). Skills of an effective administrator. *Harvard Business Review, 51,* 90-102.

Keleman, K. S., Garcia, J. E., & Lovelace, K. J. (in press). *Management incidents.* Dubuque, IA: Kendall/Hunt.

Kelley, R. (1989). In praise of followers. In W. E. Rosenbach & R. L. Taylor (Eds.), *Contemporary issues in leadership.* Boulder, CO: Westview.

Keys, B., & Wolfe, J. (1988). Management education and development: Current issues and emerging trends. *Journal of Management, 14,* 205-229.

Kidron, A. G. (1977). The effectiveness of experiential methods in training and education: The case of role-playing. *Academy of Management Review, 2,* 490-495.

Kinder, H. S. (1979). Two planning strategies: Incremental change and transformational change. *Group and Organization Studies, 4,* 476-484.

Knippen, J. T. (1988). Teaching management skills. *Organization Behavior Teaching Review, 13*(2), 39-46.

Kolb, D. A. (1984). *Experiential learning: Experience as the source of learning and development.* Englewood Cliffs, NJ: Prentice-Hall.

Kolb, D. A., & Fry, R. (1975). Towards an applied theory of experiential learning. In C. L. Cooper (Ed.), *Theories of group process.* New York: John Wiley.

Kolb, D. A., Rubin, I. M., & McIntyre, J. M. (1971). *Organizational psychology: An experiential approach.* Englewood Cliffs, NJ: Prentice-Hall.

Kotter, J. P. (1988). *The leadership factor.* New York: Free Press.

Kouzes, J. M. (1989). When leadership collides with loyalty. In W. E. Rosenbach & R. L. Taylor (Eds.), *Contemporary issues in leadership.* Boulder, CO: Westview.

Latham, G. P., & Saari, L. M. (1979). Application of social learning theory to training supervisors through behavioral modeling. *Journal of Applied Psychology, 64,* 239-246.

Lau, J. B., & Shani, A. B. (1988). *Behavior in organizations: An experiential approach* (4th ed). Homewood, IL: Irwin.

Lee, M. D., Adler, N. J., Hartwick, J., & Waters, J. A. (1987-1988). Evaluating managerial skill development. *The Organizational Behavior Teaching Review, 12,* 16-34.

Levy, A. (1986). Second-order planned change: Definition and conceptualization. *Organizational Dynamics, 15*(1), 5-23.

Lewis, C., Garcia, J., & Jobs, S. (1990). *Managerial skills in organizations.* Needham Heights, MA: Allyn & Bacon.

Livingston, J. W. (1971). The myth of the well-educated manager. *Harvard Business Review, 49,* 79-89.

Livingston, J. W. (1971). The myth of the well-educated manager. *Harvard Business Review, 49,* 79-89.

Long, J. W. (1987, March). The wilderness lab comes of age. *Training and Development Journal,* 30-39.

Luthans, F., Hodgetts, R. M., & Rosenkrantz, S. A. (1988). Real managers. Cambridge, MA: Ballinger.

Maier, N. R. F. (1976). *The appraisal interview: Three basic approaches.* La Jolla, CA: University Associates.

Mandt, E. J. (1982). The failure of business education—and what to do about it. *Management Review,* 47-52.

Manz, C. C. (1986). Self-leadership: Toward an expanded theory of self-influence processes in organizations. *Academy of Management Review, 11,* 585-600.

Marchese, T. (1987). *Third down, ten years to go. Washington, DC: AAHE Bulletin.*

Maslow, A. H. (1963). *Toward a psychology of being* (2nd ed.). New York: Van Nostrand.

McCall, M. W., Jr., & Lombardo, M. M. (1983). What makes a top executive? *Psychology Today, 26,* 28-31.

McCall, M. W., Jr., Lombardo, M. M., & Morrison, A. (1988). *The lessons of experience.* Lexington, MA: Lexington Books.

McClelland, D. C. (1973). Testing for competence rather than intelligence. *American Psychologist, 28,* 1-40.

McEvoy, G. M. (1988). A comparison of two approaches to management skill-building in an organizational behavior course: A replication. In P. Sanders & T. Pray (Eds.), *Proceedings of the Association of Business Simulation and Experiential Learning,* pp. 11-14.

McEvoy, G. M. (1989, August 14-16). *An experimental comparison of two approaches to the development of managerial skills.* Paper presented at the 49th annual meeting of the Academy of Management, Washington, DC.

McEvoy, G. M., & Cragun, J. R. (1986). *Development and use of a behavioral management skills test in an organizational behavior course.* Paper presented at the 28th annual meeting of the Mountain/Plains Management Conference, Gunnison, CO.

McEvoy, G. M., & Cragun, J. R. (1986-1987). Management skill-building in an organizational behavior course. *The Organizational Behavior Teaching Review, 11*(4), 60-73.

McEvoy, G. M., & Cragun, J. R. (1988). Management skill testing and faculty time saving in an organizational behavior course. In F. L. Patrone (Ed.), *Proceedings of the Mountain/Plains Management Conference, Denver, CO,* 82-89.

McKnight, M. R. (1979). *The universal science of the common person.* Unpublished doctoral dissertation, University of California at Los Angeles.

McKnight, M. R. (1988, March 24-26). *A holistic, skill-oriented theory of management and management education.* Paper presented at the meeting of the Western Academy of Management, Big Sky, MT.

Mead, N. A. (1986). Listening and speaking skills assessment. In R. A. Berk (Ed.), *Performance assessment* (pp. 509-521). Baltimore, MD: The Johns Hopkins University Press.

Menkowski, T., & Doherty, P. (1984). *Outcomes of the Alverno experience.* Washington, DC: AAHE Bulletin.

Michaelsen, L., Watson, W. E., Cragin. J. P., & Fink, L. D. (1981). Team learning: A potential solution to the problems of large classes. *Exchange: The Organizational Behavior Teaching Journal, 6,*(1).

Miller, J. G. (1978). *Living systems.* New York: McGraw-Hill.

Milroy, E. (1982). *Role-play: A practical guide.* U.K.: Aberdeen University Press.

Mintzberg, H. (1973). The nature of managerial work. New York: Harper & Row.

Mintzberg, H. (1975). The manager's job: Folklore and fact. *Harvard Business Review, 53,* 49-71.

Mockler, R. (1971, May-June). Situational theory of management. *Harvard Business Review,* 146-154.

The money chase. (1981, May 4). *Time,* pp. 58-69.

Morgan, G. (1988). *Riding the waves of change: Developing managerial competencies for a turbulent world.* San Francisco: Jossey-Bass.

Moses, J. L., & Byham, W. C. (Eds.). (1977). *Applying the assessment center method.* New York: Pergamon.

Napier, R. W., & Gershenfeld, M.K. (1981). *Groups: Theory and experience*. Boston: Houghton Mifflin.

Nonaka, I. (1988, Spring). Toward middle-up-down management: Accelerating information creation. *Sloan Management Review,* 9-18.

Nonaka, I., & Johansson, J. K. (1985). Japanese management: What about the "hard" skills? *Academy of Management Review, 10,* 181-191.

O'Malley, N. (Ed.). (1989). Crisis in the business schools: A question of balance. *Administrator, 8,* (Whole No. 10).

Pascales, R. T. (1985). The paradox of corporate culture—reconciling ourselves to socialisation. *California Management Review, 27*(2), 26-41.

Pavur, E. J., Jr. (1988). Personal communication. Development Dimensions International. Pittsburgh, PA:

Peters, T. J., & Waterman, R. H. (1982). *In search of excellence*. New York: Warner.

Polanyi, M. (1966). *The tacit dimension*. New York: Doubleday.

Porter, L. W. (1983). Teaching managerial competencies: An overview. *Organization Behavior Teaching Review, 8*(2), 8-9.

Porter, L. W., & McKibbin, L. E. (1988). *Management education and development: Drift or thrust into the twenty-first century*. St. Louis, MO: AACSB.

Powers, E. A. (1983). The AMA management competency programs: A developmental process. *Organization Behavior Teaching Review, 8*(2), 16-20.

Prahalad, C. K., and Hamel, G. (1990, May-June). The core competence of the organization. *Harvard Business Review,* 79-91.

Prideaux, G., & Ford, J. E. (1988). Management development: Competencies, contracts, teams, and work-based learning. *Journal of Management Development, 7*(1), 56-68

Quinn, R. E. (1988). *Beyond rational management: Mastering the paradoxes and competing demands of high performance*. San Francisco: Jossey-Bass.

Quinn, R. E., Faerman, S., Thompson, M., & McGrath, M. (1990). *Becoming a master manager: A competency framework*. New York: John Wiley.

Rackham, N. (1971). *Developing interactive skills*. Northampton: Wellens.

Rae, I., Grant, B., & Pullar, T. (1984, October). A dose of the outdoors—a new approach to management training. *Management (N.Z.)*. Wellington, NZ: New Zealand Institute of Management.

Rashford, N. S., & Coghlan, D. (1987). Enhancing human involvement in organizations—a paradigm for participation. *Leadership and Organization Development Journal, 8*(1), 17-21.

Rashford, N. S., & Coghlan, D. (1988). Organizational levels: A framework for management training and development. *Journal of European Industrial Training, 12*(4), 28-31.

Rashford, N. S., & Coghlan, D. (1989). Integrating organizational behavior and business policy through organizational levels. *Leadership and Organization Development Journal, 10*(1), 3-8.

Rasmussen, R. V. (1984). The self-analytic case method: Changing learners' attitudes about the utility of the applied behavioral sciences. *Group and Organization Studies, 9*(1), 103-120.

Redding, W. C. (1972). *Communication within the organization*. New York: Industrial Communication Council.

Reich, R. B. (1984). Entrepreneurship reconsidered: The team as hero. *Harvard Business Review,* May-June 1987, 77-83.

Remaking the Harvard B-School. (1986, March 24). *Business Week,* p. 56.

Render, S. (1985). A microcomputer revolution in the school of business. *Interfaces,* 35-38.

Robbins, S. P. (1989). *Organizational behavior: Concepts, controversaries, and applications.* Engelwood Cliffs, NJ: Prentice-Hall.

Robbins, S. P. (1988). *Training in interpersonal skills.* Englewood Cliffs, NJ: Prentice-Hall.

Rogers, C., & Farson, R. (1955). *Active listening.* University of Chicago: Industrial Relations Center.

Roman, M. (1989, October 30). B-schools: The up-and-comers. *Business Week,* pp. 168-169.

Rousseau, D. M. (1985). Issues of level in organizational research: Multi-level and cross-level perspectives. In L. L. Cummings & B. M. Staw (Eds.), *Research in organizational behavior* (vol. 7). Greenwich, CT: JAI Press.

Sandelands, L. E. (in press). What is so practical about theory: Lewin revisited. *Journal for the Theory of Social Behavior.*

Schein, E. H. (1978). *Career dynamics: Matching individual and organizational needs.* Reading, MA: Addison-Wesley.

Schein, E. H. (1981). Improving face-to-face relationships. *Sloan Management Review,* 22(2), 43-52.

Schein, E. H. (1985a). *Career anchors: Discovering your real values.* San Diego, CA: University Associates.

Schein, E. H. (1985b). *Career anchors training manual.* San Diego, CA: University Associates.

Schein, E. H. (1987). *Process consultation, Volume II: Lessons for managers and consultants.* Reading, MA: Addison-Wesley.

Schein, E. H. (1988). *Process consultation, Volume I: Its role in organization development.* Reading, MA: Addison-Wesley.

Schein, V. E. (1989). Would women lead differently? In W. E. Rosenbach & R. L. Taylor (Eds.), *Contemporary issues in leadership.* Boulder, CO: Westview.

Serey, T. T., & Verderber K. S. (1988). Students and learners: A conceptual distinction to share during first class sessions. *Organizational Behavior Teaching Review, XIII*(2), 133-138.

Sheldon, A. (1980, Winter). Organizational paradigms: A theory of organizational change. *Organizational Dynamics,* 61-80.

Sherman, J. (1988). *Interactive cases in management.* New York: Harper & Row.

Simon, H. A., & Hayes, J. R. (1976). Understanding complex task instructions. In D. Klahr (Ed.), *Cognition and instruction.* Hillsdale, NJ: Lawrence Erlbaum.

Skinner, B. F. (1974). *About behaviorism.* New York: Vintage.

Springett, N. (1987). *The evaluation of development training courses.* Thesis, Nottingham University, Nottingham, U.K.

Staw, B. (1984). Organizational behavior: A review and reformulation of the field's outcome variables. *Annual Review of Psychology, 35,* 627-66.

Steele, J. (1987, October 15). Why business schools are out of date. *Los Angeles Times,* p. 23.

Taft, R. (1959). Multiple methods of personality assessment. *Psychological Bulletin, 56,* 333-352.

Thornton, G. C., & Byham, W. C. (1982). *Assessment centers and managerial performance.* Orlando, FL: Academic Press.

Ungson, G. R., Braunstein, D. N., & Hall, P. D. (1981). Managerial information processing: A research review. *Administrative Science Quarterly, 26,* 116-134.

Vaill, P. (1983). The theory of managing in the managerial competency movement. *Exchange: The Organizational Behavior Teaching Journal, VIII*(2), 50-54.

Vaill, P. (1989). *Managing as a performing art: New ideas for a world of chaotic change.* San Francisco: Jossey-Bass.

Vance, C. M. (1986). Extending academic impact: Teaching interviewees how to teach interpersonal skills to their future subordinates. *Organization Behavior Teaching Review, 12*(3), 86-94.

Waters, J. A. (1980). Managerial skill development. *Academy of Management Review, 5*(3), 449-453.

Waters, J. A., Adler, N. J., Poupart, R., & Hartwick, J. (1983). Assessing managerial skills through a behavioral exam. *Exchange: The Organizational Behavior Teaching Journal, 8*(2), 37-44.

Weick, K. E. (1979). *The social psychology of organizing.* New York: Random House.

Wexley, K. N., & Latham, G. P. (1981). *Developing and training human resources in organizations.* Glenview, IL: Scott, Foresman.

Whetten, D. A., & Cameron, K. S. (1983). Management skill training: A needed addition to the management curriculum. *Exchange: The Organizational Behavior Teaching Journal, 8,* 10-15; 21-27.

Whetten, D. A. & Cameron, K. S. (1984). *Developing management skills.* Glenview, IL: Scott, Foresman.

Wlodkowski, R. J. (1985). *Enhancing adult motivation to learn.* San Francisco: Jossey-Bass.

Wohlking, W. (1976). Role playing. In R. C. Craig (Ed.), *Training and development handbook* (2nd ed.) (pp. 36/1-36/13). New York: McGraw-Hill.

Wollowick, H. B., & McNamara, W. J. (1969). Relationship of the components of an assessment center to management success. *Journal of Applied Psychology, 53,* 348-352.

Yukl, G. A. (1989). *Leadership in organizations.* Englewood Cliffs, NJ: Prentice-Hall.

Index

About the Authors

Cynthia Bentson is an industrial/organizational psychologist in Seattle, Washington. She earned her BA in Psychology at East Stroudsburg State College in Pennsylvania and her MS and Ph.D. in Industrial/Organizational Psychology at Colorado State University, where her dissertation research examined external factors that affect assessor judgment at an assessment center. Dr. Bentson has consulted in the private, public, and nonprofit sectors in the areas of managerial training and development, selection, and performance evaluation, specializing in the assessment center method for both training and selection. She has taught Human Resources Management at the university level, as well as a wide variety of continuing education classes and workshops on topics such as conflict management, delegation, and supervisory skills. Dr. Bentson's teaching and training repertoire emphasizes reality-based teaching, which includes actor-enhanced role-play simulations, simulated organizations, and team projects. She has presented and published in the areas of assessment centers, performance-based work-sample testing and training, reality-based teaching methods, and use of simulations to teach team skills.

John D. Bigelow is currently a professor in the management department at the College of Business at Boise State University. He received his BS in Physics in 1962 at the University of Washington and his Ph.D. in Organizational Behavior at Case Western Reserve University in 1978. He served for several years as a Peace Corps volunteer and later as a staff member, and he headed a low-cost science equipment invention lab for 2 years. He was appointed to a committee to advise the U.S. Senate on Peace Corps matters in 1987 and is a member of the executive committee of the Western Academy of Management and an enthusiastic member of the Organizational Behavior Teaching Society. His current research interests focus on managerial skills, wisdom in organizations, and uses of microcomputers in managerial learning.

Douglas Bookstaver has an MBA from the University of Illinois. During the 1989 school year he was an Associate Coordinator of the BA210 (Introduction to Management) course at the University of Illinois-Urbana.

Richard E. Boyatzis is currently a Professor in the Department of Organizational Behavior at the Weatherhead School of Management, Case Western Reserve University. Prior to joining the faculty at CWRU, he was president and chief executive officer of McBer & Co. for 11 years, and for various periods he was an executive with Yankelovich, Skelly & White, and on the Board of Directors of these two firms, as well as the Hay Group and Reliance Consulting Group. Dr. Boyatzis has consulted to many *Fortune* 500 companies, government agencies, and companies in Europe on various topics, including executive and management development, organization structure, culture change R&D productivity, economic development, selection, promotion, performance appraisal, and career pathing. He is the author of numerous articles on human motivation, self-directed behavior change, leadership, managerial competencies, power, alcohol and aggression, and value trends, and a research book, *The Competent Manager: A Model for Effective Performance.* Dr. Boyatzis has a BS in Aeronautics and Astronautics from MIT, as well as an MA and Ph.D. in Social Psychology from Harvard.

David Coghlan teaches at the National College of Industrial Relations, Dublin, Ireland. He studied management science at the University of Manchester Institute of Technology, where he was an Alfred P. Sloan Fellow. He is a Roman Catholic priest and a member of the Jesuit order. He has published more than 40 articles in such journals as *Leadership and Organization Development Journal, Long Range Planning, Journal of Managerial Psychology, Person-Centered Review, Organization Development Journal,* and *Human Development.* He has a particular interest in the application of OD to church and religious systems, works as an OD consultant in that area, and has published extensively on that subject.

Joan G. Dahl is Associate Professor of Management at the School of Business Administration and Economics, California State University-Northridge. She holds a Ph.D. in Business Administration from the University of Washington and an MBA from the University of Oregon. Dr. Dahl teaches courses in Management Principles, Human Resource

Management, and Labor Relations. She has published in such varied fields as business ethics, negotiations, and public sector contracting. She serves on the Board of Directors of several local institutions and is a community advisor to the Junior League of Los Angeles. As a consultant to industry, Dr. Dahl has worked with a diverse group of clients, including General Motors, the Los Angeles County Probation Department, Micom Electronics, and the Alternate Defense Counsel. Her current research interests focus on utilizing technology in educational settings and privatization in the public sector.

Graham Elkin has had a career that has bridged academia and management. After completing a BA (Hons) in Business and 5 years' management experience in the Human Resource Management field with British Petroleum (UK) and a period of consultancy in the West Indies, he returned to City University Business School (London) to take an MSc in HRM. Two years as a teacher and consultant were followed by 7 years as Head of Human Resources for House of Fraser plc, the British company operating Harrods and 105 other department stores. In 1983 he emigrated to New Zealand, where for 5 years he was Director of New Zealand's first MBA school, at Otago University. During that time he has established a consulting practice and developed interests in a whole range of academic and practitioner management development issues. He is currently a Senior Lecturer in Management of the University of Otago, having returned from a year as a Visiting Fellow at Cranfield School of Management in the UK. His main research at present is in industrial chaplaincy interventions and socialization processes in the MBA program.

William P. Ferris is currently an Associate Professor of Management in the School of Business at Western New England College in Springfield, Massachusetts. He has also served the College as Assistant Dean of the School of Business and as Director of the Resource Center. His undergraduate degree is from Dartmouth College, and he holds a Ph.D. in Communication from Rensselaer Polytechnic Institute. Recently, he spent a year as a Visiting Fellow in Organizational Behavior at Yale University School of Management. Professor Ferris has written articles and published papers on a variety of topics stemming from his professional interests in such areas as team-building, conflict resolution, leadership, interpersonal communication, and promotability, as well as the use of case-study and experiential exercise methodologies in the teaching of management subjects in schools of business. He is currently serving as Vice President,

Program of the Eastern Academy of Management, among other positions in various professional organizations.

Joseph E. Garcia is an Associate Professor of Management in the College of Business and Economics at Western Washington University in Bellingham, Washington. He received his Ph.D. in Organizational and Social Psychology from the University of Utah 1983. He has been teaching in the field of human behavior and organizations at the college and university level since 1974. He has co-authored three books and a number of journal articles on the topics of leadership, organization development, group decision support systems, and managerial skills. He is the conference coordinator for the 1991 Organizational Behavior Teaching Conference to be held at Western Washington University.

Michael J. Grelle is an Associate Professor in the Department of Psychology and Counselor Education at Central Missouri State University. His research interests include psychoneuroimmunology, the psychology of learning, and the psychology of teaching. He received his Ph.D. in Psychology from Northern Illinois State University in 1979. Before coming to Central Missouri State University, Dr. Grelle worked as a youth counselor at the Illinois Youth Center in St. Charles, Illinois.

Waldo R. Jones, president of Simulated Reality Systems, Fort Collins, Colorado, is a veteran of 25 years of experience in front of audiences. He attended Duke University, is a graduate of the University of Hartford in Speech and Theater Arts, and pursued graduate studies in Communication Arts at Colorado State University. His work in theater, audio, and video encompasses performing, directing, writing, set design, and construction. He has worked for Universal Studios and has provided theatrical services to international corporations such as Storage Tek and Hewlett-Packard. He is currently involved in research to assess the effectiveness of a theatrical coaching model to enhance administrative leadership skills.

Vicki S. Kaman is an Associate Professor in the Department of Management, College of Business at Colorado State University. Her educational background includes a BS in Psychology from the State University at New York—Albany and an MS and a Ph.D. in Industrial/Organizational Psychology from Colorado State University. Before joining the Colorado State College of Business in 1981, she spent several years working for the Employee Development Department of the City of Fort Collins, Colorado.

It was there, in 1975, that she first designed role-play simulations for use in employee selection. Since then, she has used simulation techniques to select employees for a variety of public sector positions, including police officer, sergeant, and personnel director. She is currently using role-play techniques for training Colorado Department of Highway managers in conflict management skills. Her other research interests are in training needs assessment, gender pay perceptions, and use of employee surveys to improve human resource management.

Ken S. Keleman is a Professor of Management at Western Washington University, where he has been teaching since 1977. He holds a Ph.D. in Applied Psychology from the University of Utah. In addition to university instruction, he has been active in conducting training sessions and management development seminars for private, public, and not-for-profit organizations since 1975. He has co-authored a management development book and a number of journal articles in the areas of small group performance, group decision support systems, and managerial skills.

Kathi J. Lovelace is an Instructor at Whatcom Community College and Western Washington University. She completed a BA in Psychology in 1986 and an MBA in 1990 at Western Washington University. She has co-authored papers and presentations in the areas of managerial skills and organizational development and has conducted training seminars for both private and public sector firms. Her research interests are in communication skills and learning processes.

Douglas R. May is currently a doctoral student in Organizational Behavior at the University of Illinois—Urbana-Champaign. He received his BA from the University of Kansas before going to work for IBM in Kansas City, Missouri. He left IBM to earn an MA from the University of Missouri at Columbia and then entered the Ph.D. program at the University of Illinois. His research interests include work teams and work environments, and he has published in *Organizational Behavior and Human Decision Processes* and the *Journal of Applied Social Psychology*. He is currently conducting research on the influence of the physical environment on work group processes and effectiveness criteria.

Renee V. McConnell received her BA from the College of Wooster and her MHRM and Ph.D. in Business Administration from the University of

Utah. She is Director of Management Communication and an Adjunct Assistant Professor in the Management Department at the Graduate School of Business, University of Utah. Her current research interests cover a variety of issues regarding management assessment, leadership, and interpersonal communication.

Glenn M. McEvoy is an Associate Professor of Management in the College of Business at Utah State University. He received his BS in Industrial Engineering from the University of California at Berkeley and his MS and DBA in Organization and Management from the University of Colorado-Boulder. He has been an industrial engineer, a manager, and an academic at five universities. Dr. McEvoy's current research interests are management selection and development, performance appraisal systems, and international and strategic issues in human resource management. He is the author or co-author of more than 50 articles and papers; his recent articles have appeared in the *Academy of Management Journal, Journal of Applied Psychology, Personnel Psychology, Personnel Administrator,* and *Group & Organization Studies.*

Melvin R. McKnight holds a BS in Civil Engineering from the University of Wyoming, an MBA from Stanford University, and a Ph.D. in Management from UCLA. He currently holds the position of Associate Professor of Management at Northern Arizona University. He has held teaching appointments at Montana State University, California Polytechnic State University-San Luis Obispo, and Pepperdine University. His industrial experience includes positions at Procter & Gamble and Atlantic Richfield. His primary research interest lies in understanding the role of caring, for both the work and the people doing it, in making management and leadership effective; he has come to believe that this is the most overlooked area in the management literature.

Ralph F. Mullin is currently Assistant Professor, Management, at Central Missouri State University, where he teaches business policy and research methods. His first career, for 23 years, was as a Chamber of Commerce executive. Before that he was an Air Force pilot and aircraft controller. His research interests, in addition to basic management skills, include the assessment center method, team learning, performance appraisal systems, charismatic leadership, and organizational culture and change. Dr. Mullin completed his Ph.D. in 1987 at the University of Florida.

Robert E. Quinn is Chair of the Organizational Behavior and Human Resource Management Department at the University of Michigan School of Business Administration. His research interests are in the areas of management, organizational theory, behavior and development, executive skill development, and group dynamics. He is currently conducting research on the following questions: What makes managers effective or ineffective? What is the impact of various types of cultures on organizational performance? What are the various types and impacts of cross-gender relationships at work? How do managers change over time? Professor Quinn has published six books, including *Beyond Rational Management: Mastering the Paradoxes and Competing Demands of High Performance* and *Becoming a Master Manager: A Competency Based Framework*.

Nicholas S. Rashford, a Jesuit priest, is President of St. Joseph's University, Philadelphia, and was formerly Dean of the School of Management, Rockhurst College, Kansas City, Missouri. He studied management, as an Alfred P. Sloan Fellow, at MIT and behavioral science in medicine at Johns Hopkins University in Baltimore. He has initiated a development of the concept of organizational levels, used it widely in teaching and consulting, and, with David Coghlan, published applications to OD, management training and education, university administration, religious ministry, and organizational change. He currently chairs the Delaware River Port Authority and is a Commissioner of the Philadelphia Regional Port Authority.

R. V. Rasmussen is Professor of Organization Behaviour in the Faculty of Business, University of Alberta. He received his BS in Engineering in 1963 and his Ph.D. in Business Administration at the University of California at Berkeley in 1970. He is considered to be one of Canada's leading experts in management development and training and has delivered training workshops to both government and private sector organizations. His books and articles include texts used throughout Western Canada, titled *Supervisory Communications, Motivation and Productivity* and *Leadership*. Dr. Rasmussen has received the 3M Award and the University of Alberta's Rutherford Award, both for excellence in teaching. In the past 6 years, the MBA Association twice named him teacher of the year. In the past 3 years he has visited 17 universities in Canada and the United States to deliver workshops on teaching to university and college instructors.

Neil B. Sendelbach is a member of the Employee Development Strategy and Planning Department within the Employee Relations Corporate Staff for Ford Motor Company. His primary responsibilities are in the area of improved organizational performance and management education and development. He is currently responsible for the design, development, and implementation of the Leadership Education and Development Program targeted at the worldwide middle management population within Ford. Starting as a Product Design Engineer, he has gone on to served with Ford as a Management Development Specialist and as a Program Associate in the joint UAW—Ford National Education Development and Training Center. He was also assigned to the Ford of Europe staff for 3 years, based in England, with responsibility for the implementation of Employee Involvement across 15 countries and the establishment of a Human Resources Development Department. Dr. Sendelbach has also worked as Group Manager: Education, Training, Development and Personnel Planning for General Instrument Corporation, where he had global responsibility for operations in the United States, Europe, and Asia-Pacific. He has also worked as a management development specialist with United Technologies, Mostek (a semiconductor microelectronics chip manufacturer), where he had responsibility for the training and development of management. He received his BS in Science Education from Wayne State University, a Master's degree in Curriculum and Instruction, and a Ph.D. in Learning and Cognition from Michigan State University.

Timothy T. Serey received his Ph.D. in Organizational Behavior from the University of Cincinnati, after a career in marketing with a major oil company. He is now Associate Professor of Management at Northern Kentucky University. He has consulted with leading organizations across the country, including the Kroger Company, several state governments, Federated Department Stores, AT&T, and Procter & Gamble. For the past 2 years, he has organized and chaired a campuswide teaching conference at NKU. His current research interests center on the investigation of factors that predict success for Japanese expatriate managers here in the United States, as well as on larger U.S.-Japan trade issues.

John W. Seybolt received his BA from Yale University, an MBA from the University of Utah, and his Ph.D. from Cornell University. He is the Dean of the Graduate School of Business and College of Business at the University of Utah, where he served as Assistant Dean and Director of

Graduate Studies in the Graduate School of Business from 1986 to 1987. He is also a Professor of Management and an Adjunct Professor of Psychology there. His major interest for research, teaching, and consulting is organizational behavior.

Paul L. Shaffer is the Dean of the College of Business and Economics at Central Missouri State University. He earned his Ph.D. in Management from the University of Oklahoma in 1974. Prior to that time he was employed by a major oil company. Dr. Shaffer's research interests include performance appraisal design and design evaluation, psychometric research, organizational change, and assessing management development programs. He has also recently been involved in working in organizational cultural change as related to acquisitions and mergers.

Gretchen M. Spreitzer is a Ph.D. candidate in Organizational Behavior and Human Resource Management at the School of Business Administration, University of Michigan. For the past 1 1/2 years, she has been involved in an extensive research program on organizational change. Her major research interest is understanding micro-macro linkages, that is, the reciprocal impact of organizations and individuals. Her current research is exploring the role of managerial change and empowerment in organizational revitalization.

Kathleen S. Verderber is an Associate Professor of Management at Northern Kentucky University. She holds a BA in Rhetoric and Public Address, an MA in Communication, and an MBA and Ph.D. in Organizational Behavior from the University of Cincinnati. She is co-author of a textbook, *Interact: Using Interpersonal Communication Skills* (5th ed.). Dr. Verderber has published articles in *Journal of Occupational Psychology, The Organizational Behavior Teaching Review,* and *The Psychology of Women Quarterly.* She reviews for the *Journal of Business Research.* Her research interests focus on the development of managerial competencies. She has recently completed a study of business meeting behaviors and their relationship to meeting effectiveness.

David A. Whetten is the Commerce Alumni Distinguished Professor of Business Administration at the University of Illinois. He received his Ph.D. from Cornell in 1974. He has written extensively on organizational effectiveness, organizational decline, and managerial skill development. He is the co-author of several books, including *Developing Management*

Skills (2nd ed.). He has been very active in the Academy of Management, serving as a member of the Board of Governors, as the Chair for the OMT division, and as editor of the *Academy of Management Review*. He has also served as Associate Dean for Graduate Programs at the University of Illinois.

Deborah Lundberg Windes is a graduate student in Organizational Behavior at the University of Illinois-Urbana. She received her undergraduate degree at North Park College in Chicago, majoring in Psychology. She is currently writing a dissertation on the relationships between state regulatory commissions, electric utilities, and consumers.